Community Organization and Development

COMMUNITY ORGANIZATION AND DEVELOPMENT
An Indian Perspective

ASHA RAMAGONDA PATIL

Associate Professor
Department of Continuing and Adult Education and Extension Work
S.N.D.T. Women's University
Mumbai

PHI Learning Private Limited

Delhi-110092
2013

₹ 195.00

COMMUNITY ORGANIZATION AND DEVELOPMENT: An Indian Perspective
Asha Ramagonda Patil

ISBN-978-81-203-4694-9

Published by Asoke K. Ghosh, PHI Learning Private Limited, Rimjhim House, 111, Patparganj Industrial Estate, Delhi-110092 and Printed by Syndicate Binders, A-20, Hosiery Complex, Noida, Phase-II Extension, Noida-201305 (N.C.R. Delhi).

To
My Sadguru
and
all those interested in
working with the community

Contents

List of Figures

List of Figures

List of Tables

Preface

In the global scenario, the professional discipline of Social Work has established its importance. Many students are lured by this field. The subject covers a vast area. One of the frequent problems voiced by Social Work students in India relates to the difficulty in getting books written by Indian authors considering Indian situation. Most of the colleges offering Social Work course have very few books available on Community Organization, which is a very prominent method of social work. Hence, this book is an effort to explain the basic concepts of community organization and development and other related issues.

In a democratic country like India, community organization and development has a great significance. Many communities/social workers are often encouraged by the government and NGOs (non-governmental organizations) to work for the uplift of the unreached people. The role of a community worker in bringing social change is pivotal. The history of India reflects the enormous role played by the community workers in bringing social change. Many professional community workers work with a voluntary zeal. Though they have diverse ideologies, objectives and methodologies, their main aim is to help people to fight for their rights.

Many social work colleges are upcoming. Several NGOs and corporate sectors are working for the welfare of different sections of society. The youth working with the communities needs to understand different concepts related to the subject. To achieve people-centred development, one needs to have a clear understanding about community development. People working in different government departments and implementing different schemes for the development of the marginalized groups need to understand the process of community development. This book aims to enrich the youth with a deeper insight and better perspective on the process of community development, which, in turn, will enhance them to work for people-centred development in a better way.

This book consists of eleven chapters, with one annexure. Chapter 1 illustrates the evolution of community organization in USA and India. The current trends in community organization explains shift in conceptualization and philosophy, changes in agencies and programmes, changes in the area of methods, changes in relation to personnel and professional practice, which have been covered exhaustively. Chapter 2 focuses on different aspects of community organization such as definition, principles, functions steps, etc. It also deals in detail with the process of community development as well. Chapter 3 deals with the concept of community mobilization covering needs, benefits, process, phases and challenges related to it. It focuses on the optimum use of local resources for the development of people. Chapter 4 explains different models of community organization practice for bringing social change, especially in the lives of marginalized people. The knowledge of these models and their combination will result in sustainable development of society.

To understand the needs and problems of the community, the community worker has to follow different methods. One of the methods is participatory appraisal, which is discussed in detail in Chapter 5. This method helps us to understand power relationships in the community. It analyzes the needs and the available resources, motivation level, values and taboos followed by the community. This knowledge is prerequisite for implementing any development programme. Meetings play a significant role in proper functioning of any organization. It is required for collective decision-making, planning and follow-up action. Chapter 6 covers in detail theses aspects of utilizing meetings for democratic and constructive discussions, which will result in total participation of community people. Conflicts are the integral part of any community. It is expected from a community worker to handle these conflicts in such a way that all the parties involved find the solutions acceptable. Chapter 7 focuses on conflict management in a constructive way. It defines and classifies conflict, focuses on the need and the strategies of resolving it. This chapter also suggests that conflicts, if dealt proactively, can bring positive changes and harmony among people. To avoid conflict, the community worker has to understand the power structure in a community. Chapter 8 explains that power is an integral part of the functioning of any type of human organization. The community worker must realize the importance of power structure to achieve the goals of community organization and development. The community worker should tap, train and involve the potential leaders in all the social activities for sustainable development.

Social action is one of the important methods to bring social change. Chapter 9 covers origin, elements, models and strategies used in social action. It clarifies the concept with the help of examples of some important movements—'*Chipko* movement' in Uttaranchal and 'Anti-liquor movement' in Andhra Pradesh, which were propagated by women. It also describes the Public Interest Litigation (PIL), *Narmada Bachao Andolan*, and *Lokpal Bill* in detail. The community worker has to perform different roles depending on the issues and problems s/he is dealing with. Chapter 10 covers different roles of a community worker to be performed, while working with the people. S/he has to play multiple roles of a guide, initiator, communicator, enabler, counsellor, motivator, facilitator, etc. A very significant task of the community worker is to maintain different records of the activities carried out by him/her. Records are very important documents which give a clear picture of the work done by an organization. They guide in planning future activities for achieving the goals of community development. Chapter 11 deals with all the aspects of documentation of these records.

Annexure I gives brief information about Saul Alinsky—a very significant figure in promoting social action all over the world. He is treated as a model for the same.

I have tried to explain the concepts of community organization and development in a very simple manner by giving examples wherever necessary. I am sure this book will guide the students of Social Work and the aspiring community workers to perform their roles successfully. This will also help those who are passionate to help people to fight for their rights.

Asha Ramagonda Patil

Acknowledgements

Writing this book became a reality due to the support of many people. This moment I wish to remember all of them with gratitude. This idea was generated during my visits as a faculty to the tribal and rural areas and the urban slums, where I went to assess the needs of the local people. While interacting with the people and students, I realized the need to put my experiences in the book form. Today, at the completion of this book, I am obliged to give my thanks to many people, but some of them deserve special mention.

First and foremost, I wish to express my gratitude to my best friend Dr. Pratima Dave for extending all the moral support. I am grateful to her for wholehearted support. She read and edited the manuscript and gave valuable suggestions. She was ever generous with her time and boosted my morale. Despite her busy schedule and family responsibilities, she was always with me, and for this, I am indebted to her.

I remember my friend Rohit Joshi with fondness, who was instrumental in writing this book. A chance meeting with him changed the course of my life.

Dr. Sushma Powdwal deserves my special thanks for her enthusiastic support and cooperation. Her encouragement and inspiration helped me in completing this book. I recognize with gratitude the extensive cooperation given by the staff of S.N.D.T. Women's University library. I am grateful to Tata Institute of Social Sciences (TISS) library for letting me use their library. My special thanks are for Mr. Ravindra Shinde, from TISS library for his untiring help, especially in locating the reference books.

I am thankful to Mr. Muneer Alavi of 'Rural Cummunes', who permitted me to use the maps of PRA, which were prepared by the staff and students of his organization. I owe a debt of gratitude to all of them. I am also thankful to the villagers residing in different padas/villages of Tal. Khalapur, Dist. Raigad. My special thanks are for the people living in Varsai-Pada, Apati village, Karambeli, Nandan-pada and Mouje-Ghote, who participated whole-heartedly in the PRA exercise. This has helped me to understand the concept of PRA and use of different tools in PRA.

I take this opportunity to thank Shaila and Ashok Shastri for their hospitality. I am thankful to Ishan for sparing his mother (Dr. Dave) whenever required. I thank all my students, who continuously asked me probing questions, which helped me in writing this book from students' and the future community workers' point of view. I am grateful to my guru OSHO for encouraging me with the aphorism—'work as meditation' to take up this endeavour and complete it within the stipulated time.

I would like to thank my publisher PHI Learning, New Delhi, for their continuous support and patience. Last but not least, my parents Vimal and Ramagonda, who are my pillars of strength. My gratitude to them is beyond words.

I dedicate this book to all those who really want to work for people-centred development.

Asha Ramagonda Patil

1

Historical Perspective of Community Organization

Community organization as a method of social work has evolved over decades. This chapter gives an overview of the history of community organization from the year 1870 onwards. It also includes the Lane Report (1939), which is considered a milestone in the history of community organization.

The term 'community organization' was not used in earlier days when social welfare services started, though these services catered to the needs of community people. The evolution and development of community organization in United States since 1870 can be grouped under four major periods as follows:

1. Charity organization period (1870–1917)
2. Rise of federation (1917–1935)
3. Expansion and professional development (1935–1955)
4. Community organization and social change (1955 onwards)

Let us see how the concept of community organization has evolved during these periods.

CHARITY ORGANIZATION PERIOD (1870–1917)

This was an era that witnessed the beginning of social welfare activities. The origin of community organization can be found in the charity organization movement. The establishment of first State Board of Charities in Massachusetts in 1863 was an important event of this period. By the end of 1870, such boards were established in six other states. Another important event which took place in 1872 was the establishment of the State Charities Aid Association (SCAA—now State Communities Aid Association) in New York. This was the first state-wide citizen's welfare planning association. In 1869, Charity Organization Society was established in London to coordinate relief giving services during a period of social and economic distress. This movement spread to other parts of the country. By the end of 1895, there were around 100 charity organization societies in the US, which were involved to coordinate the administration of relief. To do this, they established district level committees. These societies were involved in raising and administering the funds, providing direct services to individuals and families, investigating the causes of poverty and dependency, etc. These efforts, subsequently, contributed towards the development and expansion of social welfare programmes in the area of child welfare, health and recreation.

The organization of the National Conference of Charities and Correction in the US in 1873 became another landmark in the history of social welfare. The following year, it started publishing its annual 'proceedings'. In 1917, the name of this conference was changed to the National Conference of Social Work, which was renamed in 1956 as the National Conference on Social Welfare. This organization became a milestone which guided all American social welfare activities.

Later on, in 1899, the National Conference of Jewish Charities was established to serve for social welfare. In 1910, the National Conference of Catholic Charities was also established for the same cause.

The problems of relief came into focus due to the depression of 1873 in the US, followed by the civil war. Unemployment was the national problem. Due to industrial revolution, migration of population to the urban areas became an issue of major concern. In this situation, the first city-wide charity organization society in the US was established in Buffalo in 1877. The Buffalo Society was an organization of established local charities.

The charity organization movement spread to other cities as well. They encouraged a cooperative approach to the 'charitable' or special problems of the community. They promoted cooperation among social welfare agencies. They focused on community rather than individual welfare.

A number of councils of social agencies and community chests were formed during the 1920s. They took lead in the welfare programmes. The local leadership came from charity organization executives, who participated actively in these councils. The first council of social agencies was organized in Pittsburgh in 1908. Primary leadership in community organization was exercised by chests and councils. After World War I, the charity organization societies primarily focused on family rather than community. Most of the programmes concentrated on family welfare.

The social settlement, one of the pioneer organizations, was concerned with the welfare of the neighbourhood or local community within the larger city. Community organization, though not mentioned directly, was one of the major thrust areas of settlement programmes. The concern of settlement's clubs and classes was always on the well-being and development of the neighbourhood or local community. One can say this because it had emphasized on experimentation, demonstration and implementation of evolutionary programmes and self-organization of the local community people to bring out needed changes through direct efforts, mobilization of local resources and democratic social action.

Around 100 national welfare agencies were established between 1870 and 1919. A number of social surveys were undertaken by different councils and societies. The survey method gradually became popular and accepted by many national and other welfare agencies. Later, there was a shift towards comprehensive community welfare surveys.

RISE OF FEDERATION (1917–1935)

The main characteristic of this period reflected in the tremendous increase in the number and rapid growth of community chests and councils of social agencies. The first modern community chest, the 'Clereland Federation for Charity and Philanthropy' was established. The two-way purpose was joint fund raising and joint budgeting.

The United States entered World War I in 1917. This led to the establishment of several 'war chests', which were also known as *financial federations*. They were mainly concerned with War appeals. After the War, these War chests were converted into peacetime community chests (1920s). These chests and councils jointly worked for financing, community planning and coordination.

In 1917, the first modern state department of public welfare was started in Illinois. The state welfare agencies started using community organization in a vast number of services and relationships. In 1921, The American Association of Social Workers was established.

EXPANSION AND PROFESSIONAL DEVELOPMENT (1935–1955)

This period was characterized by expansion and professional development of community organization, which is continued even today. Another very remarkable feature of this period is the introduction of community organization process used in the field of public welfare.

The National Social Work Council organized a United Educational Programme in 1932. The main purpose was to foster public understanding and support for essential social services. In this period, there was a tremendous growth of public welfare agencies. They expanded their services and budgets. Governmental agencies also took lead in welfare programmes. The era witnessed a shift from local to state and federal leadership in the field of public welfare.

In addition to these changes, there was an increase in the use of community organization process by public agencies. This method was used to provide better social welfare programmes through fact finding, public education and coordination with governmental and voluntary organization.

The Social Security Act, passed in 1935, helped to develop leaderships at federal and state governmental levels. This, in turn, helped to settle the grounds of community organization. The significant feature of this Act (from community organization point of view) was that it extended child welfare services to children in rural areas. It envisaged "developing state services for the encouragement and assistance of adequate methods of community child welfare organization". This was probably the first instance of the use of the term 'community organization' in a federal statute.

Another major important event was the creation of the Federal Security Agency in 1939 to which the Social Security Board was transferred.

During the 1930s, unemployed people organized and formed a group called Workers Alliance (1935). They used different tactics such as organizing demonstrations, hunger marches, and work-relief strikes to achieve their rights.

Under the leadership of Saul D. Alinsky, in the 1930s, the organization of the Back of the Yards Neighbourhood Council was formed in Chicago. Alinsky's model on 'Community Action' became very popular and is still used for community development (discussed in detail in Chapter 4).

Development of the Concept of Community Organization

The year 1939 focused on the onset of community welfare organization. The National Conference of Social Work took up an exploratory study project in 1938–1939. This led to the Lane Report, which is known as a landmark in the history of community organization in the US.

Significance

The Lane Report (1939) was the first attempt to analyse and discuss the nature and characteristics of community organization. There was an urgent need to evaluate the process, to decide on the objectives of community organization and to accept it as a method. This report propagated community organization as a method of social work like case work and group work. The report clearly explains many basic concepts. It sets up a frame of reference for the subject. It also suggests areas for further study as well. This report had greatly influenced all those involved in the field of social work to think further about community organization. The Lane Report became a major reference point in the history of professionalization of social welfare. As stated by Dunham (1970), major conclusions of the Lane Report were as follows:

1. The term community organization refers to both—a process and a field. However, the report emphasizes the process aspect more.

2. Community organization is a generic process or method of social work. It is used in many 'settings' or types of agencies.

3. The aim of community organization is stated as 'bringing about and maintaining a progressively more effective adjustment between social welfare resources and needs'. This idea was later expressed in definitions of community organization by many authors.

4. Objectives of community organization are—

   i. To secure and maintain an adequate factual basis for sound planning and action.

   ii. To initiate, develop and modify welfare programmes and services, in the interest of maintaining a better adjustment between resources and needs.

   iii. To improve standards of social work and to increase the effectiveness of individual agencies.

   iv. To improve and facilitate interrelationships, and to promote coordination between organizations, groups and individuals concerned with social welfare programmes and services.

   v. To develop a better public understanding of welfare problems and needs, and social work objectives, programmes and methods.

   vi. To develop public support and public participation in social welfare activities. Financial support includes income from tax funds, voluntary contributions and other sources.

5. Some social work organizations carry community organization as a primary function and others as a secondary function.

6. Those organizations whose primary function is community organization do not necessarily offer help directly to clients.

7. Community organization is practiced not only at the local level but also at the state and national levels and between these levels.

Each community has certain specific needs. Community organization undertakes the tasks of fulfilling these needs. For this, the community organization uses, develops, mobilizes and creates resources. It focuses on balancing needs and resources. Accordingly, it decides the tasks to be performed.

The Lane Report was discussed and studied at length by various organizations. The National Conference again appointed a committee, whose chairman was once again Robert P. Lane. This committee discussed many different aspects of community organization—such as formation of groups, intergroup relationships, integration or coordination and adjustment of needs and resources. The committee submitted its report in 1940.

The Lane Reports greatly influenced thinking about community organization. A lot of discussion took place on these reports. It is significant that it initiated the process of defining community organization and its nature. In the 1940s, the conception of community organization focused on task goals and tried to bring equilibrium between needs and resources.

At the meeting of the National Conference of Social Work in Buffalo in 1946, the Association for the Study of Community Organization (ASCO) was organized. The main purpose was to increase and improve professional practices of community organization for social welfare.

ASCO developed a detailed programme with focus on—

1. Publication of a newsletter and a quarterly bibliographical checklist of current publications on community organization.
2. Extending encouragement to local community organizations, and discussion groups existing in different communities.
3. Promotion of publication of materials on community organization.
4. Conducting meetings and discussions of interested community organization practitioners with respect to National Conference.
5. Conducting some studies, discussions and experimentations as far as community organization records are concerned.

ASCO merged with six other professional organizations to form the National Association of Social Work in 1955.

Simultaneously, a group of teachers of community organization within the American Association of Schools of Social Work devised some activities. They had a curriculum committee under which they formed a committee on community organization. This was active from the period 1939 to 1945. They conducted a study of courses in community organization in the schools. They prepared bibliographies and also gave some suggestions in the area of course content.

The Hollis–Taylor's study in 1948–1951 helped to recognize community organization as an integral and important part of social work education. The first contemporary textbook on community organization titled 'Community Organization for Social Welfare' was written by Wayne McMillan and published in 1945.

World War II

World War II gave another dimension to community organization. Due to war, the needs of the community changed. Providing minimum amenities for decent living to the thousands of war affected people was a big challenge. The problem of providing 'day care' for children of working mothers was also very acute.

During this period, there was remarkable increase in federal leadership and participation in community organization. They served in the fields of health and welfare. Many national agencies were created to meet wartime needs. One of them was United Service Organization (USO). Six national agencies came together under this banner. They served the needs of military personnel and defence communities.

The war resulted in a close association between organized labour and social work, which gave a different dimension to the development of community organization. Tremendous growth of voluntary services became a significant aspect in community organization. Civilian Defence Councils, the American Red Cross, USO, etc. were established and are proof of this. They appointed volunteers in the field to perform different tasks. United Community Funds and Councils of America and other national agencies focused on total involvement of people and the voluntary organizations in social welfare activities.

Post-War Developments

National voluntary health agencies grew on a large scale, and carried on independent fund raising. The National Development Programmes (in the early 1950s) emphasized on community development, which attracted people who were interested in social welfare and community organization.

COMMUNITY ORGANIZATION AND SOCIAL CHANGE (1955 ONWARDS)

After 1955, the community organization mainly shifted its focus towards social change. One can divide this into four major themes. These themes are briefly discussed below.

1. **Civil rights and social/racial justice:** Civil Rights Law of 1964 resulted in many controversies. A struggle for school desegregation and voter registration in the South was also a remarkable event. Many protests, demonstrations and marches were carried out by people. Riots took place in many cities, especially in North.

At the same time, there were other problems—such as slum housing, unemployment, deterioration of school and family as institutions, delinquency and riots, which needed immediate attention.

2. **Urbanization:** The problem of urbanization was at its peak. The 1960 census showed that 70 per cent of the American people lived in the urban communities. This increased the problems of poor housing, cleanliness, racial concentration (Negroes, Mexicans, etc.), poor educational achievements, low skills, health related problems, broken families, inadequate civic services, etc. There was increase in criminal rate, juvenile delinquency and diseases.

To change this situation, a need was felt to prepare urban renewal programme, with the participation of local citizens. Wilbur J. Cohen expressed the need to involve community power structure in urban planning. He believed in participation of the affected people to bring social change. This aimed to include all the people—the poor and the rich, professionals and politicians, urban and suburban dwellers for maximum results. The crux of the matter in community organization was the participation of people from all walks of life. This was the beginning of the concept of 'wholeness' in social change.

3. **Alleviation of poverty:** This was a period of acute poverty and other related social problems in the US. Mobilization For Youth (MFY) had its beginning in New York (1957). They conducted a social study. Its findings showed an appalling increase in delinquency. Columbia University School of Social Work then was also involved in research and planning. In 1960, another study was published. The findings of this study stated the reasons of delinquency as lack of social, economic and educational opportunities. It further stated that the root cause of delinquency was poverty. From the year 1962 onwards, for a few years, MFY conducted many innovative programmes related to community organization. This included a broad approach to poverty and related problems and to community development.

In 1964, the Economic Opportunity Act was passed to alleviate poverty. The Act provided an opportunity for running a variety of programmes including Community Action Programmes (CAP). CAP was a community organization approach to solve the problem of poverty. It was based on self-help. The purpose was to provide stimulation and incentive for urban and rural communities to mobilize their resources to combat poverty through community action programmes. Technical and financial assistance was received from federal government. They adopted a flexible approach. It included mobilization of their own resources—governmental and voluntary, and focused on co-ordination with existing local, state and federal programmes dealing with poverty eradication. Various programmes included establishment of multi-purpose neighbourhood centres, manpower and job development projects, health centres, family planning programmes, housing services, adult education, foster grandparents programmes, etc.

The Economic Opportunity Act included provision that was practically revolutionary, as far as the history of social welfare is concerned. It states that a CAP should be 'developed, conducted and administered with the maximum feasible participation of residents of the areas and members of the groups served'. Optimum participation of people was expected.

4. **Emergence of trends of mass organization:** To fulfil the needs of the lower income groups or consumers forming mass organizations

became a very important issue in this period. Mass organization means organization of a large number of people to bring pressure on institutions to fulfil their needs. Usually, these organizations used conflict and confrontation as their strategies to achieve their objectives.

In the 1960s, different approaches were used for community development. The model of Saul Alinsky was one of them. It was believed that 'community action' is an essential part to bring a social change. In those days, mass organization was mainly related to the economic opportunity programme.

Another method believed that facilitation of poor people to participate in protest action will enhance their confidence and the collective effort may improve their circumstances.

Several movements took place in this period. They came to the conclusion that basic political change can come only through social movements, and not through governmental service programmes.

In 1966, the United Nations Development Programme (UNDP) was established, which also contributed to the community development programmes.

CURRENT TRENDS IN COMMUNITY ORGANIZATION

Let us now deal with recent developments in community organization. Dunham (1970) has divided trends in community organization in the following four parts:

1. Shift in conceptualization and philosophy
2. Changes in agencies and programmes
3. Changes in the area of methods
4. Changes in relation to personnel and professional practice.

Let us discuss each part in detail.

Conceptualization and Philosophy

After 1955, there was a persistent effort to develop adequate conceptual basis for community organization. There was a felt-need to have a sound theoretical foundation. It was also realized to have a proper and definite content and structure of community organization in courses in schools of social work.

The major achievement was that community organization as a method was accepted by all. The objectives of community organization—process goals as well as task goals—were also accepted by the teachers and practitioners. Murray Ross (1955) interpreted these tasks in the following words:

'Task goals are concerned with meeting specific needs, performing definite tasks and achieving certain concrete objectives. Process goals mainly include helping the people in a community or a particular area by strengthening their qualities of participation, self-direction and co-operation.' Jack Rothman (1964) mentions 'process' approach to increase 'gross functional capacity' of the community.

An adult education report (1948) described community organization as a process of balancing community needs and resources. It further states that community organization involves two things: (i) correlation or inter-organization of the activities of many community agencies and groups and (ii) active participation of people in solving problems concerning community.

Several approaches were incorporated in community development such as involving residents in programmes and considering their 'felt needs', emphasis on self-help, focus on total life of the community and an interdisciplinary approach to community problems. However, in the following years, the importance of community organization in urban development, civil rights, and mass organization was realized.

Lots of discussions on the acceptance of objectives of community organization were held. Meanwhile, the objective of community organization—changing of relationships and of decision-making patterns in the community—was also accepted.

Followed by this, one of the most remarkable developments in the area of community organization is the emphasis on social change. In 1962, Roland Warren stated that community organization was concerned with 'system-maintenance' and 'problem-solving'. He made difference between community organization and community development. Today, social change has become a part of community organization—the change may be in institutions, programmes, policies or decision-making patterns.

Agencies and Programmes

During the 1960s, the emphasis on the community organization approach and method increased enormously. There was a major change in programme implementation. Programmes concerned with elimination of poverty, urban redevelopment, struggle for civil rights, etc. increased. Along with this change, there was a substantial shift from voluntary to governmental leadership in planning. This led to an increase in federal leadership. This resulted in availability of large amount of federal funds for various programmes. This constituted a major change in the setting for community organization.

Four major types of community organization programmes received recognition in this period, namely social planning, community organization (emphasising local people participation and consensus), social action and fund-raising and allocation.

Methods

Several major changes took place in the methods of community organization. Now, it includes thorough planning and implementation through organization, negotiation and social action. The techniques and strategies of social action can vary from community to community. Sometimes direct action is required. People and the community workers have to make a choice between non-violent and violent approaches. Instead of conflict and confrontation, many people prefer and emphasise on communication and the education of the community. Education comes in process goals. One has to study it thoroughly if one wants to practice it.

Personal and Professional Practice

Personal and professional practice in understanding the importance of community development has increased the demand for community organization workers. There was six-fold increase in the number of students concentrating in community organization in graduate schools of social work over a period of five years. There was also increase in the number of schools of social work offering thorough specialization in community organization.

So far, we focused on the US studies. Now, let us deal with the Indian scenario.

HISTORY OF COMMUNITY DEVELOPMENT IN INDIA

It is difficult to trace exactly when community development programmes started in India. It is due to lack of proper documentation. The roots of the community development programme seem to lie in the *Vedic* period religious practices. Basically, the values attached to the worth of an individual may be the basis for starting community development programmes. This was also the essence of the Gandhian movement. Gandhi stressed on reconstruction of rural life.

The Gandhian ideology can also be seen in Vinoba Bhave's movement for *Gramdan* and *Gram Swaraj*. Details of these movements are given later on in this chapter. At Sriniketan in 1921, Rabindranath Tagore started rural reconstruction work with an emphasis on self-reliance and self-respect. During the independence period, many states (Bombay, Madras, Uttar Pradesh, etc.) started rural development programmes. This definitely influenced the community development programmes. There were a few individual level experiments as well. All of them made a great contribution in shaping the concept of community development in India.

The report of the 'Grow More Food Campaign-Inquiry Committee' (under the chairmanship of Shri V.T. Krishnamachari) gave a strong foundation to the community development projects. The report suggested establishment of Extension Services for farmers, where they could get information and knowledge on subjects related to agriculture.

Let us deal in detail with some of these movements, which laid a foundation of Indian community development programmes. Community development came to be recognized as an effective and powerful device for promoting rural improvement in underdeveloped and developing countries.

In pre-independent India, to some extent, community development was restricted to the government departments of agriculture, animal husbandry, health and education. These departments carried out many activities for the betterment of people. But these programmes were not fully successful due to lack of unity of purpose and coordination. Further, the officials of these departments were inadequately trained. The welfare services of provincial government did not offer any sustained programme of development during pre-independence period.

The efforts of community development during pre-independence period are mostly related to rural reconstruction. Numerous attempts were made by various agencies and individuals for the improvement of the lives of people, especially the rural. They were pilot experiments. A brief account of the same is given here.

1. **Shriniketan experiment:** Dr. Rabindranath Tagore initiated this programme for rural reconstruction. The main objectives were to study the rural problems, and to help the villagers develop their own resources (namely agriculture and cottage industry). The elementary education aimed at the overall development of people. It also covered areas of health and sanitation. It also focused on the development of local leadership. To achieve these objectives, activities were mainly focused on agriculture, village welfare, cooperation and education. Night schools for women were also started.

2. **Gandhian movement:** The programme was started first at *Sevagram* (1920) and then was also implemented at Wardha (1938) for the welfare of the masses. Gandhiji had prepared a list of tasks to be performed by his trained workers for the uplift of underprivileged and rural people. This included promotion of village industries, basic and adult education, rural sanitation, uplift of backward classes, welfare of women, education in health and hygiene, propaganda of mother tongue, etc. These objectives were realized through self-help, dignity of labour, self-respect, simple and honest living.

3. **Gurgaon experiment:** This was the first development programme that was launched by government in pre-independent India. This rural welfare programme was conceived and implemented by Mr. I.L. Brayne in 1920. This was launched in Gurgaon district of

Punjab. It aimed to motivate rural people to involve in self-development and the development of their village with the help of government agencies. This project focused on increasing agricultural production, rural sanitation, education, cooperation, improvement of health, etc.

4. **Marthandam project:** This was a collaborative project of YMCA (Young Men's Christian Association) and Christian Churches, started in 1921 in Kerala. The objectives of this project included imparting education, improvement of health and economic conditions of rural people, social development, etc. It was a need based project. Trained workers were involved. It used different methods including demonstration and discussions for the development of people through self-help. This provided a guideline for rural workers.

5. **Rural development programme:** It was a government funded programme started in 1935–1936 for economic development and improvement of rural parts of India. The aims of this programme were to encourage village industry, improve village communication services, improve rural sanitation and recreation, provide medical aid, improve agricultural production, etc. To achieve them, rural reconstruction centres were established. Various non-official organizations and educational bodies also supported them.

6. **Sarvodaya scheme** (also known as Bombay sarvodaya scheme): Based on Gandhian ideology, this scheme was launched in 1948. It principally covered tribal areas. It emphasized on cooperative principles and methods. It tried to inculcate the habits of self-help, mutual aid and thriftness among the people. The main objectives of this scheme were to raise the standards of living, scientific development of agriculture, promotion of cottage industries, imparting adult literacy and development of village *Panchayats*. In other words, the scheme worked for the overall development and welfare of the people. It achieved success to a large extent. It helped to draw attention of the government towards rural areas.

7. **Etawah pilot project:** This project was started after World War II by Mr. Albert Myer and Mr. Horace Holmes in Etawah district of Uttar Pradesh in 1948. The concept of *Gramsevak* (village level worker) evolved in this project, which means a multi-purpose extension worker. It had a multi-objective purpose. In addition to the main objective of agricultural development, there were other objectives as well. They included improvement in health, eradication of illiteracy, improving communication, etc. This project became a guideline and showed the necessity of inclusion of rural economy in development programmes. It also focused on

developing people's capacities and skills. The success of this project encouraged the government to extend it to other villages as well.

8. **Firka development scheme:** The Intensive Rural Reconstruction Scheme, popularly known as the Firka Development Scheme, was another government programme, launched at Madras in 1946. It was based on Gandhian ideology. It involved various departments to achieve its objectives. It recognized the importance of rural development. It aimed at making rural people self-reliant and self-sufficient by providing them educational, economic and social facilities. This scheme was implemented under the chairpersonship of the Collector of the respective districts with the assistance from rural welfare officer. With the help of government funding and by using local resources, a great success was achieved.

Initially, the scheme was started in 34 selected Firkas which later on extended to 108 Firkas by the end of 1953. The Firka Development Scheme later on merged with the Community Development Programme.

All these experiments, schemes and projects helped to conceptualize community development in India. Some of them were successful in achieving their aims. The community development programme started in post-independent India (1952 onwards) was an evolution from these projects. It has helped to develop the present concept of community development. It aims at overall and sustainable development. It has rights-based approach.

Rural reconstruction was then included in all Five Year Plans. Attempts were made to achieve social change in a planned manner. The Planning Commission, constituted in 1950, realized the importance of socio-economic growth and modernization of people, especially the rural, and decided to allocate some funds for community development programmes in each Five Year Plan. The first Five Year Plan envisaged a Welfare Approach. This stressed on participation of people to improve their own conditions. The second Five Year Plan added one more element to this approach. It included participation of official and non-official workers. This was known as integrated community approach. Working of *Panchayati Raj* Institutions (PRIs) for the welfare of people was stressed in the third Five Year Plan. The fourth Five Year Plan had the target of production of enough food grain to be achieved through community development programmes. The basic objective of the fifth Five Year Plan was removal of poverty and attainment of self-reliance. The sixth Five Year Plan envisaged development of Below Poverty Line (BPL) people, especially from Scheduled Castes and Tribes under community development programme. This was known as Integrated Rural Development Programme. The seventh Five Year Plan mainly focused on anti-poverty programmes. Promoting social welfare measures like improved health care, sanitation, communication and provision for extensive education facilities at all levels were the main focus areas in eighth Five Year Plan. The ninth Five Year Plan emphasized on rural development creating adequate employment opportunities. One of its objectives was to provide the basic infrastructural facilities such as education for all, safe drinking water, primary health care, social issues like empowerment of women. The tenth Five Year Plan focused on reduction in gender gaps in literacy and wage rates, unemployment and other social issues. Till this time the focus was mainly on development. In eleventh Five Year Plan, rights-based approach was promoted.

The involvement of non-governmental organizations (NGOs) in community development programmes was noticeable after 1970 onwards. Till this period, the community work was mainly welfare-oriented. After globalization, more and more industries and corporate sectors are participating in community development programmes. They have Corporate Social Responsibility (CSR), under which they take up different community development projects/activities. International and national corporates (for example, TATA, Larson and Tubro) have taken up many projects. The current trend in community development involves maximizing participation of people, prioritizing their needs, finding local resources and jointly working to solve the problems. Sustainable development is at the centre of all programmes.

To summarize, we can say that these are the major events which took place in the development of community organization as a method of social work. As seen in the foregoing discussion, the idea of community organization originated from the Charity organizations in the US. Needs of the people were recognized and services were provided. It included fund raising, enactment of different social legislations and coordination of welfare activities. The main aim behind all these activities was charity. This concept went through many phases and the concept of community organization developed. There were revolutionary changes in traditional ideas about models of community organization. The difference between community organization and community development, models and approaches of community development and methods are discussed in detail in the following chapters.

In the present situation, a number of international and national agencies have entered in the field of community organization. They provide services to the underprivileged people for their overall development. The current trend in community organization focuses on self-help and sustainable development.

The community development programme in India concentrated on the overall development of the people. It has gone through different phases. Earlier, only rural area was focused. Now, it covers the urban area as well. The basic aim of all community development programmes is sustainable development, achieved by reaching to the unreached. Chapter 2 deals with community organization and development.

Review Questions

1. Briefly describe the evolution and development of community organization in the US.

2. How did the concept of community organization evolve in the US during the years 1870–1935?

3. Explain the expansion and professional development of community organization in the US since 1930.

4. State the major conclusions of the Lane Report. Explain its importance in today's context.

5. Illustrate the evolution of the concept of community development in the Indian context.

6. Explain the Sriniketan experiment and state its importance from the point of view of community development.

7. Explain the efforts of community development that took place during pre-independence period of India.

8. Different approaches were opted in Five-Year Plans for the community development. Illustrate.

CHAPTER

2

Community Organization and Development

Globalization has brought the world closer. Development in all the sectors, both at macro and micro levels, has taken place very speedily. It has to keep pace with the society which is changing very fast. Society's proper develop-ment requires meticulous planning. It is rather mandatory that people should participate in the initial stages of planning of the programmes, which affect their lives. On the one hand, community participation is increasing, and, on the other, more and more industries are getting involved in the process of community development as part of Corporate Social Responsibility (CSR). Earlier, community organization followed a charity based approach, especially towards the development of the deprived people. This has been replaced now with a rights-based approach.

Industrialization and urbanization have created a wide gap between cities and villages. Metropolises like Mumbai and Delhi have huge migrant population, staying in slums, and on footpath, without any sense of belongingness or identification with other people. This puts lots of questions before us such as: Can we call them a community? Is there any common thread which runs across the concept of community development? Which particular model of community development would be applicable? etc. In such a situation, one needs to develop a meaningful and functional definition of community, where people with common needs or interests and a sense of belongingness reside together. Here, they should have control over their environment. While working with such groups, one has to consider the political and economical power equations working over there.

As stated earlier, the impact of globalization can be seen everywhere. It has affected people's lives. Unfortunately, the poor are becoming poorer and

17

the rich richer. Now, the top priority is to rethink and restructure the poverty alleviation programmes. Those who are working with the people, both in the government and non-governmental organizations, have to adopt new techniques for economic empowerment of people. In other words, new ways need to be adopted for community development. First we need to understand the concept of 'community' and then that of 'community development'. We need to focus on the characteristics and main approaches of community development. In this chapter, we will discuss these issues in detail. Let us begin with community first.

COMMUNITY

It is very difficult to define 'community' comprehensively. People are changing fast due to rapid changes in the environment, economy, industrialization, information technologies and communication explosion. This change has affected the physical and social structure of the community. A community can be defined as a group of people, living in the same area, may be having the same occupation, religion, language or culture. They have some common purpose for living together. At the international level, many communities have come together due to common objectives/aims. For example, 'United Nations' is a community with a common belief in equality, peace and universal development.

Community can be defined in many ways, as the context changes the concept. A community is an organized group of people based on some criteria and common values that are shared by different people. The different criteria for identifying a community could be a geographical area (village, town, city, district, state, etc.), caste, religion (Hindu, Jain, Sikh, Parsi, Christian and Muslim), language (Marathi, Hindi, Urdu, English, French and Japanese), occupation (business, teaching, labour, farmers/agriculture, doctors, lawyers, etc.), ethnic origin (European, Asian, African, etc.), etc.

When we demarcate community as a geographical boundary according to the population size, political regions, industrial areas, etc., we find a major component of 'common interest' missing there. As a community worker, one has to remember that the prerequisite for community development is the 'common interest' of people.

Let us understand this with an example. The government wants to provide safe drinking water to rural people. This requires a considerable financial contribution from each family, who would be a beneficiary from it. For this purpose, the village chief (*Sarpanch*) calls a meeting to discuss this issue in detail.

In this meeting, the heads of the families and representatives from *Mahila Mandals, Yuva Manch, Kishori groups*, cooperatives (*Patpedi's*), religious *mandals,* etc. are invited. The representatives of past inhabitants (who are now living in the city), locally elected *panchayat* members, religious leaders, esteemed members and other groups will participate in it. They will decide the further steps to be taken to solve the problem of drinking water.

In this example, the village acts as a community. It has the following features:

1. A common land—the drawn boundary of the village
2. A recognized administrative structure—the chief (*Sarpanch*) and the organized groups
3. Invitees—members of the village
4. Common goal—access to safe drinking water
5. Common values—participatory decision making process
6. Common property—schools, temples, mosques, playground, grazing land, etc.
7. Common culture and history.

In the case of a cooperative, the following things will be common:

1. Common activities
2. Common interests
3. Common property (office, etc.).

The World Health Organization (1998:5) has defined community as follows:

'A specific group of people, often living in a defined geographical area, who share a common culture, values and norms, are arranged in a social structure according to relationships which the community has developed over a period of time. Members of a community gain their personal and social identity by sharing common beliefs, values and norms which have been developed by the community in the past and may be modified in the future. They exhibit some awareness of their identity as a group, and share common needs and a commitment to meeting them.'

Thus, one can say that different criteria can be used for the identification of a community. They could be a geographical territory, language(s), religion, caste, culture, profession, values and codes of conduct, common interests, etc. Let us understand the concept of community organization, its need and principles in detail.

COMMUNITY ORGANIZATION

Community organization is one of the methods of social work. Basically, it focuses on developing the capacities of local people in the community to solve their own problems. Community organization increases interaction among people. It tries to integrate and coordinate with existing organizations/groups for helping people to identify their needs and fulfil them. Before going into further details, let us deal with the definition of community organization.

Definitions of Community Organization

Following are some of the definitions given at different times (1939 onwards). The common factor in all these definitions is, helping people "to identify and solve their problems by themselves".

1. Community organization may be described as the art and process of discovering social welfare needs of creating, coordinating and systematizing instrumentalities through which group resources and talents may be directed towards realization of group ideas and the development of the potentialities of group members. Research, interpretation, conference, education, group organization and social action are the principle tools in this process. He further elaborates: Community organization is the process of dealing with individuals or groups who are or may become concerned with social welfare services or objectives, for the purpose of influencing the volume of such service, improving their quality or distribution or furthering the attainment of such objectives. (McMillan, 1939)

2. Community organization is a technique for obtaining a consensus concerning both the values that are most important for the common welfare and the best means of obtaining them. (Sanderson and R. Polson, 1939)

3. Community organization is a broad field of endeavour directed towards "a progressively more effective adjustment between social welfare resources and social welfare needs." (Lane, 1939)

4. Community organization refers to the process of building and maintaining a community of interest or a common interest group. Someone has called this 'the development of association to meet need.' (King, 1948)

5. It is the process by which people of communities as individuals, citizens or as representatives of groups join together to determine social welfare needs, plan ways of meeting them and mobilize the necessary resources. (McNeil, 1954)

6. Community organizations has been defined as the process of bringing about and maintaining a progressively more effective adjustment between social welfare resources and social work needs within a geographical area or functional field. Its goals are consistent with all social work goals in that its primary focus is upon the needs of people and provision of means of meeting these needs in a manner consistent with the precepts of democratic living. (Ross and Lappin, 1955)

7. Community organization for organizing marginalized groups into a self-sustaining cohesive entity whereby they exercise their collective power to negotiate and gain control over forces that affect their

lives. (Definition evolved in a workshop organized by ICOR towards an understanding of Human Development, ICOR Mumbai, 1998)

8. Community organization includes the activities, organization and processes through which, by concerted action, a community secures the services and facilities it desires. (Community welfare organizations, community physical planning and community industrial planning are all parts of community organization). (Warren, 1955)

9. Community organization is a process by which a community identifies its needs or objectives, orders (or ranks) these needs or objectives, develops the confidence and will to work at these needs/objectives, finds the resources (internal/external) to deal with these needs/objectives, takes action in respect to them and in doing so extends and develops cooperative and collaborative attitudes and practices in the community. (Ross, 1951)

10. Community organization is the process by which the social system of the community provides for integration and adaptation within the community. (Gangrade)

11. Community organization refers to various methods of intervention whereby a professional change agent helps a community action system composed of individuals, groups or organizations to engage in planned collective action in order to deal with special problems within the democratic system of values. (Kramer and Specht, 1975)

These definitions give a broad picture of community organization. They basically reveal that community organization leads to finding needs and resources, building-up social relations (interpersonal relationships, interaction and cooperation). Community organization helps people improve their quality of life. It is a participatory method of problem solving.

It is important for us to understand that the community organization is a process which helps people to remove all blocks hindering their growth, development, utilization of potentialities, optimum use of resources and build-up capacities of people.

Community organization is a long-term approach. People affected are supported in identifying problems and taking action to achieve solutions. The community worker helps people to bring social change through collective action by changing the balance of power equation. The tactics and strategies used may include timing the issue, deliberate planning, getting attention, framing the issue in terms of the desired solution, and shaping the terms of the decision-making process.

Need for Community Organization

Community organization helps to bring out many voices to add collective power and strength to an issue. Community organization is a key to bring changes in a community that are widely felt, and that reflect the wishes of the people, who are directly affected by problems. Thus, the community worker should help community residents develop the skills necessary to address their own issues in an ongoing way. At the heart of community organization, there should be inclusion, ownership, relationship building and leadership development. Community organization changes the balance of power and creates new power bases. We need to focus on its functions to understand this.

Functions of Community Organization

Community organization functions can be broadly divided into nine sectors, namely planning, programme operation, fact finding and research, public relations, fund raising and allocation, community development, neighbourhood work, social action and miscellaneous.

Planning includes planning of activities/programme development, coordination, improvement and maintenance of standards and related activities.

Fact finding and research includes the knowledge of actual needs of the people and available resources. This helps us to realize whether people have worked on these problems, and if so, then try to gain from their experiences.

Public relations include interpreting social welfare needs, programmes, services, developing and maintaining public relations, etc.

Fund raising and allocating in a proper way is an important task. Fund raising may be carried out by organizing a campaign or individually putting efforts. Once the funds are raised, budgeting and allocating them to groups becomes a crucial step.

Community development includes consultation regarding programmes of development. Helping people to meet their needs and to develop attitudes of self-direction, self-help, and cooperation are important aspects of development.

Social action includes carrying on legislative observation, analysis and promotion in a selected area adopted for the work. This may include confrontation, conflict and militant direct action to attain the goals.

While performing these entire tasks, one may require doing consultation as well. We also need to follow a principled approach to it.

Principles of Community Organization

Various sets of principles are given by various authors. Ross (1967) has grouped those under twelve headings; Dunham (1958) presented 28 principles under seven headings. Siddiqui (1997) in India has given the following eight principles:

1. Principle of specific objective
2. Principle of planning
3. Principle of people's participation
4. Principle of inter-group approach
5. Principle of democratic functioning
6. Principle of flexible organization
7. Principle of optimum utilization of indigenous resources
8. Principle of cultural orientation

These principles are implemented in different stages.

Stages in Community Organization

They can be broadly divided into six stages, namely:

1. Assess the community.
2. Form an active functional team.
3. Develop plan of action.
4. Mobilize the action.
5. Execute/implement.
6. Evaluate.

Assess the community

It is very important for a community worker to know the community where s/he has to start the process of community organization. It is very important to know the history and background of the issues that s/he will address. To do this, one has to spend two to three months in the community before starting the actual work and get familiar with people. Collect information about the history, demography, geography, and economic, political and power structure of a community. For this, one needs to establish individual contacts in the initial phase. Listening to people and gathering detailed information is the first step. This is explained in detail in the following chapters.

Form an active functional team

While interacting with individuals, tap potential people who can be useful later on in your work. Choose members from all strata, who can represent the entire community. Make sure the list is manageable. Choose only those passionate and dedicated members who can devote time and energy. Most importantly, they must be bestowed with the 'can do' attitude.

Develop plan of action

Prepare a plan of action with the help of people. This includes major problems faced by the majority of people, policies to address that problem, decision-making group members, action needed to take, etc. Once the plan is ready, call a meeting of people and discuss it with them. Take consensus of all people whose lives will be affected, give time schedule for each action, assign duties and responsibilities. Remember, the plan of action should be flexible, feasible and realistic.

Mobilize the action

Community support is the base of any action plan. Participation of all people is very important in community organization. Hence, make an effort to seek support of maximum number of people, make presentations, appeals, conduct campaigns, meetings. If possible, meet the elected representatives and try to get their support. This may help in getting government support in implementing programmes. As a community worker, your role is to keep the action moving forward. For this, assign different duties to the people and engage them in plan of action. See that the group remains on the track and focused.

Execute/Implement

According to the plan of action, one needs to implement activities in the community. Make sure that all the people participate in these activities.While implementing the tasks, ensure that you achieve the desired results.

Evaluation

It is important to carefully review the ongoing work from time to time and check the progress during the whole process. It also helps to check whether we are on the right track or not. It helps to know what went wrong or right and learn lessons for future.

COMMUNITY DEVELOPMENT

People are one of the basic resources for any development. Hence, the main objective of development should be welfare of the people, which, in turn, will result in community development. True development means development of the people, which can be brought by the people themselves. In other words, it is the development of the people, by the people, for the people. Community development is a structured intervention. This does not solve all the problems faced by a local community. However, it does build confidence to handle problems effectively.

Community development is a skilled process and an art in itself. It is one of the means of initiating change. A variety of programmes can be organized for the development of the community. The nature of these programmes varies as per the situations from country to country, state to state and from community to community. Actually, the situations can be the defining features of this development.

Community development provides an opportunity to individuals as well as communities to grow and change according to their own needs and priorities. It also allows them to grow at their own pace. While realizing this, it also pays attention to the fact that this development does not take place at the cost of oppressing other groups or communities. It encourages participation, involvement and sharing.

Definitions of Community Development

At different times, different authors have defined community development in various ways. Following are some of the definitions of community development:

1. Community development is a process designed to create a condition of economic and social progress for the whole community with its active participation and the fullest possible reliance upon the community initiative. (The UN Bureau of Social Affairs, 1955)
2. Community development is a movement designed to promote better living for the whole community, with the active participation and if possible on the initiative of the community, but if this initiative is not forthcoming spontaneously, then by the use of techniques for arousing and stimulating it in order to secure its active and enthusiastic response to the movement. (Mukherji, 1961)
3. Community development is a process of social action in which the people of a community organize themselves in planning and action, define their common and individual needs and problems; make group and individual plans to meet their needs and solve their problems; execute these plans with a maximum of reliance upon community resources, and supplement these resources where necessary with services and material from governmental and non-government agencies outside the community. (Jain)
4. The term 'Community Development' designates the utilization under one single programme of approaches and techniques which rely upon local communities as units of actions and which attempt to combine outside assistance with organized local self-determination and effort and which correspondingly seek to stimulate local initiative and leadership as the primary instrument of change. (Ross)

In all the above definitions of community development, there is a common thread focusing on community development as a continuous process. It is a process which facilitates the community to become aware of the factors and forces affecting their quality of life. It also empowers the people with the skills needed for improving their living conditions. In this process, people get together, communicate and discuss their problems, prioritize their needs, plan accordingly and take actions to overcome the problems. In short, Figure 2.1 explains the process of community development.

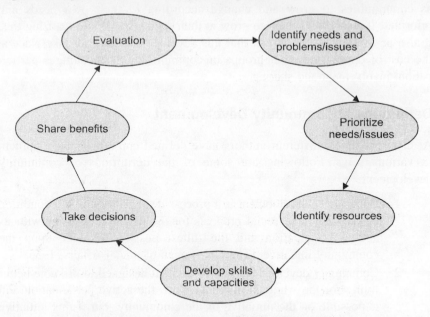

Figure 2.1 Process of community development.

Community development is an organized effort of people to improve their lives. It focuses on self-help, voluntary participation and cooperation of people from the community.

People's participation ensures a planned change and development of the community. This change affects people in a better way. Participation of people refers to their involvement in decision making process and problem-solving methods. All the members of that selected community can express their voice of discontent—a voice which should be heard.

Community development may be viewed as a means by which unnecessary super ordinate domination may be eradicated, personal alienation reduced as much as possible and individual dignity and importance may be realized.

Need of Community Development

Billions of people in the world, and especially in India, live in underdeveloped and rural areas. They do not have access to basic amenities, forget about modern technologies. Even today, children are malnourished. Diseases like diarrhoea, malaria, and dengue are rampant. Babies are delivered by traditional and mostly untrained midwives. Infant mortality rate is high;

exploitation by moneylenders is very common. Illiteracy is highly prevalent. Due to ignorance and poverty, the size of the family is big. The status of the woman is very low. Violence against women and backward class still exists.

However, for centuries, this bleak picture has remained unchanged. To change this picture, one has to execute a plan systematically and comprehensively. Efforts should be made for these people to get minimum essential facilities to make their life comfortable. From this point of view, the Indian government has made some efforts by implementing community development programmes through Five Year Plans. Programmes related to social and economic development of people, such as Twenty-Point programme to eradicate poverty, National Literacy Mission for eradication of illiteracy, technological mission, etc. were included in these Five Year Plans. They were implemented at the national level. To bring a change much faster, there is a need to carry programmes at local levels. Attempts should be made to improve socio-economic status of local people by implementing programmes on improving agricultural production, animal husbandry, developing village industry, improving health facilities, reducing infant and maternal mortality, providing educational facilities, etc. Here the role of community development is significant to realize these dreams.

In short, community development includes the following five elements:

1. Focus on the total needs of the community
2. Encourage self-help (main theme)
3. Secure technical assistance—from government or voluntary groups/ NGOs, may be in the form of financial and/or infrastructure
4. Plead advocacy on various areas—agriculture, health, education, etc.
5. Execute programme—based on felt needs of community.

Objectives of Community Development

The primary objectives of community development are:

◆ To initiate
◆ Give direction to
◆ Sustain community action.

In this process, the target group remains the same throughout the process. The development takes place towards the defined goals. Community development demonstrates a mode of community action, where it has to face conflicts, power, economic and social pressures.

The main aim of community development is to develop the competence of a community, so that it may solve its own problems. It is challenging. It requires involvement of community more effectively in initiation, planning and organization of services and programmes at the community level. In all these activities, every member of the community plays a meaningful and significant role. In other words, community development is a viable means of facilitating the great change in the first place and subsequently of responding to the consequences.

Community development is a process. It is a systematic approach to change. Each phase of the process is well defined and measured. For this, specified criteria are developed. For example, in this process of community development, the cooperation and participation of the community members is desired. This can be measured on the basis of the extent of involvement in decision making, awareness and utilization of local resources—both human and material.

Community development enables people to recognize their own ability to identify their problems and use the available resources to earn and increase their income, and build a better life for themselves. In this process of community development, people must be enabled to develop their capability to identify their problems and devise means of solving them. In addition, people must be helped to develop their capacity and enhance their desire to participate in decision making related to greater social and economic development.

Community development is also viewed as a method of achieving specified goals. The whole process of achieving these goals can be viewed as methods. This refers to centrally designed programme. This programme may be planned to fulfil the needs of the whole society or may be to fulfil the needs of certain groups of people.

If we look at the practical aspects of community development, we realize that these programmes are mostly planned outside the community. Hence, at times they may not address the needs of the community. Sometimes, they also impose specific goals on the community, which may be of use to the outside agency and not to that particular community.

However, community development has been characterized as a process, a method and a programme. It requires formulating a series of planned programmes or activities to achieve its goals. These planned programmes may take into consideration either a single need or interest or problem of the community or can focus upon many interests/problems/needs of that community. For example, it may simultaneously focus on issues related to agriculture, health, nutrition, education, industry, housing, etc., or emphasize only on one particular issue.

Assumptions

Community development is based on the following assumptions:

1. Every individual has worth and dignity.
2. Every individual has something to contribute towards community.

3. People have an ability to learn and grow.
4. Through conscious cooperation, appropriate planning and its execution (action), one can promote community change.
5. Community development can provide an individual an opportunity to contribute and to learn through it.

The ultimate aim of community development is to make it possible for everyone to have at least minimum basic amenities to live like a dignified human being.

Due to its unique features, community development has become a distinguished method of social work. It has certain characteristics.

Characteristics of Community Development

Following are the characteristics of community development:

1. It focuses on the whole community rather than on any one area or a group or a segment or of population. However, all the people need not necessarily participate in community development activities/ programmes.
2. It concentrates on the overall development of the community and attends the needs of the whole community. Usually, it does not attend any need in isolation.
3. It is always concerned with bringing social change.
4. It promotes problem-solving approach.
5. The foundation of community development is self-help and participation of local people, in whatever manner they can.
6. Community development usually involves utilization of local resources along with the help from governmental and voluntary agencies, NGOs. This help may be in the form of money/fund, infrastructural facilities, expertise, etc.
7. Community development considers both task goals and process goals. As a result, it strengthens the qualities of participation, self-direction and cooperation.
8. Community development is an ongoing process, and not a short period programme.
9. Community development is concerned about 'felt needs'. This involves community action, which is not forced but is realized with common consensus. Hence, it does not have programmes, which are conceived outside or inside the community by outside agencies or government departments, without participation of community people.

Let us focus on the elements of community development process.

Elements of Community Development Process

Following are the elements of community development process:

1. **Community:** As a whole, it is a unit of action. The definition of community varies from a geographical demarcation to an interest demarcation. It may vary in size, occupation, religion, and so forth. In other words, it explains the complexities and variables that need to be intervened in any community development process.

2. **Local initiatives and leadership:** They are very important factors in the community development process. The issue of the extent of importance given to local participation, and for the development of grass-roots level people, leadership plays a significant role in the overall development process. Involvement of local people in the development process includes identifying and defining the needs of the communities' and taking necessary actions to fulfil these needs. This process aims at meaningful participation of the local people not only for their overall development but of the development of the community itself. In other words, it tends to increase the competence of grass-roots level people in managing their own affairs. In this process, people learn by doing and gain experience.

3. **Utilization of resources:** Community development process requires utilization of local as well as outside resources at the optimum level. Sometimes to fulfil their needs, the available local resources can be used. Take, for example, the problem of unemployment, the unemployed youth can be given vocational training and be encouraged to start their business. For this, all the available resources within the community should be utilized.

   There are certain problems which can be dealt with at the community level itself. For the alleviation of poverty in the community, economic and social resources can be made available to people. Sometimes there arises a need to take the help of outside resources. In such a case, the community workers should take the responsibility to find out how these outside resources can be made available to the community without diluting the determination and strength of the community.

4. **Participation:** Community workers should ensure that all individuals and groups participate, get accommodated in the development process. Their participation is of immense use.

Community development is nothing but a means of bringing social change. Hence, proper attention must be paid to the intangible, qualitative, process oriented community development.

Community development can be successful only with the citizen's total participation. It also depends on the size of the community, scope of the endeavour across community sectors, extent of participation and relation between the existing power structures. One has to take into consideration the socio-economic aspects of the society as well. It is difficult to challenge social and economic injustices and actively confront the power hierarchy. When there is a necessity to take the support of the power structure, the community worker has to work out a way of ensuring social change without antagonizing "the hand" that can feed it.

In order to achieve community development, people must be enabled to develop their capacity to identify their problems and plan ways of solving things. In addition, people must be helped to develop their capacity and enhance their desire to participate in decision making related to greater social and economic development.

Indicators of Community Development

Although community development is a product of many elements, including changes in thinking, cultural beliefs, traditions, etc. the following indicators can generally be used to show the levels of development and welfare in a community:

1. Increases in social services such as good housing, health, education, nutrition, clean environment and sufficient clean and safe drinking water, etc.
2. Increase in income that enables families in a community to meet their needs.
3. Decrease in infant and maternal mortality.
4. Demand for modern technology.
5. Sustainable use of environment.
6. Eradication and/or reduction in poverty.

This shows that community development is a joint venture. It can include efforts and support from the government departments, NGOs, donors and the community as well. Remember, community development is always concerned with bringing about social change in the community.

It is the responsibility of the community to identify their members' problems or needs, formulate plans to solve them and implement these plans by utilizing to a large extent their own resources on a self-reliant basis.

In order to implement community development activities successfully, without discouraging the people, there must be transparency in the activities through regular exchange of information. This can be done through holding official meetings. There should be a strong leadership, which responds to the needs of the people. Leaders should be accountable to them. The community workers should—

1. Remain with the people. If possible, live with them (live in the community itself).

2. Learn from the community.
3. Identify the development priorities with them.
4. Plan together with people.
5. Look together for resources to implement the plans.
6. Collaborate with experts from other sectors to implement the plans.
7. Evaluate together with the people.

People are one of the basic resources for any development. Hence, all the common causes of development should be for the welfare of the people which in turn leads to community development.

Community development is an art. It is one of the means of initiating change. A variety of programmes can be organized for the development of the community. The nature of these programmes varies as per the situations from country to country, state to state and from community to community. In other words, situations can be defining features of this development.

The concept of community organization and development has changed over the years. Emphasis has changed in each decade since pre-independence and post-independence.

In 1930–1940s, the emphasis was on collaboration, consensus, co-operation, working together and adjustment.

In 1940–1950s, it was more on meeting needs, service delivery, welfare, process and integration.

In 1960–1970s, the emphasis was on social and economic progress and participation.

From the 1970s onwards till today, the emphasis is on expanding opportunities, power and political support.

The community worker should understand the power dynamics and social relations that govern the relationships between various structures. S/he should work towards social justice by bringing social change.

The backbone of the community development is people having the innate capacity to improve their lives. As people have the first hand knowledge of their problems and situations, it helps them to take action to bring the desired change.

Let us see the difference between community organization and community development.

DISTINCTION BETWEEN COMMUNITY ORGANIZATION AND COMMUNITY DEVELOPMENT

1. Community organization (CO) is a method of social work whereas community development (CD) is a programme planned to bring social change.
2. In CO, the emphasis is on process, but CD focuses on end/goal.

3. CO is a continuous process, without any time binding, and is achieved as per the pace and participation of people. CD is time-bound and one has to take action within a stipulated time to achieve the goals.

4. CO emphasizes people's participation whereas CD focuses on people's development.

5. Assistance of government and/or other agencies does not matter in CO. In CD, external assistance is sought and considered as important.

6. In CO, people are involved in planning and executing the programmes to solve their problems. In CD, external agencies plan the programme. People's participation is optional.

7. Very importantly, CO is universal to all communities but CD differs from community to community, people to people, according to the nature of the problem, needs, situations, etc.

8. Community organizers are usually people who bring social change (social change agents). CD personnel can be from any professional field other than social work such as economics, sociology, expert from agriculture, animal husbandry, technology, etc.

CO and CD are interrelated, though there are some differences. In other words, they are two sides of the same coin. It is better to use CD and CO for the betterment and development of human beings.

To summarize, both community organization and community development focus on fulfilling the needs of people. Both are concerned with problem-solving, working with people. To do this, they use many methods and approaches. There are a few differences between community organization and community development. As stated earlier, community organization focuses on the welfare areas of community life. For example, urban development, education, civic rights, etc. Community development focuses on total community life and its needs. It does not deal separately with only one aspect such as either health or shelter. Community development usually deals with basic needs such as adequate water supply, ration, etc. Methods used in community organization are fact finding, analysis, planning, conference, negotiations, etc. Community development uses many more methods in addition to these. In community organization, it is the agency which, with a representation of community, carries out services. It has some staff and workers. In community development, community people, those who wish to participate, can directly participate. In other words, community organization uses representational devices and delegates duties whereas community development emphasizes direct participation of community people. To live a peaceful life by fulfilling all basic needs is a basic right of all human beings. Everyone has a right to get equal opportunities for the economic and social development. Hence, it is necessary to have both community organization and community development programmes. The next chapter deals with community mobilization.

<h2 style="text-align:center">Review Questions</h2>

1. Define community. Explain different types of community.

2. Give any three definitions of community organization. Explain the need for community organization.

3. Illustrate different functions of community organization.

4. Define community organization. Explain the principles of community organization.

5. Explain in detail different stages of community organization.

6. Define community development. Illustrate the process of community development.

7. Illustrate the necessity of community development.

8. Explain the objectives of community development. Explain the characteristics of community development.

9. What are the assumptions of community development?

10. Illustrate different elements of community development process.

11. Distinguish between community organization and community development.

3

Community Mobilization

Community mobilization is the process of building community capacity to identify its members' priorities, resources, needs and solutions in such a way as to promote representative participation, good governance, accountability and peaceful change. It helps the people to bring positive social change. In community development, people's involvement in designing, planning, implementation and evaluation of the programmes and activities leads to sustainable development. Even if the development agencies leave the place, the development continues.

The communities, where development programmes are usually implemented, have typical background of chronic poverty, bad governance, conflict, power imbalance, insufficient facilities, etc. Hence, involving people right from the beginning of the development programmes helps them to prioritize their problems and needs. When members of the community participate directly or through their representatives in designing, implementing and monitoring the programme, it becomes their own programme. This sense of belongingness motivates them. This also gives an opportunity to all the people, irrespective of their gender, age, physical disability, ethnicity, religion, language, their minority or majority status, to share their capabilities, experiences and skills.

Peoples' participation can be in different forms, namely:

1. Passive participation
2. Participation as an informant
3. Participation by sharing knowledge and skills
4. Active participation.

Governance in general is related to the process of decision-making and its execution. Accountability is an essential characteristic of good governance, where the community workers/NGOs are accountable for their decisions to people affected by them. An ideal governance is accountable, transparent, just, responsive and participatory. Hence, good governance is a condition for all development activities. Good governance does not simply mean strong leadership and efficient administration. It refers to people's involvement, trust, honesty and a vision for the future. It is the responsibility of the organizations working with the community to avoid the pitfalls of jealousy and competition over scarce resources within communities. This can happen when aid or development opportunities are not carefully planned and communicated.

Community mobilization promotes:

1. Sustainable use of natural resources.
2. Access to information for all members of the community.
3. Opportunities for economic advancement.
4. Healthy practices and well-being for each community member.
5. Knowledge by awareness of their rights and the ability to advocate for themselves.

While mobilizing the community, one comes across different attitudes, norms, practices and behaviours of individuals as well as of groups. In all these circumstances, a community worker has to work. The community worker should be able to assess people's needs, help them to prioritize them, identify options for addressing them, and find solutions by using local resources. Often, such processes lead to structural changes within communities.

NEED FOR COMMUNITY MOBILIZATION

Community mobilization is a process of capacity building. It is a participatory partnership of organization and community who, together, plan, implement and evaluate the activities to improve the life of the people. Each community has a wide range of problems. Problems can be individual and/or collective. Problems such as social injustice and inequality often exist in most of the communities. There are situations when all kinds of resources are exhausted, the community worker has to assist the affected people, as this is the goal of community mobilization. Community mobilization involves strengthening the existing agencies and programmes and building community's resources. In other words, the organization has to work till the community becomes independent and sustain the activities.

The government or the NGOs are outsiders. They do not understand the needs and problems of a community in totality. If programmes are implemented without seeking participation of local people, there are less chances of success. The following four cases will help you understand the importance of community mobilization:

Case 1: An NGO, working for the development of people, decided to start an adult literacy class in a remote village. They approached the community and explained their plan. There was no proper place to conduct the literacy class. They put a condition that the community should participate in building literacy class. It was decided that the NGO will provide material required for the construction of classroom and people will provide the land and their labour.

Case 2: The village X has literacy rate below 30. An NGO approached this village and organized a meeting of local people to explain the importance of literacy. For this, the NGO used the audio-visuals and gave practical/live examples. People were convinced and understood the importance of literacy and decided to participate in this programme. But, there was no place to conduct literacy class. It was decided that the young people of this village would go to collect the wood needed for the construction of the literacy centre. Women decided that they will fetch water required for the construction and will help in plastering the walls. The NGO decided to sponsor metal sheets required for the roof of the centre. Due to the active involvement of the people, the centre was ready within three months.

Case 3: In village Y, the NGO decided to start a literacy centre, but could not do so. The reason was lack of proper place to conduct the activity and the community could not mobilize everybody's contribution.

Case 4: In another village, a literacy centre for women was started. Within a few days, it was realized that young mothers could not attend the literacy class, as they had nobody to take care of their babies. The NGO organized a meeting of local people and put the problem before them. After discussion, the community decided to set up a separate place, near the literacy centre, where the young children could be kept. The question of looking after these children was also solved by the elderly women. A few grandmothers came forward and volunteered their services. The NGO decided to train these grandmothers in child development.

The above four cases explain us the importance of community participation in achieving the common goals and objectives. In Cases 1 and 2, we see how community mobilization has helped in implementation of the programmes. From Case 4, we learn that it is important to involve not only those who are directly concerned with the problem (young women learners who had children), but also other people in the community (the grandmothers) who could be of immense help.

In short, community mobilization promotes:

1. Participation and involvement of everyone living in the community.
2. Mobilization of community resources.
3. Local ownership and the sustainability of the activities.
4. Empowerment and self-management.
5. Commitment of the people.

Usually community mobilization is possible if the objectives or goals of the programme are useful and beneficial to majority of the people in the community. In the beginning, the community worker has to take initiatives and try to implement new ideas with the help of the people. If people are convinced that the programmes are for their betterment, they will come forward and contribute.

Community mobilization is a planned process. It encourages the active commitment of one or several members of the society in order to achieve a common goal. It also gives an opportunity to people to come together, understand the common issues that affect their lives. This helps them to mobilize resources—human, material and financial—needed to achieve the common goal.

BENEFITS OF COMMUNITY MOBILIZATION

Community mobilization is an organizational endeavour. More than one organization can work simultaneously in one community and participate in the process of enabling communities to become self-sustaining. Each and every organization has something to contribute to the process. Each organization is responsible for doing what they do best and integrating their services with other organizations. Remember, the ultimate goal of community mobilization is to build up local leadership and make them self-reliant.

Community mobilization has long-term as well as short-term benefits, which are as follows.

Long-term Benefits

1. Active involvement of community helps us to understand its needs and concerns in a better perspective. The community knows its needs and is aware of availability of resources. People know each other and are familiar with their culture. When people participate in identifying problems, prioritizing them, planning an action and taking decisions, this will increase the sense of belongingness, ownership and responsibility for the programme.
2. Community partnership leads towards sustainable development.
3. It increases transparency and easy accessibility to information and services.
4. It is also more cost-effective as outside and local resources are utilized. The coordination increases cooperation among them.
5. It reduces the dependency of the community members on outside aid, as they are able to identify and solve their problems.
6. Communities respond very fast during crisis or disaster period as they have learned not only to identify needs but prioritize them as well.

7. Political leaders, especially at the local level, gain greater credibility in their constituencies as they are familiar with local needs. This can be used in building a better lobby at the national level with decision makers for bringing more development plans/programmes. Hence, they may get more local support.

Short-term and Immediate Benefits

1. Utilizes local resources—both human and material.
2. Includes the excluded groups, such as women, youth, and persons with disabilities, the elderly and religious or ethnic minorities.
3. Fosters strong relationships between local self government, community members, business community, local organizations and NGOs.
4. Increases participatory decision making process by bringing people with diverse interests, needs, and problems together.
5. Ensures local ownership of development.
6. Promotes active participation of people.

Community mobilization involves building up local leadership, strengthening their capacities and building confidence so that local people can take more responsibilities.

Community mobilization is a process where community worker and local people work together with mutual understanding to address the local needs and problems. The objective is to support and strengthen the community's natively available (local) resources. This, in turn, increases a sense of ownership. This also increases the chances that the community will continue to work together even after the outsider agency departs after winding up its programme.

The community worker's role is to coordinate the services and programmes with the local people and the outside agencies, if needed. Taking active and willing participation of community people is at the heart of community mobilization.

PREPARING FOR COMMUNITY MOBILIZATION

Community mobilization is often initiated by an external agency or organization. The external organization may be governmental or non-governmental organization. They may be from local, district, state, national, and international levels or may be a combination of the above levels. They respond to the needs or problems of the community.

PREREQUISITES FOR STARTING MOBILIZATION

1. One should know whether the community is interested in receiving outsider's help. It is very important in community mobilization that

the community should be willing to take help from outsider and invest in participation. Once community gives its green signal or acceptance, the organization can start working with them. Meanwhile, the organization can see and assess the sources and magnitude of the problems.

2. As an outsider, the organization must understand the political structure in the community. It is difficult to work in an unstable political environment. Working in an unstable political environment may lead to failure. However, the chances of support from political parties increase if there are strong political alliances.

3. The study of socio-cultural context is a must in community mobilization. One should thoroughly understand the culture of a community. Develop a plan which is sensitive towards their beliefs and attitudes. While doing this, one should also pay attention towards the diversity of a society. One should try to include the excluded people as well. The diversity of cultures increases cultural differences, which creates hurdles in smooth functioning. Still, it is necessary to address the problems in a culturally appropriate manner.

4. It is a necessity to know community's resources. This includes the identification of the owners and providers of resources. This also gives a clear picture of the people deprived of these resources. This information helps to coordinate services at local, state, national and international levels. It is also important to examine how the community organizes itself.

5. One should realize the accessibility of the community. It is important to know the barriers and remedies to deal with them.

INITIAL CONTACT WITH THE COMMUNITY

Before starting any programme or activity, it is very important to know the community. Understanding community practices, traditions, culture helps the community worker in identifying appropriate approaches to be used for community development.

The community worker should take every opportunity to meet people informally at different locations and different occasions. For example, *panchayat, mandir, masjid, samaj mandir*, cooperatives, youth, *mahila mandals*, common place where women gather for fetching water, school, *anganwadi*, etc. Festivals such as *Ganeshotsav, Navratri*, Eid, X'mas, and marriages in the community provide occasions for interacting with people.

One can find out the natural gathering points and traditions related to social gatherings and tap them. This is an excellent way to identify the key persons and leaders and build a relationship/rapport. For example, tea time is a common practice in most of the communities. So 'tea meeting' at tea stalls is the best place to meet people and start initial contacts. This effort helps in building community contact. Another very striking place is grocery shop. This place is useful for getting and disseminating the information. You can reach to a large number of people through these places. In some places, there are bulletin boards installed near these stores, where you can find notices put up about various programmes/activities taking place in a community. Another important juncture of meeting people is cultural programmes, festivals, celebrations, where a large number of people gather. At these occasions, the community worker can meet people, talk to them and gather detailed information about the community.

The community worker can build an informal network with women by approaching them at different places such as grocery shops, vegetable shops, schools where their children study, wells/bore wells, hair salon, etc. There is a possibility that you may be able to identify a few women who can give you information about the community, its problems, power structure, etc.

Try to meet the youth separately. They are the ideal bridge in most communities. They can explain the problems of the community along with their causes/sources. Remember, building trust and relationships are fundamental aspects of working with communities. This is necessary when you are working in a new culture or in a set up where you are less familiar with that culture and different forms of oppression are prevalent there. Establishing rapport and gaining trust of people requires time. Hence, the community worker should be patient and should not be in a hurry. The community worker should make frequent visits to the places where majority of people gather and spend time with them.

One can collect information about the selected community through newspaper articles. The Internet is also an important source of information. The community worker should make all attempts to get maximum information about the community where he wants to work.

Explore whether any organization is already working in the same community/area. If yes, try to get access to the community through this organization. Meet the authorities and workers of this organization and explore on which issues they are working, and if there is any possibility of coordinating with them. Through them, you can reach the community and establish rapport with people. After discussing and in consultation with the key persons and leaders in the community, you can organize the first meeting. Here, you can explain about your organization, its aims and objectives, funding nature, reason/s for working in that particular community and what cooperation you want from the community, etc.

The meeting should be organized as per the convenience of people. The community worker should make sure that s/he arrives on time for the meeting. Never make people to wait for you. Use a simple and unambiguous language which everyone can understand. It should be culturally sensitive to be correctively perceived and understood. Make sure that information delivered reaches to each and everyone, whosoever attends meeting.

Remember, first impression is very important while working with the communities. People may draw conclusions about you and your organization based on how you conduct the meeting, how you speak and deliver the information, your overall behaviour in and after the meeting. Show respect towards community people (especially to those who are in problem). Your behaviour should reflect your earnest desire and sincerity to do something for people. Consistency and transparency are essential qualities for building trust and confidence between organization and the members of the community. The community worker must ensure that after the first formal meeting, the follow-up action is immediately taken.

COORDINATING COMMUNITY MOBILIZATION

Coordination is essential if more than one organization is working in the same area or community. This avoids duplication of services. Sometimes, organizations feel threatened by others. Instead of seeking cooperation as an opportunity to reach more people, rivalry arises. They prefer to work in isolation instead of extending cooperation. In such a situation, services may be duplicated; other services and needs may be overlooked. There is a possibility that a few people may take benefit from all organizations and some needy people may be deprived of these facilities. As a result, the ultimate goal of community development may be defeated. Hence, it is very essential to coordinate and cooperate with each other. If possible, the organizations can form an inter-agency team or a group. The main responsibility of this group would be to see that the duplication of work does not take place.

COMMUNICATION

Communication plays a vital role in seeking coordination. There should be an open channel of communication. Communication should be in both forms—written and oral. An ongoing dialogue with all the people is the key to achieve success.

ENTERING THE COMMUNITY

Before starting actual programmes/activities, it is very important to know the community. The initial visit plays a vital role in establishing rapport with the people. The success of the programme depends on how you enter in the community, the people you meet, and the way you convince them about your plans. The initial contact also helps to set expectations and gather information which may be important in planning the programme and activities. Decisions made at this phase influence the entire mobilization process. Let us see its utility with the following examples.

Case 5: A community worker arrives in a community which is dominated by a particular religion. S/he meets a few women and invites them to an information giving meeting to be organized the next day. The next day when s/he arrives for the meeting, s/he finds herself/himself alone at the venue of the meeting. S/he waits but no one turns up. S/he talks to a few passersby, who advise her/him to meet the religious leader.

The community worker meets the religious leader and explains about the objective of his/her visit and informs about the organization. S/he also explains how the literacy classes will help the women to acquire literacy along with some income generating skills. At the end of the discussion, the community worker requests the leader to appeal to the people, especially women, to attend the programme.

A few days later, the community worker once again organizes a meeting, where s/he invites the leader as well. This automatically attracts a large crowd.

Case 6: In another example, in a village, the community worker wanted to organize a meeting of women at *panchayat's* office. Women did not turn up. When s/he met the *sarpanch*, s/he came to know that the *panchayat* office is always crowded with men, where women cannot come. S/he changed the venue and organized the meeting at *anganwadi*. Many women attended this meeting.

Cases 5 and 6 make us re-think over the following issues:

1. Why the community worker did not get a response from the community, especially from women, on the first day of the meeting?
2. What really went wrong?
3. How did s/he finally solve the problem?
4. What approach one has to follow while entering in a new community?
5. What are the important things a community worker needs to remember while entering in a community?

The community worker should always remember that s/he cannot organize meetings directly without respecting the customs of that community. One needs to respect the culture and social practices of the people. It is essential to take support of recognized power of authorities, as and when needed, to carry out the activities smoothly and successfully. In the above examples, the community worker was an outsider. Even if the community worker is from the same community or village, it is important that s/he should respect the local cultural norms. S/he should know and respect the social values and taboos of the community and should avoid challenging them.

Therefore, entry into a community is not always that easy. The community worker must realize the need to identify the right people in the community, who can explain to her/him the codes, taboos and rules of the com-munity. S/he must also identify the people who can introduce her/him to the most influential members of the community.

While working with the people, the community worker should be:

1. Humble
2. Tolerant and self-restrained
3. Honest
4. Open
5. Persuasive
6. Patient
7. Convinced about what s/he is doing.

It also depends on the community worker's attitude, body language and verbal communication as it determines whether the community accepts or rejects him/her. The community worker must have good listening skills and accommodative nature, while working with the people.

Hence, one can enter into the community by contacting following one or more people, depending on the type of community (tribal, rural or urban):

1. *Bhagat*
2. In-charge of *mandir*/mosque/church/*gurudwara* person
3. *Panchayat* head/members
4. School teacher/headmaster/principal
5. *Anganwadi* worker/*balwadi* teacher
6. Health worker (ASHA worker)
7. President/members of different *mandals* such as youth, *mahila*, *ganesh*, gymkhana, etc.
8. Presidents/members of cooperatives, *patpedhis*, *dairy*, etc.
9. SHG members
10. Local political leaders or *dadas*
11. Any influential person/s.

Before conducting any formal meeting, the community worker needs to pay two to three visits and more if required. S/he should talk to the people informally to find out the local customs, traditions, and problems of that area.

Functioning of the Community

Each community has its own way of working. It has unwritten rules and regulations, which are followed by the people residing in that particular area or community. There are certain powerful people who are the decision makers. This power is unequally distributed. Without understanding these factors, if someone tries to work, then there are chances of conflict. By using appropriate tools and techniques, one can understand the functioning of community. The following examples will help us to understand this in a better way.

Case 7: The village 'X' is located in a drought-prone district. Every year, they have less rainfall, which results in scarcity of drinking water.

The youth group from this village meets an international NGO, working at the district level, explains the problem and requests them to do something to overcome this problem. After a couple of meetings with youth, the NGO agrees to the proposal of constructing a well. The representatives of the NGO visit the village. Without consulting the elderly members of the community, they select a site for the construction of well. The work begins. Within a few months, the work is completed.

They organize a function after completion of the work. Representatives of the NGO and government officials attend the function. But none of the elders of that community turns up.

The representatives of the NGO get surprised. After the function, they meet the seniors, elderly people of the community to find out the reasons for non participation. The elderly person, who was also the spiritual leader, told the representatives that, the site chosen for digging the well was a burial place in earlier days. According to them, it was a taboo to drink water from that place. Hence, they will not use the water.

The NGO representatives realized their mistake of not consulting the elderly people before starting the construction of the well. Even the youth group realized their mistake for not taking into confidence the elderly people. The overenthusiasm of showing that they can work on their own was futile.

One can learn a lesson from this example. Before starting any work in a community, one should know:

1. Who are the decision makers in that particular area?
2. Who holds the power?
3. Who are the power groups?

In the above example, the NGO was an outside agency and they entered into an unknown territory. Though the youth group from the village approached them, the NGO did not make any efforts to know the community. The NGO was neither aware about the social, cultural and administrative structure of the village, nor the real power structure. At the end, it had to face a failure. Though the well was constructed, the problem of drinking water scarcity was not solved. It was just wastage of funds, time and resources. By using participatory tools and techniques, one can collect information about the community.

Following are some of the tools and techniques for collecting information about the community. How to do community mapping through participatory appraisal is discussed in Chapter 5.

1. Survey
2. Questionnaire

3. Observation
4. Group interviews
5. Focus group discussions
6. Community mapping
7. Listening to people
8. Interviews—structured and unstructured
9. Brainstorming
10. Stories, proverbs
11. Secondary data such as records, reports and studies, etc.

For example, if one wants to know the history of a particular village, one can collect chronological events data such as significance of the name of the village, the people who founded it, major events that have occurred through time, etc.

Following are some of the participatory tools mostly used in understanding the community:

1. Mapping (e.g. community mapping)
2. Calendars (e.g. seasonal calendars)
3. Matrices (e.g. simple and preference ranking matrices)
4. Diagrams (e.g. Venn diagrams).

The details of these tools and how they are used are given in Chapter 5.

Challenges

Entering a new community and establishing contacts is a challenging task. The community worker should keep in mind the following important things:

1. While establishing contacts with the community and gathering information, you come across the key informants. They will supply you information and in turn expect many things. Some of them may take an advantage and seize an opportunity to meet other leaders. They themselves start thinking and behaving as if they are your leaders. As a community worker, you must remember not to make any false promises about anything. Just listen to all self-declared leaders. Do not share what one person has shared about other leaders.

2. It is impossible to know everything about every group within a community and their culture. Remember, you are an outsider. Try to get information as much as possible. Do not be afraid of showing ignorance. You can always say that, 'I know very little about your culture and customs. I would like to understand and learn it so that it will help me in building community and working with you.'

3. If you are working in a community where multi-cultural people reside (for example, slums of Mumbai city or any other metropolis),

you have to use many skills. For example, linguistic skills. There will be several sub-groups with different political affiliations, socio-economic backgrounds, original resident and migrants, etc. As a community worker, it is challenging to work in this situation as you should remain careful not to create further tensions. Remain neutral, even though you belong to the same culture or same political party. Remain impartial. This will help in avoiding potential conflict situations.

TECHNIQUES FOR MOBILIZING A COMMUNITY

The success of any programme depends on community participation. Many times, problems are there but they are not viewed as 'problems'. They become hindrance in the overall development. For successful mobilization, one can focus on the following steps:

1. Identify the problem.
2. Plan and select a strategy to solve the problem.
3. Identify key actors and stakeholders.
4. Mobilize these key actors and stakeholders for action.
5. Implement activities to work towards a solution.
6. Assess the results of the activities carried out to solve the problem.
7. Improve activities based on the findings of the assessment.

The following case will help you to understand how to follow the above steps.

Case 8: In a village, the community worker realizes that there is an absenteeism of women from many programmes, even though they are directly related to them. The community worker decides to pay home visits and find out the reasons.

In the home visit, the community worker came to understand that there were no toilets in the village and people used open space for this purpose. Women faced lots of problems, especially during summer; they could not go for toilet during the day time, as all the crops were removed from fields. Water scarcity was also a big problem during summer and women had to walk long distance for fetching water. Due to this, most of the women had health related problems such as headache, backache, stomach upset, vomiting, etc.

The community worker wrote a play. With the help of women, they performed this play in the village. It touched the hearts of the members of the community, especially the males and many cried.

This was performed for a few times. This was followed by conducting meetings of different groups. The community worker personally met the prominent people (decision makers) such as *panchayat* members, religious leaders, heads of families, chairpersons of cooperatives, etc. The community worker also gathered information about government schemes for constructing toilets in the village and shared this information with people. After two months, a special *Gram Sabha* was called by *Sarpanch*. A unanimous decision was taken to construct toilets and to dig *bore wells* and *hand pumps* in the village. The strategy was decided democratically for the welfare of the people.

In the above case, the community worker used folklore drama (street play) as a technique to mobilize community, creating an emotional reaction. The drama, followed by meetings, made it clear that there was a need for change in the community. Other tools used were home visits, dissemination of information on government schemes, etc.

The community worker followed the following steps:

1. Identify the problem (toilets, water scarcity).
2. Plan and select a strategy to solve the problem (wrote a play for sensitization on the issue, performed it with the involvement of local people).
3. Identify key actors and stakeholders (women, village chief, *panchayat* members, religious leaders, cooperative chairpersons, heads of families).
4. Mobilize these key actors and stakeholders for action (discussions, meetings, dissemination of information, calling special *Gram Sabha* and planning on what to do and how).
5. Implement activities to work towards a solution (taking democratic decision of construction of toilets and digging wells and hand-pumps and working on it).
6. Assess the results of the activities carried out to solve the problem (follow-up of decision).

The community mobilization process should answer the following questions:

1. What is the nature of the problem?
2. What is the extent of its seriousness?
3. What is the scope of the problem, i.e. how many people are affected by it?
4. When and where does the problem manifest itself?
5. Is it an emerging or a chronic problem?
6. What are the causes of the problems? One should find out immediate and basic causes of the problem.
7. What are the long-term causes?
8. What resources are available within and outside the community to address the problem?
9. Is there any agency that is addressing this problem or programmes relevant to the problem? If yes, what are the reasons that people are not receiving benefits of these programmes?
10. What action the local people are taking on their own?

11. How public, voluntary resources could possibly be used to deal with this problem?

The community worker must be able to guess as to who will be influential in reducing the problem, in what way influential people can participate in the problem reduction process, etc.

The community workers who are working at the community level must remember that mobilization becomes easier when the problem or issue is common and people want to resolve it. Several methods of community sensitization and mobilization exist. Community workers should choose the most effective and appropriate methods which can address the issue. Solving any problem requires effective planning. It also requires distribution of different roles to community people and their active participation in implementation of the plan.

The community worker also integrates marginalized groups of individuals in development activities. Marginalization can be caused by several factors such as:

1. Extreme poverty
2. Physical and mental disabilities
3. Sex/gender discrimination
4. Class or caste
5. Ethnicity or tribal
6. Religion.

The integration of marginalized groups in development activities depends on the observation skills of the community worker along with his/her thorough knowledge of the community. The community worker should make special efforts to establish contacts with these groups, build up rapport with and confidence in them. While planning activities, the community worker should involve marginalized people, so as to ensure that their special needs are addressed.

PHASES OF COMMUNITY MOBILIZATION

As stated earlier, community mobilization is a process which goes through different phases. It must be conducted with trust, participation and inclusion of all people. The community worker must listen to their views and opinions, which help to create a trust and a sense of ownership in the process. This takes time, especially if the organization is new in that area/community. The broad phases are discussed here in detail.

1. **Assessment:**   The assessment of community needs and resources is the first phase in community mobilization. It is essential to find out the needs and problems, their causes and effects. Once you know and understand the problem from all angles, it becomes easier to

plan actions/to take further steps to solve them. While assessing the needs, it is also important to find what resources the individuals and community have. This will help you to understand what is still needed. The assessment must be inclusive and should cover all aspects—economic, social, religious and cultural factors.

The assessment of needs and resources should be done with the involvement of community people. To do this, different methods are adopted. This is discussed in detail in Chapter 5. The involvement of community people in the process since the beginning gives a feel of ownership of the programme, which ensures sustainability. They feel empowered. Through assessment, one needs to gather geographic and demographic information, which is a prerequisite for developing a community based programme.

The gathered information should be analyzed based on the following aspects:

    i. Demographic features of population
   ii. Economic activities
  iii. Social stratification and power relations
   iv. Political structure
    v. Leadership style and its influence, impact
   vi. Cultural aspects (traditions)
  vii. Health status
 viii. Educational/literacy status
   ix. Any other organizations working in that area, its objectives and activities
    x. Critical issues, problems and needs of the community
   xi. Resources available.

The above information will help the community worker to understand the community in a better manner.

2. **Programme planning:** Once the assessment is over, one needs to analyze the data. Based on the available resources, one should plan the programme and activities. Planning helps to execute programmes in an efficient manner. This is a very crucial phase. One can use existing resources from the community. In addition to this, the community worker can have a network with other agencies, may be from outside and coordinate with them. It is essential to have networking and coordination with governmental agencies and NGOs working in that area. The organizations should find out the expertise of the people, their capacities and abilities, so that they can be involved in the programme. The community worker should remember that people often work at different speed, for many reasons. Accordingly, planning is done. This will ultimately help in estimating the needs and solving the problems. The community

worker should make maximum utilization of local resources—human as well as material.

3. **Preparation of action plan:** The action plan should include the current status of the community and where it intends to lead. Involving people in preparation of action plan means involving people in decision-making process. By doing this, people can discover their potential to address their own problems by themselves. By involving community people in preparation of action plan, their priorities get reflected in the plan. The community worker's main role in this phase is to ensure and facilitate the people's participation. In planning, one should have clear vision, where do the communities want to go? They should be able to answer the following questions:

   i. What do we/you want? (goal)
   ii. What do we/they have? (resources)
   iii. How do we use? (for optimal use)
   iv. What do we have to get? (outside resources)
   v. What will happen when we take action? (implementation)
   vi. How are we going to assess the results? (evaluation)

The draft action plan should be presented before the whole community for refinement and final approval. Getting consensus from all people is very important. The duration of the action plan depends on the issue and involvement of people to solve them. For example, it may require one year, two years, and five years or may be more. The action plan should include description of activities and its tentative duration. Some people call this the calendar of activities. It contains work distribution as per the activities and different strategies to be adopted to complete different tasks. Work plan is essential in all development programmes. This helps to answer the inevitable questions from the community members about the outcome and the time required for the accomplishment of the task. It is also a good tool for coordinating among team members as well as other departments. The plan should be flexible. For example, you have decided to have a training programme for local people in this month. Due to natural calamities, say, flood, it is not possible to conduct the training programme. In this situation, you can postpone it and attend to the present problems and help people affected by this disaster.

The work plan should be based on the information collected from the community showing selection of target areas, organizations with whom networking and collaboration is possible and number of beneficiaries, strategies to be used, etc. Coordination with other agencies including government agencies at international, national, state or district level, civil society, etc. should be mentioned in the plan.

The draft action plan should be presented to the whole community to get comments and final approval.

4. **Implementation:** All the programmes should be implemented with the help of local people. This is a very delicate phase in community mobilization process, because conflicts and power challenges may arise in this phase. Through community mobilization process, you are reaching to the unreached. So, it may challenge the established people. Hence, the community worker should be very alert. Such issues are very sensitive and should be handled very carefully, tactfully and respectfully before they become big ones, and go out of control. How to handle conflict is discussed in detail in Chapter 7.

5. **Monitoring and evaluation:** Monitoring and evaluation are very important components of any programme, especially if it is related to development. Monitoring means "regularly collecting, reviewing, reporting and acting on information". In monitoring, information is systematically collected throughout the process for the purpose of management and decision-making. Monitoring is generally used to see performance against targets. While planning the programmes, one needs to work out the methods of monitoring and evaluating the different aspects of the programme. It should be an integral part of planning. Monitoring gives direction to the programme. It tells us the progress of the programme, whether we are on the right track or not. Monitoring is much more than data collection. The data collected should be reviewed and processed, which can help in decision-making. Monitoring is an internal learning tool. It helps in maintaining the quality of work. It also promotes accountability. Based on monitoring reports, if required, one can make changes in implementation strategies and methodologies as well.

Monitoring helps us to know the strengths and weaknesses of the programme. It informs us whether the resources, money and time are wasted or utilized properly. Monitoring also tells us whether it is moving in the right direction or not. It ensures people's participation, helps to know the areas where people require training. It helps to identify the emerging problems, which need attention. Monitoring always helps to know whether we are moving towards achieving our goals. It helps us to avoid getting off the track.

Evaluation is assessment of impact of the action. It helps us in decision-making and designing future programmes. Evaluation answers how it was carried out, what should have been planned instead of present action, etc. It tells us what worked and what did not? Evaluation also gives reasons for the same. It tells us whether the needs of the community are fulfilled or not. It also suggests emergence of new needs of the community.

In this process of evaluation, one needs to take into consideration the participation of the community. The community worker should also monitor the capacity building of the people. This ensures the future sustainability of the programmes. Monitoring and evaluation should focus on the whole process, and not only on programme outcomes. It should also examine the conflict situations and power struggles. Certain strategies should be decided and used to handle the conflict situations. This will determine the success of the programme.

6. **Phase out stage:** The purpose of community mobilization is building capacity and empowering people. Making people self-reliant is the goal of this process. Once this is achieved, the outside organizations should start phasing out of the community. The organization must inform the community people about different development schemes to be offered by national and international organizations. This will help the community to sustain even after the withdrawal of the organization.

Table 3.1 explains the stages, tools and activities to be conducted during community mobilization. This is a general outline. One may add or delete a stage as per the local situations.

Table 3.1   Tools and activities for community mobilization

Stages	Activities	Tools	Description
Pre-visit	• Initial visit to community • Rapid assessment (informally) • Focus groups • Target area selection • Introductory meetings	• Initial visits • Checklist • Focus group— guidelines	• List of things to be observed/inquired about • List of things that can be obtained remotely
Understanding community	• PRA • Preparation of community profile • Field-based observations	• PRA tools and interview schedules (semi-structured)	• Transect walk, ranking, mapping, matrix, Venn diagram, etc.
Implementation of activities/ programmes	• Selection of target groups • Prioritizing needs/problems • Preparation of action plan • Developing local leadership • Capacity building • Community contribution • Budget management • Advocacy and networking	• Mapping • Action planning process • Meetings	• Prioritizing issues and selecting target groups as per the objectives • Steps for action how to go about • Defining the roles and responsibilities
Evaluation	• Con-current evaluation • Formative evaluation • Summative evaluation	• Evaluation tools—written and oral • Assessment of impact (scoring sheet)	• Based on objectives, evaluation tools be developed • Concrete indicators of project impact
Handover	• Community members and local self-government	• Exit strategy checklist • Leadership hand-over checklist	• Sample list of roles and responsibilities and coordination

COMMUNITY CONTRIBUTION

Each activity requires some element of community investment. It reflects community's commitment and the value they attribute to the activity/programme. Community contribution may be in the form of cash or in kind, or in the form of labour and time.

CHALLENGES OF COMMUNITY MOBILIZATION

There are many challenges in community mobilization. In today's globalized world, everybody has to struggle to live in better condition. So, time is a major challenge in community mobilization. People are busy in earning their bread and butter for their survival. Community mobilization is an ongoing process. To succeed, there must be a collective, organized and cooperative effort among the participants. This requires a lot of time. People from different backgrounds need to come together, participate in activities and programmes, reach a consensus and take decisions on what action to be taken. This requires a lot of time. People should be ready to devote their time in all these activities.

Communication is another challenge in community mobilization. A community is a mixture of different cultures, with multi-lingual people. Reaching people by using modern communication techniques is a challenge. Technological advancement, at times, is also responsible for miscommunication. For example, phone may not be reachable due to disturbance in network or traffic jam prevents a person in reaching his/her venue on time.

Coming to a **consensus** and taking decision is often a challenge as a large number of people are involved in community mobilization. Their priorities and goals may vary. Each one has a different perception. It takes a lot of time to reach to a consensus and decide for their immediate needs. Hence, it is very important to establish a common vision built on **common goals**. **Cost** is another very important factor in community mobilization. If the time spent is too long, it increases the cost as well. It may lead to lack of financial support. Hence, a **good coordination** is required. Coordination of services can prevent duplication of work and be more cost effective.

LEADERSHIP AND CAPACITY BUILDING

For sustainable development, it is necessary to develop local leadership and build their capacities. Whether it is a governmental project or NGO working in the community, finally, they have to hand over the project to the community people. It is the community which continues the work. Hence, developing local leadership and building their capacities is a part of community development programmes. It is necessary to involve people and assign them some responsibilities. This involves allowing them to use their knowledge and skills and train them in areas where they lack expertise. Building their capacity slowly helps the community to sustain the programme in future, even if the organizations withdraw.

Capacity building is a continuous process. It involves demonstration, training, mentoring and technical assistance. NGOs working in the community should identify a few people. The selection process must start from the day the organization enters the community. Through observation and continuous dialogues, people with leadership potentials can be tapped. Once the community worker has enough confidence in these people, s/he assigns them certain tasks, puts responsibilities on them and observes and then accordingly develops their capacities.

Demonstration involves showing what is possible and what is expected. Generate enthusiasm in them. Take them to different projects by organizing expository visits.

Capacity building helps the people to empower themselves. This can be possible if they are involved in facilitating the process such as conflict resolution, collection and analysis of data, problem-solving, programme planning and implementation, resource mobilization, motivation of people, etc.

Empowerment is an outcome. Power within the people should be recognized and promoted. People should be encouraged to take decisions and implement their decisions. For this, they should be equipped with proper knowledge and information about problems. Their abilities can be developed through training.

The main motto of the community mobilization process is to develop the capacity of people. Do not undermine, overlook or neglect this. Instead of entering a community with prescribed plans, it is essential to build upon the strengths and resources that already exist there. By training the local community, they will be able to manage and sustain the programme over time.

Training should mainly focus on developing different skills such as communication skills, negotiation skills and decision making skills. If it is an experiential training, it is the most useful one. People can learn theory and practice it immediately in the field and then the theory inputs can be given to enrich their experience. So, learning is concretized. They get an opportunity to practice newly acquired knowledge and skills, apply them in practical settings, assess their own attitudes and reflect the experience.

Training content varies from community to community, and the needs of groups and programme objectives. Most of the trainings are related to administering the project. Regular trainings are needed in the following areas:

1. Proposal writing, budgeting, finance and accounting
2. Management
3. Monitoring and evaluation and reporting
4. Networking and advocacy
5. Legal formalities.

COMMUNITY PARTICIPATION

Community mobilization is not possible without community participation. Their participation is very much essential in assessing needs and problems, planning and implementation of action and evaluation of the programme outcome. The involvement of community people varies. It is the responsibility of the organizations to maximize people's participation.

The organization/s working with the communities must understand their political, social and cultural issues. They should be able to identify the power structure, community leaders and decision makers, the process of decision making, etc. This will help to plan their strategies for executing different activities.

The organization and the community worker should focus on political leaders' views and opinions about the problems of the community. They should try to find out whether the leaders have taken any action to solve these problems. They must understand the role relationship between men and women. The knowledge of the status of the women, their economic conditions, health and educational status in the community helps the worker to plan activities in a better way. In addition to this, the community worker should explore other issues such as unemployment, poverty, water, transportation, etc.

BARRIERS TO PARTICIPATION

Community mobilization needs participation of all people. Sometimes only a few people participate in all the activities whereas others do not. None can force people to participate. The organizations and community workers should find reasons of/barriers to non-participation and make efforts to seek their participation. Following are some of the reasons for non-participation of people:

1. **Physical limits:** The distance between the venue and people's residence can be a major cause for their non-participation. This may also be the reason for not receiving any information (non-communication). They have to travel a long distance to participate and no public transportation is available. Physical disability can also be one of the reasons for non-participation.

2. **Cultural restriction:** This is a very important factor for less or non-participation of people. There are many communities which culturally prohibit men and women to meet publically on the same platform. In some communities, only the community leader participates in decision-making and others are not allowed to give their opinions. This restriction demotivates them to attend the meeting. At times, the family and husbands forbid wives to participate. This results in the lower attendance of women in the

meeting. Certain people feel that their primary responsibility is towards family, and not community.

3. **Language and literacy:** Language can be an important barrier to participation in the meeting. Those who do not speak the common language, or are illiterate, may feel intimidated by large groups. They feel left out. They lose interest as they cannot understand the proceedings. They may feel that they do not have anything to offer. This may affect their self-esteem very badly.

4. **Misunderstanding:** Lack of complete information about the purpose of the meeting, the issues to be discussed and the lack of clarity about the target beneficiaries may result in misunderstanding in people. This affects the attendance at meeting.

5. **Time:** Time could be a major constraint for participation. People have to prioritize their attendance according to their family responsibilities, personal/official/business work. At times, the community takes a backseat.

The organizations and community workers should try to understand these barriers and use certain strategies to overcome them so that people's participation can be sought, which is a necessary prerequisite for the overall development of the community.

TRUST BUILDING

Mutual trust is crucial for working in the community. Building this trust is an important prerequisite for community mobilization. The individuals should feel safe to share their opinion/s, feeling/s. Building trust is a continuous process and can be built up throughout the process of community organization by observing the following factors:

1. Being punctual
2. Keeping promises (words)
3. Taking into consideration the opinions of people and acknowledging people's contribution, inputs
4. Being transparent in all processes including decision-making, finance, sharing information about the programmes, policies, etc.
5. Being accountable for inputs as well as outputs, success as well as failures
6. Being accountable and open about finances by sharing income, costs, donations, sponsors, etc.

WORKING IN TEAMS

Once the tasks are decided, it is better to delegate responsibilities to each group. Teams can be formed. Each team should have community members, representatives of marginalized people, women and representatives from the organization. Working in small teams helps in completing the tasks faster. Whenever needed, the community worker can call a meeting of team leaders and ask them to share information about task progress, and difficulties faced by them. This sharing helps to know all the teams about each other's progress and difficulties.

Each team should have a cocoordinator who can be called team leader. The role of a team leader is to:

1. Get the assigned work done from team members.
2. Keep group members united and maintain transparency among them.
3. Resolve conflicts, if any, within and outside the team.
4. Recognize power structure and manage accordingly.
5. Manage smooth flow of communication with team members and others.
6. Build the capacity of self and the group members (using their knowledge and skills and training them in areas where they lack expertise).

The community worker should give a chance to people to share their experiences with each other. Sharing informs us what works and what does not work. This helps to plan new strategies for achieving goals. Sharing experiences helps in capacity building. As stated earlier, community mobilization is a process that empowers community people to organize themselves and solve their problems on their own. Working in small teams and sharing with each other helps people to cooperate and coordinate.

While the people are working in the teams, the community worker should provide opportunities to team members for public speaking, to organize meetings, planning actions, etc. The community worker should boost their morale. Encourage them to try out new things. The community worker should remember that the problems can be solved or reduced only through combined efforts of local people.

Remember, the whole process of community mobilization is dependent on people's participation. Hence, it is very important that the community teams should be formed for various activities to make them self-reliant and to take decisions independently. Hence, community mobilization can also be seen as an approach and tool that enables people to organize themselves, pool resources and take collective actions to resolve common problems and work towards the overall development of the community.

NETWORKING

Networking is a very important part in community organization and development. It offers an opportunity to exchange timely news and information, and learn from each other's experiences. It also helps in exchange of common assets. It avoids repetition as well.

The following points help in determining the objectives of networking:

1. Purpose of networking
2. Benefits of networking—may be at the organization level or community level
3. Benefit to the networking agency
4. Utility in bringing changes in the community
5. Benefits of joining together (saving on time, energy, infrastructure, funds, etc.).

The following self-explanatory framework (Figure 3.1) explains the process of community mobilization.

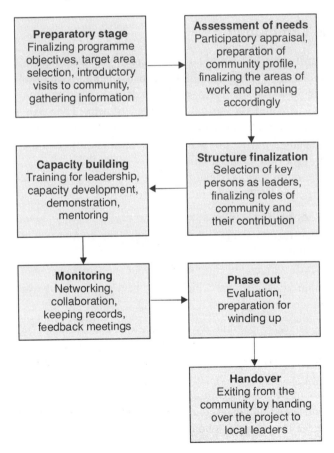

Figure 3.1 Process of community mobilization.

(*Source:* Adapted from Guide to Community Mobilization Programming, Mercycorps, mercycorps.org.)

ROLE OF A COMMUNITY WORKER IN COMMUNITY MOBILIZATION

The community worker is a catalyst between the NGO and the community. Hence, his/her role is very significant. S/he has to act as a facilitator and mobilizer to help the community members to identify their issues and needs and prioritize them and overcome by finding solutions for them. For this, the community worker should:

1. Know the community thoroughly.
2. Work with the existing leaders.
3. Ensure regular and clear communication.
4. Develop strong facilitation skills.
5. Find ways to motivate communities.

Know the Community

The community worker should understand the community for which s/he intends to work. It is very essential to know the interests and motivation of the people for their active involvement. In doing so, they should know the local culture, festivals, and day-to-day activities of life. This will help them to design intervention activities. For example, people gather once a week on a regular basis at a particular place. This opportunity can be exploited to disseminate information about NGO and its activities.

The community worker can use such occasions to collect information on the following aspects through informal discussions:

1. What really motivates the community?
2. What resources and local knowledge the community members value the most?
3. Whose voices are missing from decision-making?
4. What are the things which may harm or be useful while working in the community?

For an effective community mobilization, one needs to know the details of the community in general and the target group in particular. One should know in detail about social organizations, economy, languages spoken, problems and political powers functioning in the specified community. This information can be collected through formal and informal talks with people. This is a continuous process and one should never assume that the information collected in the beginning is enough forever.

Work with Existing Leaders

Leaders are required for successful implementation of the programme. Using existing leadership and simultaneously building new leadership potential in people is very essential. This involves understanding local self-government system and its decision-making process. The community worker should be a keen observer to locate an unexpected, but highly respected leader from among women and minority groups.

Ensure Regular and Clear Communication

There should be regular communication between the community worker and the people. Communication gap hampers the development process. All the elements of the programmes, especially about finance, should be communicated to people. Try to keep more transparency. This builds trust and results in support and cooperation from the people. This should be mutual. This involves lots of interaction including question-answer and discussions. The community worker should listen attentively to people as, at times, they may not speak directly. S/he should understand the undertones. The community worker should make sure that people understand correctly and clearly.

Develop Strong Facilitation Skills

The community worker should always remember his/her role of the facilitator and not helper. S/he may have many ideas from her/his experience but s/he has to allow the people to take the lead.

Find Ways to Motivate Communities

Motivating people to involve in development task is the first step. But, sustaining their motivation is the biggest challenge. People are busy with their own routine. Initially, they may participate enthusiastically, or even lead some activities or programmes. Over a period of time, the motivation level goes down especially if it is a long and time-consuming project. When the immediate results are not seen, or there are delays in finance, people get demotivated. The community people, involved in the project, need to explain to other members of their community about the progress/ delay in the activity/ programme. At times, ridicule by the community people may discourage those who are directly involved in the activity. Hence, their participation is also affected. This becomes a challenging task for the community worker to convince them about the long-term benefits of their work. In such situations, one should organize field visits of community people in other neighbouring communities, where similar work is being carried out successfully.

Skills of a Community Worker

The community worker has a very important role in community mobilization process. Usually s/he plays the role of a facilitator. To be a successful facilitator, s/he requires different skills. The community worker must be a good communicator. S/he needs to learn how to be a good public speaker. S/he should be an effective leader and a good mobilizer. The community worker must learn how to draw information from people. This requires full understanding of the community. To acquire these skills, the community worker must be honest, enthusiastic, patient, tolerant, should have positive attitude and motivation as well. The community worker should have skills in planning, managing, observing, analyzing and writing. S/he must have good listening skills and understand the motive behind people's talk. The community worker should have sharp wit to understand the accuracy of the information. S/he should be able to reach to the level of people and should illustrate her/his view point in a simple language so that people can understand her/him. S/he should give interesting examples from their day-to-day life for easy identification. The community worker must try to avoid giving lectures but use participatory approach. S/he should always use dialogue format and should be able to face many people confidently. The community worker should be sensitive towards people's problems. S/he should know how to lead discussion in a democratic way during dialogues with community people. S/he can learn and master these skills.

To summarize, community mobilization is a continuous process. The local resources must be utilized in this process. The efforts will reduce and/or solve the problems, depending on their nature. This whole process increases cooperation, develops team work and builds capacity and promotes local leadership, which ultimately results in sustainable development. The next chapter deals with models of community organization.

Review Questions

1. What do you understand by community mobilization? Explain with example the need for community mobilization.

2. Illustrate the short-term and long-term benefits of community mobilization.

3. What are the prerequisites for starting community mobilization process?

4. Explain the importance of communication in community mobilization based on your field work experience.

5. How will you establish your initial contacts with the community before starting actual community mobilization process?

6. Visit a nearby community. Write a report including the following points: who are the decision makers? Who holds the power? How are the government development programmes implemented?

7. What are the challenges faced by a community worker in mobilizing a community?

8. Before starting actual work in the community, what are the different aspects of a community the community worker should know?

9. Comment on different techniques of community mobilization by giving suitable examples.

10. Illustrate the phases of community mobilization.

11. How can a community worker seek the participation of local people in the process of community mobilization?

12. Explain the barriers to community participation.

13. Explain in detail the process of community mobilization.

14. Explain the role of a community worker in community mobilization.

15. 'Community worker requires different skills for mobilizing a community.' Endorse this with suitable examples.

4

Models of Community Organization Practice

The development of any nation depends on the development of its people. Hence, most of the governmental and the non-governmental organizations devise different developmental programmes for their communities. For proper planning and implementation of these programmes, they need to understand different models of community organization. This knowledge will help them to design strategies for ensuring the participation of people, foresee prospective problems that may come across while working with communities and their probable solutions, etc.

Let us understand the meaning of model. Model is nothing but a window through which a community worker looks at the complex nature of community. Those who want to work with communities should have a theoretical framework of knowledge. It helps in working smoothly. It facilitates them in deciding and adopting different strategies to achieve the ultimate goal of community development. It also helps the community worker to decide what skills and techniques are to be used during different meetings with people, roles to be played, etc.

MODELS OF COMMUNITY ORGANIZATION

Jack Rothman (1974) has given the following three models of community organization:

1. Locality development model
2. Social planning model
3. Social action model.

Let us discuss in detail the definitions, themes, effects, problems, solutions and roles of community worker in each model.

Locality Development Model

Locality development model presupposes that community change may be pursued optimally through broad participation of a wide spectrum of people at the local community level in goal determination and action. One of the major U.N. Publication (1955) defines community development as a 'process designed to create conditions of economic and social progress for the whole community with its active participation and the fullest possible reliance on the community's initiative.'

Locality development model emphasizes the process of community building. In other words, its main focus is on the whole community or on a part of it. It believes that communities have some common needs and interests. Once the people realize their needs and interests, they come together to solve them to improve the quality of their life.

According to Dunham (1970), this model is based on five elements, namely:

1. Democratic procedures
2. Voluntary cooperation
3. Self-help
4. Development of local leadership (indigenous leadership)
5. Education.

If this model is used while working with the communities, one can see increase in local people's participation in all the programmes. It increases the capabilities of local people. The cooperation among the people also improves. This promotes the development of local leadership. The ultimate result of this model shows empowerment of people.

The main challenge to the community worker using locality development model is how to increase the community participation. For understanding the community, s/he has to use different strategies and techniques such as meeting and interviewing key informants and conducting focus group discussions. The community worker should make special efforts to involve community and political leaders, members of agencies working in that area and other professionals. S/he should also ensure that marginalized people also participate in the assessment of common needs and interests. The community worker also has to create opportunities for equal participation, especially during the process of problem-solving and decision-making. Identifying common interests and needs, and accordingly deciding common goals/objectives for development is an important part in the whole process.

The locality development model believes in people's participation at all levels. It believes that people have capacity to overcome the problems. Hence, the community worker should ensure that people get involved since the beginning, i.e. identifying needs, problems, prioritizing them, and selecting one or more problems to work on, planning activities and implementing them, and also thinking of evaluation process. In doing so, if any problem arises, the community worker can organize a meeting/s of people, discuss and come to a consensus. Involvement gives them greater satisfaction—both at the individual and collective levels.

The major role of the community worker in implementing locality development model is that of an enabler and a catalyst. S/he brings people together (organizational skills), initiates communication (problem solving), and develops understanding to promote interpersonal relationship among the community members.

The NGOs who want to implement various schemes and programmes to fulfil the needs of a particular area or community may use this model. It involves networking and coordination with various agencies who offer different services for the welfare of communities. In India and many other developing countries, this model has been used while implementing developmental activities.

Social Planning Model

Social planning model is basically concerned with social problems. Its main goal is to solve community problems. It emphasizes a technical process of problem-solving with regard to social problems such as housing, health, etc. As stated by Rothman (*op. cit.*), rational, deliberatively planned and controlled change has a central place in this model. The community worker can collect information regarding the needs of the community and services available in that particular community/area. Based on this, he can suggest solutions to get the maximum benefits from these services. For example, problems of housing, illiteracy, non-availability of appropriate health services, etc. are important issues which need attention.

Once the data is collected, the analysis of the data may be done by the worker or professionals. Accordingly, decisions are taken by professionals. Issues are prioritized by service providers. At this stage, the involvement of community people in planning is almost negligible. In other words, the power remains with planners and service providers. In this process, conflict may arise between the community and service providers. In this model, planning is done **for** and not **with** community people. Somewhere the feeling of 'donor' and 'receiver' comes. This also increases dependency on outsiders. In short, capacity building and empowerment of community people for development is not a major goal of this model. Fostering radical or fundamental social change is not a central part of this model.

The planner normally establishes contacts with the organization and/or government body and makes arrangement to deliver services which fulfil the needs of the community. By using this model, there might be either consensus or conflict with the people.

There are various services to cater to the needs of a society such as health, education, housing, sanitation, employment, etc. These services are routed through certain systems and sub-systems. Due to various reasons, many times these systems become defunct and people suffer. For example, cities have better employment opportunities than rural areas/villages. This creates disparities and adds to the feeling of inequality. In such a situation, the community worker develops certain strategies, either with the help of outside agency or tries to modify or restructure the situation individually.

Social planning model presupposes that change requires expert planners. Through experts' technical abilities and skills of dealing with bureaucrats, they can bring the desired change. The focus here is on establishing, arranging and delivering goods and services to people who need them.

The role of a community worker in this model is that of a researcher (who can collect data), programme implementer, and spokesperson (if required) with bureaucrats.

Social Action Model

Each society has small communities and groups. They are directly controlled by the governments' (central and state) policies and laws. Informally, they are controlled by the customs, traditions and beliefs of the respective community as well. All these factors decide the social rights of an individual. The macro level policies affect the micro level people. This model aims to change decisions, societal structures and cultural beliefs. Social action is a strategy used by groups or communities who feel that they have inadequate power and resources to meet their needs. This model presupposes a disadvantaged segment of the population that needs to be organized, in order to make adequate demands. They are deprived of resources. To give them social justice and bring democracy, equality in the real sense of the word, this approach is practiced. To bring equality, one has to confront the power structure. It aims at making basic changes in major institutions or community practices. This model emphasizes on social justice, equality, redistribution of power and resources, participation in decision making and/or changing basic policies of formal organizations. It demands for improved treatment. Conflict, as a method, is used to solve their issues related to inequalities and deprivation, especially for the issues like women's liberation, reservation policy, right to information, etc.

Social action model focuses on the review of social policies and practices that continue to disempower and oppress the marginalized people. It aims to achieve social progress by modifying social policies and changing social legislations (if required) and welfare services.

The community worker collects the data from the community and presents the facts related to the deprivation of the rights of marginalized people. This would include evidences, its impacts, etc. This collected data can be used to challenge the existing system.

The role of the community worker may be of an activist or advocate. S/he creates opportunities for marginalized people to participate, be heard and makes decisions on activities that affect their quality of life.

The community worker using this model helps people to identify issues, to help them know their enemy and the person responsible for their problems. By creating awareness among the deprived people, the community worker tries to organize them and prepare them to take a mass action against the oppressor, who may be a government body or organization or people.

Social action model uses change tactics of conflict or contrast, such as confrontation and direct action or negotiation. Some of the tactics usually used in the social action model are campaigns, appeals, petitions, boycotts, strikes, picketing, sit-ins, etc. But some tactics are non-violent, yet illegal and represent a form of civil disobedience. In this model, the community worker uses all means to pressurize the power structure to give justice to the people. The role of a community worker may be that of an advocate, activist, agitator, broker, mediator or negotiator, depending on the issues and situations. This is a long process which goes through different stages. It is very difficult to predict the success rate. However, the community worker can sow the seeds of social change. The role of a community worker also changes at every stage. The well-known examples of this model are *Narmada Bachao Andolan, Lokpal Vidheyak* and Right to Information Act.

The practice of each of these models may require certain techniques and skills. Many community workers use a combination of more than one model. For example, a community worker may require drawing up a social plan in order to get funds/financial help for the desired project from the government, either state or central. In this case, s/he can use social planning and social action model.

In another case, the social planners want to change the attitude of people towards 'girl child'. To change the traditional attitude of people towards a girl child, the community worker may organize discussion forums, participate in local rituals and festivals to understand their culture. In this way, the community worker uses both models—locality development and social planning.

Table 4.1 gives detailed illustrations to get a deeper insight into these three models of community organization practice.

The distinction of each of these models as per different variables is as follows:

1. **Goals:** Each organization works in different types of community with different set-ups, with various goals of welfare of people. Accordingly, they have to perform various tasks.

Table 4.1 Comparison of three models: According to selected practice variables

Dimension of comparison	Locality development model	Social planning model	Social action model
Goal categories of community action	Self-help; community capacity and integration (process goals)	Problem-solving with regard to substantive community problems (task goals)	Shifting of power relationships & resources; basic institutional change (task of process goals)
Assumptions concerning community structure and problem conditions	Community eclipsed, anomie; lack of relationships and democratic problem-solving capacities: static traditional community	Substantiate social problem: mental and physical health, housing, recreation	Disadvantaged populations, social injustice, deprivation, inequity
Basic change strategy	Broad cross sections of people involved in determining and solving their own problems	Fact-gathering about problems and decisions on the most rational course of action	Crystallization of issues and organization of people to take action against enemy targets
Characteristic change tactics and techniques	Consensus: communication among community groups and interests; group discussion	Consensus or conflict	Conflict or contest: confrontation, direct action, negotiation
Salient practitioner roles	Enabler-catalyst, co-ordinator, teacher of problem-solving skills and ethical values	Fact gatherer and analyst, programme implementer, facilitator	Activist-advocate; agitator, broker, negotiator, partisan
Medium of change	Manipulation of small task-oriented groups	Manipulation of formal organizations and of data	Manipulation of mass organizations & political processes
Orientation towards power structure(s)	Members of power structure as collaborators in a common venture	Power structure as employers and sponsors	Power structure as external target of action: oppressors to be coerced or overturned
Boundary definition of the community client system or constituency	Total geographic community	Total community or community segment (including 'functional' community)	Community segment
Assumptions regarding interests of community subparts	Common interests or reconcilable differences	Interests reconcilable or in conflict	Conflicting interests which are not easily reconcilable; scarce resources
Conception of the public interest	Rationalist-unitary	Idealist-unitary	Realist-individualist
Conception of the client population of constituency	Citizens	Consumers	Victims
Conception of client role	Participants in interactional problem-solving process	Consumers or recipients	Employers, constituents, members

(*Source:* Adapted from J. Rothman, Three Models of Community Organization Practice, in Cox, F.M. and others (Eds.), *Strategies of Community Organization*, F.E. Peacock Publishers, Illonois, 1974, pp. 26–27.)

There are two types of goals usually mentioned in community organization, namely task goals and process goals. Task goals refer to the completion of a particular task or the solution to a particular problem faced by the community, such as delivery of a service/s, establishment of new service/s, passing of new legislation to overcome that problem, etc.

Process goals mainly focus on system maintenance and capacity building. For example, the formation of a group to solve community problems themselves fosters collaborative attitudes and practices, increasing indigenous leadership, etc. They are mainly concerned with building capacity of the community to function over a period of time.

In locality development model, more emphasis is given on process goals. It builds capacity of the community to such an extent that it becomes functionally integrated. It promotes cooperative problem-solving on a self-help basis. Democratic decision-making is encouraged in this model.

Task goals are more emphasized in social planning model. It aims at the solution of the problem. A concrete social problem is dealt herewith.

The social action model may either use task goals or process goals. For example, trade unions emphasize upon obtaining specific legislative outcomes on changing specific practices (e.g. bonus). Usually, this model intends to modify the current policies.

2. **Assumptions regarding community structure and problem conditions:** In locality development model, the local community is usually seen as oppressed, overshadowed by the large society of dominant people. The oppressed groups do not have problem-solving skills and hence, are vulnerable. They follow old traditions as they are ruled by conventional leaders. Mostly, they are illiterate or less educated. They are unaware of democratic processes, equality rights, etc.

The social planning people usually have different viewpoints. They are likely to see that the community has substantive problems of illiteracy, unemployment, poverty, which need immediate attention.

The social action practitioners have totally different attitude towards these problems. Community, for them, reflects a hierarchy of privilege and power, where powerless people are oppressed, deprived and ignored. They suffer social injustice, as they are exploited by the dominant people.

3. **Basic change strategy:** In locality development model, the change strategy is democratic. People are called together to discuss issues and take decisions with common consensus. Efforts are taken to seek participation of all people from different strata and then their felt needs/problems are identified.

In social planning, the change strategy is 'let's get the facts and logically decide steps'. They first gather all the facts related to a particular social problem. Then they decide rational and feasible course of action. The community worker has an important role in gathering information, analyzing it and determining services/programmes/appropriate actions to be taken. S/he may or may not involve the community.

In social action, the change strategy may be, 'let us organize (unite) to destroy/demolish/defeat our oppressor'. Through this, people become aware of their oppressor. By uniting together, they get strength to fight for their rights. This also helps them to create a pressure group to fight against oppressor.

4. **Characteristic change tactics and techniques:** Tactics used in locality development are generally chosen by mutual consensus, which is mostly achieved through open-minded communicative discussions with different groups in the community.

In social planning, tactics used are either conflict or consensus, depending on the issue and the type of community. This is because most of the work is based on finding facts, analyzing them and planning action. The planners may have different attitudes and approaches than local people.

In social action, conflict is the most often used tactics. Confrontation and direct action, these two tactics, can also be used. For this, the community worker should have an ability to mobilize people on a large scale, may be by organizing rallies, marches, boycotts and picketing.

5. **Practitioner's roles and medium of change:** In locality development, the community worker plays the role of enabler and/or encourager. The community worker acts as a facilitator. S/he facilitates the process of problem-solving, helps people to express their opinions/discontents freely and openly, and builds interpersonal relations.

In social planning, the community worker has to play a technical role. This includes fact finding, analyzing, implementation of programmes, establishing networking with various NGOs/institutions/bureaucracies, various professionals with varied specializations. In addition, the community worker should have research skills, analyzing skills, knowledge of technical information and different evaluation methods.

In social action, the community worker has to play the role of 'advocate' and/or 'activist'. S/he has to act on behalf of the people's interest. The community worker has to create and manipulate mass organizations and movements. Also s/he has to influence political processes.

6. **Orientation towards power structure/s:** In locality development, the whole community is included in the target group. So, the existence of a separate power structure is not taken into consideration. Hence, all the people are considered to be the part of the power structure within that particular community. Due to this

assumption, incompatible interests are ignored or discarded as inappropriate.

In social planning, the power structure either remains with the donor agency/sponsorer/government/employer or may be community worker himself/herself.

In social action, the power structure exists outside the community. It is a challenge to the community worker to make the best use of this power structure for the benefit of the people. In order to attack existing bureaucracies, possessing resources, the community worker needs an autonomous power to use, which the parent organization where s/he works, can give/provide.

7. **Boundary definition of the community client system or constituency:** As stated earlier, in locality development, the whole community is the client system. It promotes unity.

In social planning, the client system may be the whole community/ society or sub-groups, part of the community.

In social action, the client is the suppressed people of a particular community. They suffer due to the dominance of the oppressors and need a special support from the community worker. In social action, the task of an activist/community worker is to organize the oppressed groups/voiceless people and strengthen their capacities to pursue their interests and rights.

8. **Assumptions regarding interests of community sub-parts:** In locality development, the interests of various groups and factions are taken into consideration. Every community has conflicts, which, if properly handled, can be used creatively. Mutual agreements can help in taking further steps to solve or overcome the problems or issues. When people are allowed to express their differences freely, they become more responsive and responsible. They consider the interest of the whole group.

In social planning, community involvement is less. The planner cannot be expected to be attuned to the factional situation. By the time planners plan programme/s, community might lose its interest.

The social action model assumes that the community is divided into sub-groups, each one having different interests. They have to apply different tactics such as legislation, boycotts, political and social upheavals. Those who hold power will not easily give up their rights. It is foolish to expect them to do so. Rather, by using their power, they will threaten the oppressed ones to castigation, public and private smears and/or sometimes attack on their very existence.

9. **Conception of the public interest:** The public interest can be grouped under three categories—the rationalist, the idealist and the realist. The rationalist view means common interests of a

community, derived through democratic discussion. It is in the wider interest of the majority of the people.

The idealist view means public interest arrived through an exercise of judgement and conscience on the part of knowledgeable and compassionate advocates of the public interest.

The realistic view considers the community as a group of people with conflicting interests, which endlessly contend with one another.

With this background, we can apply these views to our models in the following manner:

The locality development has a rationalist-unitary conception of the public interest. It focuses on general welfare by using a cooperative decision-making process.

The social planning model has an idealist-unitary view of the public interest. With the help of actual facts, planners always place pressure on power structure.

In the social action, the activists are well acquainted with the conflicting forces. They take a realist-individualist view of the public interest. They have the ability to face whatever comes in the confrontation.

The practitioners of social action model are predetermined, specialized and have vested interests. They place greater stress on pluralistic values. They are tough minded. They try to respond to the world in terms of how it functions, rather than how it ought to function.

10. **Conception of the client population or constituency:** In locality development, the whole community is the client. They have capabilities and skills, which are not fully developed and they need some help from outsider/community worker. It is expected that the outsider/community worker will develop their capabilities to solve their own problems. The assumption is that each person has under-developed abilities, which can be cultivated and strengthened.

In social planning, the community is considered as consumers of services. They are at the receiving end. They will utilize the services given through different programmes.

In social action, the community people are considered as the victims of the system.

11. **Conception of clients or constituent role:** In locality development, the community is viewed as an active participant. It is involved in different interactions to know the issues/problems. Through this, people express their felt needs, determine desired goals and take appropriate action to achieve them.

In social planning, the community is a recipient of services provided by outsiders. They are inactive in determination of policy and goals. They are active in consuming services.

In social action, the benefiting group is employers or constituents. They are in a position to determine broad goals and policies (for example, trade unions).

The above discussion gives a detailed comparison of three models based on different practice variables. In short, the locality development model's goals of action include self-help, building community capacity and integration. Through small group discussions and effective communication, among all groups including the excluded ones, people come to a consensus for common problem/issues. The role of a community worker is that of enabler, problem solver and catalyst. S/he should have skills in manipulating and guiding small group interaction.

In social action model, goals include the shifting of power, resources and decision-making. It emphasizes on changing the present policies. System change is viewed as critical. Community is considered as deprived of resources, suffering from social injustice. The basic change strategy includes organizing people to take action on their own behalf against the suppressor/ system. Change tactics include conflict techniques such as confrontation and direct action (rallies, marches, boycotts, etc.). The practitioner of this model plays the role of activist, agitator, broker, negotiator, partisan, etc.

Use of one or a combination of more than one model depends on the type of situation. There is no rule of thumb guideline for use of these models. When community is homogeneous or consensus exists among different groups within a community, locality development model can be used. When sub-groups are hostile and interests clash, even through discussions consensus is not reached. In such a situation, social action can be used. When problems are fairly routine and common, and can be solved through factual information, social planning model can be applied. The community worker should understand the utility of each model, acquire knowledge and skills required to apply these models and use them appropriately for optimum results.

The community worker should also become sensitive to the mixed uses of these models. Within any given model, aspects of other models may play an important part. For example, in social action, the community worker can employ locality development techniques and come to a fruitful resolution of issues through discussion or negotiation. A combination of locality development and social planning may be more effective.

As we have talked about mixing of two or more models, there are also chances of shifting from one model to another. The community worker can start with social action and can then switch over to social planning model. For example, through social action, one achieves success and attains resources. Then, they can opt for social planning model. Get some funding from outsiders and continue activities for the welfare of people. To do this, the community worker must have appropriate decision-making skills to decide to shift from one model to another.

APPROACHES TO COMMUNITY ORGANIZATION

History witnessed a variety of approaches to community organization. We discuss here certain important approaches implemented during twentieth century onwards, that is, neighbourhood organizing approach. The feature of this approach is that people of the community put efforts to solve their day-to-day problems and help those in need. There are three approaches:

1. **The social work approach:** The main focus is on the whole society. It pays more attention towards building a sense of community. This approach was used in USA during social settlement movement and war on poverty alleviation programme in the 1960s. In this approach, the community worker plays the role of an enabler and/or advocate. S/he helps the community in identifying their problems and tries to overcome them by gathering existing resources from the community and getting some help from the people who are in power.

2. **The political activists approach:** Saul Alinsky is the founder of this approach. Philosophy behind this approach is, 'more the representatives in the organization, stronger the organization'. In this approach, he looked at the community as a political entity. The approach says that most of the problems are due to unequal distribution of power and resources. Power is concentrated in the hands of a few people and the majority of the community is deprived of it. Hence, they focus on gaining the power. In doing so, they face conflict with the groups with vested interests. The role of a community worker, at times, is that of facilitator, sometimes of a leader as well. S/he has to help people to understand the problem in terms of power, make them understand how it is directly and/or indirectly affecting their lives and how they are denied of their rights and help them to take necessary steps to resolve these issues. This approach has the potential of bringing equality as it emphasizes on rights-based approach.

3. **Neighbourhood maintenance/community development approach:** This approach is a combination of earlier two approaches. It uses peer group pressure to provide services in the community. The strategy includes pressurizing the officials to deliver the services to the community.

To summarize, we can say that these models should be applied to foster and support social change. There is a need to redistribute resources and give justice to the unreached population, especially oppressed minorities, women and children. Appropriate phasing and mixing of these models can be done to bring sustainable development.

The next chapter deals with understanding the community through participatory appraisal.

Review Questions

1. Explain the different models of community organization given by Jack Rothman.

2. Describe locality development model and social planning model. How are they different from each other?

3. Compare the three models of community organization given by Jack Rothman based on different dimensions.

4. Explain various approaches to community organization.

5. Which model will you use while working with community? Justify your choice.

5

Understanding the Community through Participatory Appraisal

Understanding the community is the prerequisite for starting any developmental or welfare programme. Before 1970, survey was the most commonly used method to understand community. Realizing its limitations, new approaches were developed. It was realized that people's participation is an important factor in estimating the needs of the community. People's participation is an informal way of learning quickly from local people about their problems and opportunities in a specific area.

Participation, basically, is a political process, which helps redistribution of the financial, administrative powers and legal information. Meaningful participation refers to the power of decision-making that affects individuals' life and the development of the whole community as well.

Participatory appraisal is one of the methods to understand the community. There are other methods such as conducting focus group discussions, semi-structured interviews, staying in the community to understand it, etc. All these methods help to prepare a community profile. In this chapter, we discuss the participatory appraisal in detail which will help in understanding the community.

RATIONALE

Participatory approach has the following rationale:

1. **Reduction in development cost:** The actual needs of the people are understood before implementation of the programme. Naturally, it increases the utility value of the programmes and the goal is realized. There is no wastage of finance resulting in reduction of cost.

2. **Increase in perceived and actual benefit:** As the organizers know the exact needs of the community, they also understand the outcome of the programme to be organized. It reaches to those for whom it is meant. Hence, the actual number of beneficiaries increases. There is no need to imagine who will benefit, how much it will be beneficial, etc.

3. **Correction of design mistakes:** The development plans are prepared with the help of people. Hence, the mistakes get rectified before the programmes are implemented.

4. **Reaching benefits to all:** As participation of each and every individual is sought, their needs are considered. Hence, the benefit also reaches to everyone.

5. **Decrease in dependence on government:** People's participation helps to understand the needs and problems. In addition to this, they realize the available resources—both human and material. Understanding these things help them to solve their problems collectively. Hence, many times they do not have to depend on the government to solve their problem.

6. **Access to control of resources:** Most of the times the resources are available within the community, but people are unaware of them. Participatory approach helps them to gain access and avail them in the community itself. Sometimes the resources are controlled by a few people. Participatory approach helps all members of the community to have access to these resources.

7. **Mobilization of local resources:** Participatory approach helps to mobilize local resources and utilize them for the development of individual as well as the community.

8. **Empowerment of the oppressed classes:** In participatory approach, people from all the religions, castes, and classes participate. Due recognition is given to each person. This helps oppressed class people to express their views, opinions, needs, problems, etc. They get due consideration as well.

FACTORS AFFECTING PEOPLE'S PARTICIPATION

Obstacles existing within the programme, the community and the society affect the participation of the people. Following are some of them:

1. **Easy availability of grants/subsidies:** There are certain pro-grammes for which direct government grants are available. The organizations just use them without bothering whether the people need them or not. They get funds easily. Hence, they are least concerned about people's participation and development.

2. **Biases/discriminations:** Many a time, the government and the voluntary organizations underestimate people's intelligence. They are marginalized. So, the participation of women, people from oppressed class, people living below poverty line is ignored.

3. **Illiteracy/ignorance:** In rural areas, more than 40 per cent people are illiterate, so they are ignorant of different development schemes and funds. The outsiders think that they "do not know". Hence, their participation in planning, implementation and/or decision making is just neglected.

4. **Parties/groupism/variations in population:** Usually groupism is prevalent all over the country. Power either lies with rich people or with the ruling party. The powerful people, though in minority, enjoy and exhaust all the benefits.

5. **Social status/income differences:** People belonging to higher castes, with good economic status, dominate others. They change decisions according to their convenience. This affects the develop-ment of the deprived class and minority people.

RAPID RURAL APPRAISAL

Rapid Rural Appraisal (RRA) emerged in the late 1970s. This method was used to understand and learn about rural life and conditions as an outsider. In this method, an outsider could get quicker information, which was found to be more cost-effective than surveys. It was also realized by outsiders (development professionals) that rural people were more knowledgeable on many subjects related to their lives. During the 1980s, RRA was accepted in many parts of the world. Mostly, agro-based studies started using RRA. It was found to be very useful for an outsider to gain first hand information and insight from rural people about their conditions.

EMERGENCE OF PARTICIPATORY RURAL APPRAISAL

In the mid-1980s, RRA started using the words 'participation' and 'participatory'. In 1985, Khon Kaen International Conference was organized. In this conference, 'participation' was used with RRA. New typologies were generated in this conference, one of which was participatory RRA. This referred to stimulating community awareness, with the outsiders' role as catalyst. In 1988, the team of International Institute for Environment and Development (IIED), London, listed participatory RRAs as one of the four classes of RRA methodologies.

Parallel to this, there were developments in the areas of RRA in India and Kenya. As stated by Robert Chamber (1997), the National Environment Secretariat in association with Clark University, Kenya, conducted an RRA in Mbusanyi. It adopted a Village Resource Management Plan. This was subsequently described as participatory rural appraisal. Around the same time (1988), the Aga Khan Rural Support Programme in India showed interest in developing participatory RRA. Hence, it invited experts from IIED. With the help of these experts, participatory RRA was facilitated in the village of Gujarat. Both the experiments of Kenya and India contributed to the development of a new concept called participatory rural appraisal (PRA).

Subsequently, a number of innovative programmes were taken up in India. NGO sector and government agencies took initiatives and trained their senior staff in conducting PRA in early 1990. These people then conducted training programmes in other countries and continents. They contributed to the spread and evolution of PRA and its methods. PRA methods were introduced by India to Nepal and Sri Lanka. Trainers from India and, later on, from Kenya and other countries conducted a number of trainings in other countries and continents. PRA approaches and methods, spread from South to North, especially in industrialized world. By the mid-1996, PRA was accepted and practiced in more than 100 countries. NGOs and government departments were already using PRA. Now, training institutes and universities have also started using PRA methods and approaches.

PARTICIPATORY RURAL APPRAISAL

Participatory Rural Appraisal (PRA) is the most commonly used set of participatory assessment tools. It describes a growing family of approaches and methods for learning about rural life and conditions.

Robert Chambers (1997) describes PRA thus: 'PRA is a growing family of approaches and methods to enable local people to share, enhance and analyze their knowledge of life and conditions, and to plan, act, monitor and evaluate'. PRA is being extensively used in natural resources management, agriculture, health and nutrition, poverty and livelihood programmes and urban contexts.

PRA is still evolving. At one stage, it was 'an approach and methods of learning about rural life and conditions from, with and by rural people', with emphasis on learning by outsiders. The prepositions—'by, with and from' then were reversed as the analysis, and learning shifted from 'us' to 'them'. Then, PRA extended to analysis, planning, action, monitoring and evaluation.

Different approaches were evolved in different countries. It had different contexts. To include all these, in 1994, PRA was described as 'a family of approaches and methods to enable rural people to share, enhance and analyze their knowledge of life and conditions, to plan and to act' (Absalom et al., 1995).

The philosophy behind PRA is that community members are the best experts of their own situations. PRA is an easy method to collect information about a community. To do this, outsiders must establish a good rapport, build trust and then use different techniques and tools to collect the right and factual information.

Always remember, people's participation changes according to local situation. Though it is a participatory approach, the percentage of participation, its type/method, quality differs from place to place, even within the same community. Hence, the advantages and disadvantages of participatory process vary according to the local situations. Unless you practically implement all the techniques, you will not understand which works in a particular situation and which does not. PRA helps the outsiders as well as villagers to learn more about village. The experiences of people who implemented PRA tell that local people have more knowledge about their village. If the community worker, who is an outsider, takes people in confidence and explains the purpose behind PRA, convinces people that they can learn new things by doing this, and explains its benefits, then people definitely cooperate. The community worker should make an attempt and ensure that everybody participates in the PRA including illiterates, literates, women, children, backward and minority communities, etc. As an outsider, the community worker should always be eager to learn from people. S/he should be ready to accept mistakes committed by her/him. S/he should avoid giving unsolicited suggestions/advice. It is really beneficial if the community worker undergoes training in how to conduct PRA.

Dimensions of PRA

Table 5.1 explains different dimensions of PRA.

Table 5.1   Dimensions of PRA

Area/focus	Dimensions
Emphasis	From stressing methods to stressing behaviour and attitudes
Impact	From methods to professional change
	From behaviour and attitudes to personal change
	From applications to changes in organizational procedures & cultures
Focus	From appraisal to analysis, planning, action, monitoring & evaluation
Location	From rural to urban
Analysis	From practice to theory, finding what works and then asking why

(*Source:* Adapted from Chambers, Robert, *Whose Reality Counts? Putting the first last,* Intermediate Technology Publication, UK, 1997.)

PRA is a good method which can be used to understand the village/area. The role of an outsider/community worker is that of a facilitator, who should guide the discussion and help community members tap their own knowledge and resources and use them effectively. As stated earlier, PRA helps to analyze local problems and formulate tentative solutions with local stakeholders. It makes use of a wide range of visualization methods such as mapping, diagramming, etc. These tools can be very effective for getting detailed information from large groups. As most of these methods are visual, they can be used with illiterates or who have very low literacy. This also encourages the participation of all members of the community.

The community worker should act as a catalyst and a convener to enable local community people to identify and investigate their exact problems/needs, analyze them, plan and implement solutions. It also helps people to face the outcome. That is why PRA is considered both attitude and methodology. It serves as a tool for outsiders to understand village system, its dynamics and politics using combination of techniques.

The unique feature of PRA is that it enables local people to participate actively, express their views, opinions and make them aware of their hidden potentials. It changes and reverses the role, behaviour, relationships and learning. Here, outsiders do not dominate and lecture or impose their ideas/programmes on local people. They just facilitate the process by sharing with local people, listening to them and learning from them. Outsiders do not transfer any technology, but they share methods, which can be used by local people for their appraisal, analysis, planning, implementation, evaluation, and uplift.

As stated by Robert Chambers (*op. cit.*), PRA has three pillars, namely:

1. Partnership and sharing of information, experiences, food and training, between insiders and outsiders, and between organizations.
2. The methods include closed to open response, from verbal to visual, from individual to group and from measuring to comparing.
3. The behaviour and attitudes of outsiders, who facilitate, not dominate.

Sharing between organizations helps create a culture of openness. The information generated spreads over government departments, NGOs, university departments and others. This results in learning not only at the field level but it also increases interaction among the villagers. PRA creates a spirit of sharing—of food, of living together, of learning—resulting in establishing rapport. The whole process strengthens the methods of PRA.

It is astonishing for outsiders when they see local people use PRA methods. Mere observation of local people (who are illiterate, semi-literate) doing participatory mapping, affects the attitude and beliefs of outsiders. People come together in a group, where a lot of knowledge, ideas and values are shared. This generates commitment, cross-checking, enthusiasm and even the fun element among people. In a way, lots of knowledge and information get shared between local people and outsiders, who are facilitators.

The third pillar, behaviour and attitude, is the key to its success. Good facilitators (outsiders or community worker) avoid dominant behaviour. They should be respectful, relaxed, unhurried, interested and be able to establish rapport. They should listen attentively and not interrupt the conversation, learn patiently to initiate the process. Such behaviour facilitates the methods. It also encourages the sharing amongst people.

How these pillars work in PRA is shown in Figure 5.1.

According to those who have practiced PRA, it helps to empower the lower strata of society, that is, women, minorities, the poor, the weak and the vulnerable. It has helped to make power reversals real.

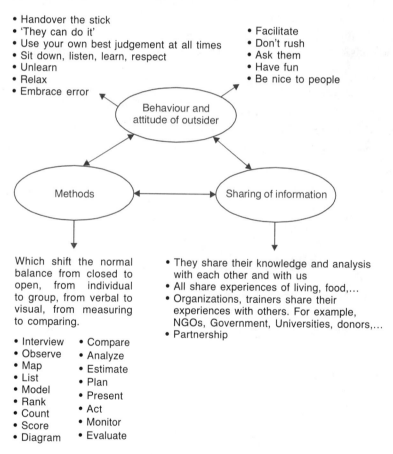

Figure 5.1   The three pillars of PRA.

(*Source:*   Adapted from Mascarenhas, James et al. (Eds.), Proceedings of the February 1991 Bangalore PRA Workshop, PRA Notes 13 August, in Chambers, Robert, 'Whose Reality Counts? Putting the first last', Intermediate Technology Publication, UK, 1997, p. 105.)

Need for PRA

In early days (before 1970s), mostly the development plans were based on secondary data (such as files, reports, maps, aerial photographs, articles, books and surveys). The authenticity of the data was doubtful. Survey method was the most widely used method as it was easy to collect quantitative data and analyze it. But the participation of the people used to be less as compared to the participation in PRA. Survey is a time-consuming method. It is not cost-effective and flexible. Information collected through the questionnaire has to be analyzed and stored in computer. If the questionnaire is faulty, the information collected remains incomplete. It is impossible to correct the lacunas once the data is collected. The major drawback of survey is its limitations of collection of qualitative data. PRA helps to collect qualitative as well quantitative data/information.

Table 5.2 will help to understand the difference between PRA and other methods of research (data collection) as explained by Chambers (*op. cit.*).

Table 5.2 Comparison of PRA with other research methods

PRA	*Other methods of research*
Less expensive and requires less time	Expensive and time-consuming
Flexible process	Typical framework
More people's participation	Less people's participation
On the spot analyses of data	Collected data, analyzes in office
Qualitative information	Mostly quantitative data
Informal, semi-structured interviews and group discussions	Use of informal questionnaire
Group of variety of approaches and methods	Researcher's domination
It is helpful to understand from rural people about their behaviour, attitude, and opinions and learn from them	Arrangement of representatives and useful to collect quantitative data

Planning of any developmental activity requires accurate information, especially to address the needs and problems of weaker sections. PRA helps people to:

1. Bring sustained/sustainable change
2. Collect accurate and timely information
3. Find solutions to their problems
4. Cut down biases
5. Make the programme cost-effective.

The main purpose of PRA is to understand local priorities by developing direct contact with local people. Hence, it increases the responsibility of a community worker. One has to understand the diversity and try to bring equity and empowerment among the marginalized, excluded, deprived people, including women.

Before going into details of how to conduct PRA, let us understand the differences between RRA and PRA.

Comparison of RRA and PRA

As stated earlier, RRA uses secondary sources for data collection, including the technique of observation and verbal interactions. Semi-structured interviews and focus groups are also used in RRA. PRA stresses on shared visual representations and analysis by local people. This is done through mapping on the ground or paper, listing, sequencing and card sorting, estimating, comparing, scoring and ranking with seeds, stones, sticks or shapes. It also uses Venn diagramming. The community representation is always there for checking and validation. The major areas of difference between RRA and PRA are explained in Table 5.3.

Table 5.3 Comparison of RRA and PRA

	RRA	*PRA*
Major development	Late 1970s, 1980s	Late 1980s, 1990s
Major innovators	Universities	NGOs
Main user	Aid agencies, universities	NGOs, government field organizations
Key resources earlier overlooked	Local people's knowledge	Local people's capabilities
Main innovation	Methods	Behaviour
Outsider's mode	Eliciting	Facilitating
Objectives	Data collection	Empowerment
Main actors	Outsiders	Local people
Long-term outcomes	Plans, projects, publication	Sustainable local action and institution
Outsider's role	Investigator	Facilitator
Information owned, analyzed and used by	Outsiders	Local people
Mode	Finding out—elicitive	Facilitating—empowering

(*Source:* Adapted from Chambers, Robert, Whose Reality Counts? Putting the first last, Intermediate Technology Publication, UK, 1997, p. 115.)

The major differences between traditional research method, and RRA, PRA refer to methods of data collection, analysis, presentation, roles, behaviour and attitudes. In RRA, data collection is done by outsiders, who dominate the scene. They determine the agenda and obtain information. They possess the information, remove it, if they feel it is irrelevant, and analyze it from their perspective. Accordingly, they write papers and reports. They 'own' the information.

On the other hand, in PRA, the outsider encourages local people and allows them to take the lead. People determine much of the agenda. They are actively involved in gathering the information, express freely and analyze information and plan accordingly. The outsider acts as a facilitator, learner and consultant. The outsider has to establish rapport, convene, catalyse and enquire. S/he has to help people in using different methods and tools of PRA. S/he encourages people to choose and improvise methods, if required. Once people start working, the outsiders just watch, observe, listen and learn. In other words, in the whole process, the authority remains in the hands of the people.

PRA has opened a new world for people's development. Local people and outsiders play complimentary roles. Every time you conduct PRA, there is a different outcome, as it involves creative interactions.

Implementation of PRA

As stated earlier, PRA is a group of methods and approaches. Before starting PRA, one needs to understand its nitty-gritty. To get better results, one has to follow the following steps:

1. **Pre-field work:** Once you have decided to conduct PRA, the first step is to prepare a team of five to ten people. The team should be multidisciplinary in nature. The team should include a few local people as well. While selecting team members from your own organization, you should remember that they need to have good listening, communication, observation and writing skills. They should be ready to work before and after office hours, should adjust to village situations/discomforts, have faith in people, should be keen and willing to learn new things especially from local people (illiterate/semiliterate), etc. Team members should be culturally sensitive. Selection of local people should be done carefully. Select such people who have good knowledge and awareness about their own village, have better understanding about local problems/needs. They must have good knowledge of available resources and should be willing to devote time to be with you. The team must have representation of both the sexes, if possible in equal number. But, women representation is a **must**. Before staring actual PRA, one needs to collect following information about that locality/village population. This information can be collected through secondary data as well as by paying two-three initial visits to that village.

(i) Language/s spoken by the people
(ii) Economy (main occupation and other issues)
(iii) Culture
(iv) Social and political organizations working.

This would give a preliminary idea for line of inquiry and choosing potentially important topics. Before conducting the actual PRA, the community worker should select the methods and tools, pay visit to the village and explain the process to people and seek people's involvement/participation. The date and timings of the PRA should be decided after consulting with the people according to their convenience.

Location: While deciding the location of the PRA exercise, the community worker should consider the following points:

(i) Purpose of the exercise
(ii) Number of households
(iii) Programme terrain
(iv) *Others:* Such as the capacity of the village to host the outsiders (group of 10–15 people) for 4–6 days-food, water, accommodation, etc.

Logistics: It is advised to stay in the village till the PRA gets over. In such a case, it is very important to see the accommodation facilities available in the village. One can explore the possibility of staying in the houses of local people. If not, the team has to travel every day. In such a case, explore available transport facilities and their feasibility. This is essential so that the team can stay in nearby city/town and travel every day to the desired place of PRA. In addition, the food arrangements, space for working on presentations and notes, space for evening meetings and group presentations, etc. should be explored.

Materials and kit: Followings are the few important items which the community worker should carry for exercising PRA:

(i) *Rangoli* powder (at least one kilogram) (minimum six different colours of *rangoli* powder in which red, green and blue are essential) or chalks in different colours
(ii) Brown paper sheets (for charts and presentations)
(iii) Coloured felt pens (the thick ones are better)
(iv) Gum, cello tape, scissors, coloured papers, pins, note books, pens, etc. (general stationary)
(v) Seeds and counters
(vi) Board- for presentations
(vii) Substitute for electricity. For example, petromax, torches, candles, etc.

2. **Actual field activity:** PRA requires minimum 5–10 days to complete, depending on the local situation, purpose/objective of the programme, the information needs to be sought, etc. Accordingly, one can select the methods and tools of PRA to be used. Then all the required preparations, as stated in phase I, should be made. One of the first issues in starting PRA is deciding on who should be involved to get the best possible picture of the community. One should try to involve all the people irrespective of their religion, caste, institutions, social status, etc. Listen to everyone. Different perspectives give useful information. Listen for emotional, physical and spiritual needs. Try to gather information on what has already been done to solve problems.

Briefings: The group should be divided into sub-groups. Each sub-group should be formed in such a way that it has people with technical competencies and skills of PRA. This enhances the quality of the interaction and affects the output. Each sub-group will use different techniques of PRA depending on the objectives of PRA. The sub-groups be briefed on:

(i) How to draw maximum information from the people?

(ii) Which method should be used for a particular topic?

The group members should remember the following questions:

(i) Why are we doing this exercise? (purpose)

(ii) What do we want to get out of it? (outcome)

(iii) How do we go about it? (strategy)

The group members should decide the roles of its members which includes interviewer (who asks questions), observer and recorder.

3. **Presentation of report to the local people:** It is very important to call a meeting of the local people and present the information gathered through PRA. People must be told about needs, problems, resources found by using PRA techniques.

Presentations: Evening timings should be kept aside for presentations of the day's findings. This helps to understand, scrutinize the information and, if required, to do the correction/s. It is also helpful in getting an end product of every day that is accurate and reliable.

Documentation: One can take:

1. Photographs, prepare slides and films (video shooting).

2. Individual and group write-ups.

Following are some of the practical tips for those who want to conduct PRA:

Before PRA

1. Meet villagers with open and frank mind a few days before the actual exercise begins.
2. Build personal rapport.
3. Identify villagers who are willing to share experiences.
4. Show full interest and enthusiasm.
5. Relax tension of the interviewee.
6. Sit down with the villagers on the same floor, at the same level.
7. Decide the suitable timings for PRA.

During PRA

1. Listen carefully.
2. Show empathy.
3. Observe intensively and carefully.
4. Understand villagers' way of reasoning.
5. Do not interrupt, suggest or prescribe.
6. Be polite, gentle and accommodative.
7. Try to adjust with the villagers' convenience.
8. Do not lecture.
9. Respect villagers as human beings.
10. Avoid head nodding.
11. Follow existing social customs.
12. Participate whole heartedly.
13. Accept hospitality, if offered.
14. Be patient and do not be too inquisitive.
15. Lead towards sensitive issues.
16. Ask simple questions.
17. Take detailed note of all answers, discussion and information generated.
18. Tackle gatekeepers carefully.
19. Do not prolong discussion unnecessarily.
20. Revolve discussion around main issue.
21. Change topics smoothly.
22. Intervening group should not be prolonged.
23. Use Kipling's seven servants—What, When, Where, Who, Which, Why and How.
24. Identify potential resource persons.
25. Intimate the group formally while going out during the course of interview/activity.

After PRA: Once you complete the PRA, you should thank all the villagers individually. Decide, if possible, the time when you will be sharing the information collected through the whole process and the plans for the development/further action. Remember, information must be shared in an honest and realistic manner, without making false promises that cannot be kept.

Important Things for Exercising PRA

Following are a few things which should be practiced by all those who wish to exercise PRA:

1. **Protocol:**   The success of the PRA exercise depends on how you follow the 'required' protocol in the village. Each village has its vested interests, power structures and the establishments. Try not to interfere with them. Hence, it is very useful to have a few meetings initially with the village elders, opinion leaders, chairpersons and youth leaders, women representatives, etc. This should be done a few days before the PRA exercise begins. This gives a sanction of legitimacy. Legitimacy refers to participation of villagers from all categories either directly by attending sessions or indirectly through interviews. Legitimacy is also for the 'outsiders' to move freely in the village (of course respectfully and sensitively).

2. **Village camping:**   This is a must in all PRA exercises. Staying in the village with local people helps to break down the barriers between the outsiders and the villagers. A great degree of access to the villagers and vice versa is achieved.

3. **Ice breakers:**   On the first day of PRA, one can organize a few games in introductory session itself. Beginning with games help in breaking down the barriers and establishing rapport. Every day some light games can be organized. You can make games an integral part of PRA. It helps people to feel refreshed, to become more energetic, and they continue their participation whole-heartedly. The whole atmosphere becomes friendly. This helps to bridge the gap between the outsider and the insider (local people).

Games should be used very carefully. It should not give the impression that you are not serious towards your activity and simply trying to kill the time. Hence, use games according to the situations.

4. **Friendly approach:**   Lecturing must be avoided as it is disastrous in PRA. The aim of PRA is to gather accurate and relevant information. Hence, an effective inquiry mode should be adopted. Lecture is one-way communication. Always remember, never interrupt a person who is talking. Many times, we miss important

information due to frequent interruptions and interventions. First, listen to them and, if required, ask questions.

Types of PRA

Following are the different types of PRA widely used all over the world (Sharanagat, 1996):

1. **Exploratory PRA:**   This method is used to understand different practices, rituals, important events happened in a particular village. This helps in future planning.

2. **Topical PRA:**   The main objective of this method is to collect maximum information on a particular point. Each village has different problems. Concentration on a very particular issue out of the many problems and studying it in detail is known as topical PRA. Different seasons and its related issues can be studied by this method. Exploratory PRA is supplementary to this method.

3. **Deductive PRA:**   For studying the hot issues of a village, this indirect method is used. The issues such as casteism, religious riots, common disputes, corruption at local level, etc. can be studied by using this method. Instead of collecting information directly on such issues, one can study its effects on local people. By collecting this information, one can understand direct correlation between effect and intense issue. Many times people do not share information if asked directly on hot issues. In such a situation, this method is used to collect information.

4. **Training and research PRA:**   This method is useful for training people who are going to use PRA. For example, personnel involved in development work, workers of NGO, government employees, especially department of rural development. These trained people use PRA in their work or further training of people from their respective field.

5. **Planning and implementation PRA:**   New projects can be started by using participatory appraisals. To start a project, we need to have an exact picture of the needs of a particular group, and the utility of the project for them. This can be verified by using this method. One can also assure the feasibility of a project due to people's participation since its inception. People's participation is needed in working out its layout and planning. By using this method, people's participation may increase in implementation and monitoring.

6. **Monitoring and evaluation PRA:**   Monitoring and evaluation of any programme or project can be done by participatory appraisal. By understanding the problems faced by the community or a group

in implementation of a project or errors/lacunas they came across, one can plan actions to resolve it. Suggestions are given to improve administration of the project. Certain guidelines are prepared locally to implement the project properly. In case, due to certain difficult situations and unavoidable circumstances, local people cannot implement the project, they can take the help of other people related to the project. They include technical personnel, planners, and facilitators. By consulting them, people can decide the next step to be taken. With the help of outside people or the local, people themselves can study the effects of the project.

Practical Application of PRA

PRA is widely used in the following five main areas:

1. **Natural resources management:** Watershed, soil and water conservation, forestry including social and community forestry, degrades forest assessment, protection, nurseries and plantation, coastal resources and fisheries, wild-life conservation, rural energy assessment, land tenure and policy, etc.

2. **Agriculture:** Crops, livestock and animal husbandry (participatory research), irrigation, integrated pest management, markets, etc.

3. **People, poverty and livelihood:** Women and gender, livelihood analysis, poverty assessment, credit, selection, income earnings, adult literacy, IRDP, DWCRA,etc.

4. **Health and nutrition:** Food security and nutrition assessment and monitoring, water and sanitation assessment, health assessment and monitoring, etc.

5. **Urban:** Needs assessment, community participation, urban poverty and violence, etc.

Principles for Participatory Learning and Analysis

For getting good results from RRA and PRA, the practitioners and facilitators have to follow certain basic principles. Following are some of the principles evolved over time:

1. **A reversal of learning:** This includes learning from local people, i.e. learning from people directly, on the site and face to face as well. It also aims at gaining insight from their local, physical, technical and social knowledge.

2. **Learning rapidly and progressively:** During PRA, one has to be flexible. One cannot follow a blueprint of a programme but be

adaptable in a learning process. It is a process of conscious exploration, flexible use of methods, improvisation and cross-checking.

3. **Offsetting biases:** All those involved in PRA should go to the community with an unbiased mind, like a clean slate. They should be relaxed, and not rush to finish one activity. They should listen and not lecture. They should ask probing questions. At no point should they impose any of their ideas, thoughts, values and suggestions on local people. They should seek out the participation of marginalized people including BPL (Below Poverty Line) people, women, ethnic minorities, children, and those people who are isolated and remote. It is very important to know their concerns and priorities.

4. **Crossing in the field:** It is very important to cross-check the collected information in the field itself. Compare the information and gain insight.

5. **Handing over the stick (or pen or chalk):** The facilitators must have confidence in local people that **they can do it**. They must believe that the local people are able to map, rank, score, diagram, analyze, plan and act. In this process, the local people generate and own the outcomes and also learn. Hence, in PRA the facilitator should just initiate the process and then sit back and keep quiet.

6. **Self-critical awareness:** The facilitators should continuously and critically examine their own behaviour. They should always keep in mind that this is a learning opportunity for them. This includes facing failures positively, correcting dominant behaviour, being critically aware of what is seen and not seen, shown and not shown, said and not said, etc.

7. **Sharing:** It is very important that whatever information is collected through PRA should be shared with the local people and outside facilitators by photocopying and translating, and sharing with other organizations as well.

Tips for Conducting PRA

The community worker has to play the role of a facilitator in conducting PRA. S/he must have full faith in local people. Facilitators are often not aware of their own lack of knowledge. They should build confidence in local people that they can do this activity. The facilitator should not strive for 'getting it right' information. Remember, local people know the things much better than you, as you are an outsider. Sometimes, they do not see any rationale behind an exercise. They may be tired, are short of time or are simply playful. It is possible that they may bias your views as their perception could be different.

But usually, in visual representation this risk is minimized. At initial stage itself if people know that they have to analyze, prioritize, plan and take an action, they will strive to 'get it right'.

Those who have facilitated PRA comment that people find the process as creative, fulfilling and often enjoyable. The process generates lots of energy and commitment. People do it as they enjoy it.

In practice, it has also been observed that, the PRA facilitators usually do not devote much time to it. They want to finish this activity very fast. As a result, they forget to explain their identity, their purpose, their actions and inherent limitations. They just rely on methods mechanically, without taking any trouble to establish rapport and earn trust of the local people. At the end of the activity, they do not even thank people sincerely. Such behaviour leaves a bad impression on people. As a community worker, one should always avoid such behaviour.

The whole process of PRA requires a lot of time. Local people get engaged for a long period in these activities. Naturally, people's expectation regarding future action increases. Many times, the outsiders/agencies are unable to respond to the local needs. They do not honour their promises made to people. As a community worker, one should respect the local people and should not keep them hanging. What you and your organization can do for them should be explained to people in the initial meeting itself.

Robert Chambers (1997) has suggested very important behaviour patterns and attitudes for those who want to conduct PRA. Briefly, it is discussed in the following lines:

1. Sit down, listen, watch and learn. Change behaviour. Learn not to dominate, not to wag finger, not to interview, and not to interrupt.
2. Use your own best judgment at all times. Rely on personal judgments and not on manuals and rules, fostering flexible and adaptable responses and accepting responsibility.
3. Unlearn. Be open to discarding beliefs, behaviours and attitudes.
4. Be optimally unprepared. Enter unknown participatory situations with a repertoire but without a detailed preset programme. This allows you for creative improvisation and an open interactive process.
5. Embrace errors. Be positive about mistakes. Do not bury them. Recognize and learn from them.
6. Relax. Do not rush. Take time. Enjoy things with people.
7. Hand over the stick. Facilitate. Hand over the pen, pencil, chalk, *rangoli* powder to people. Initiate participatory processes, and then step back. Listen and observe, without interrupting.
8. They can do it. Assume that people can do something until proved otherwise.
9. Ask them. Ask local people for information and advice.
10. Be nice to people.

By keeping in mind the three pillars of PRA, the methods and above-mentioned principles of behaviour and attitudes, one can successfully complete PRA. This will open up a new range of experiences.

PRA Methods and Approaches

The PRA related approaches and methods continue to unfold. It is a powerful and popular method to understand the community. This process empowers the local, marginalized and vulnerable people. Groups and individuals express, share and analyze the realities of their conditions and lives. This helps them gain confidence to plan action and act on it. Most commonly used methods are discussed in the following paragraphs. These methods can be grouped under two major headings:

1. Methods promoting participation
2. Methods seeking actual participation.

Methods promoting participation

1. **Primary and secondary data review:** It is necessary to have background information of a particular area/village where you are going to conduct PRA. This information gives an idea about different interests of people, their culture, and their living style. It also helps us know how they have changed over a period of time. This information can be collected in two ways—either through old records, notes, diaries, court correspondences, etc. or through newspaper articles, research centres, archeology departments, market *sammittes*, universities, government offices, survey reports, etc. Such information helps a lot especially in the earlier stages. For example, one gets an idea about where to go, whom to contact, how to clarify doubts/contradictions or gaps in the information received, etc. One should be careful in using the information collected by these secondary sources and should check the reliability.

2. **Observing directly:** This can be the most effective method, if used properly. It also happens that we tend to be selective in our approach and we focus on certain aspects (see what we want) and neglect other things. While living with the people in the community, if you observe carefully their different cultural background (programmes), their life style, day-to-day activities, you learn a lot. This also helps to recognize their potential and skills and the efforts they make to solve their problems. This gives us an insight into the prevalent power structure and decision-making patterns of the community.

Methods seeking actual participation

1. **Interview:** Semi-structured interviews play a great role in PRA. Open-ended questions help us to understand the locality in a much better way. Remember, the interviews should be conducted in a very friendly, fear-free and informal environment. This can be conducted wherever people are available, i.e. at farm, temple and home, or outside the *panchayat* office. Try to interview people from different occupation like farmers, *sarpanch*, elected representatives, post-master, school teacher/headmaster, police-*patil*, housewives, etc. If you are interviewing *sarpanch* or elected representative, ask questions related to development such as transport, marketing, health facilities, drinking water, schools, etc. Following are some guidelines for conducting an interview:

   (i) Name of the village/community, block, district, state

   (ii) Area/location—tribal, rural, urban

   (iii) Total population (source of information)

   (iv) Nature—*pada*, village, city, town

   (v) Occupations/how people make their living

   (vi) Power structure/who is the decision maker in the village

   (vii) Major political parties

   (viii) Resources available in the village—educational, health and medical, cultural, entertainment facilities, religious, transportation, housing pattern, drinking water sources, sanitation, electricity, and so on

   (ix) Major problems—alcoholism, unemployment, untouchability, casteism, unequal distribution of above resources, draught, non-availability of grazing land, significant conflicts and tension situations, etc.

   (x) Possible solutions to above problems.

2. **Seeking out the experts:** Outsiders must remember that local people also have expertise. They may have expertise on various topics and may guide us about medicinal plants, underground water identification, changes in sources and types of fuel, agro-ecological history, changing values and customs, fodder grasses, animal diseases, kitchen garden, etc. You need to ask people to suggest the name/s of the experienced and the most respected people in community, whose advice will be unanimously accepted in conflict resolution. Through social mapping also, one can find the names of the experts.

3. **Case studies and stories:** This is also a good way to understand the practices followed in the village. One can prepare a household history and profile as well. A detailed case history can give us a

clear picture of the prevalent crisis management and conflict resolution patterns in the community.

4. **Transect walks:** This is a systematically walking through a village. It offers a profile of the village. Transect is an observatory walk through a village living area and/or the area surrounding the village such as fields, hillocks, forests, grazing land, etc. Transects are used as prerequisites for mapping. It can be used to locate areas in a village, which need to be developed. This exercise can be done with the help of persons, who are staying for a longer period of time in that village. They can become your leaders and guides. It not only helps to locate and pinpoint various physical aspects of the village but also helps to understand and discuss with the people the backgrounds of these items. For example, causes of deforestation, use of common land, other indigenous practices, etc. can be studied in this way. Figure 5.2 is self-explanatory.

This is not just based on walking, but it also includes observing, listening, asking, discussing, learning about different zones, soils, land uses, vegetation, crops, livestock, local technologies, new introduced technologies, seeking problems' solutions and opportunities, resources and findings. The amalgam of all these techniques makes it a very useful method.

Transect allows you to get a quick view of the characteristics of a village. It is used to help the villagers to understand their socio-economic environment in a better way. It is important to let people carry out the visualization process themselves. This promotes discussions and dialogues.

5. **Focused group discussions:** If time is limited and one wants to collect more information, focused group discussions can be organized. If it is managed properly, such activity often becomes powerful and efficient.

6. **Do-it-yourself:** Here, the role of experts/outsiders and local people is reversed. Local people become experts and teachers and the outsiders act as novices and learners. Local people supervise and teach skills such as how to transplant, remove, weed, plough and level a field, mud a hut, fetch water from a well/river, carry water on head, fetch firewood, wash clothes on the banks of river or near a well, cook meal on stove, etc.

7. **Time lines and trend and change analysis:** It refers to a chronology or sequence of events that has taken place in a particular village or a specific area. Listing major local events with approximate dates, people's accounts of the past, how customs, practices and things close to them have changed, changes in land use and cropping patterns, population, migration, fuel uses, education, health pattern, and the causes of changes and trends, etc. is very useful.

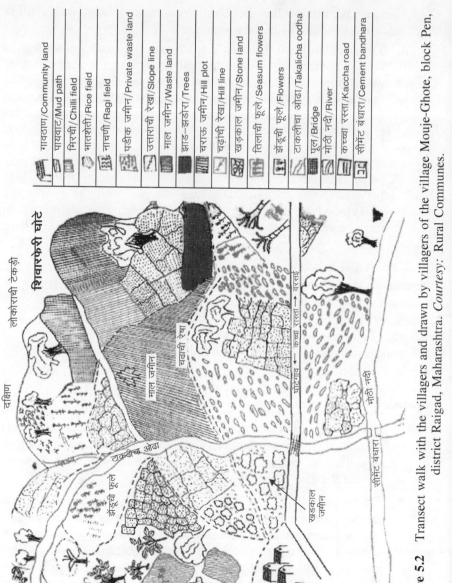

गावठाण/Community land	
पायवाट/Mud path	
मिरची/Chilli field	
भातशेती/Rice field	
नाचणी/Ragi field	
पडीक जमीन/Private waste land	
उताराची रेखा/Slope line	
माळ जमीन/Waste land	
झाड-झुडोरा/Trees	
चराऊ जमीन/Hill plot	
चढाची रेखा/Hill line	
खड़काळ जमीन/Stone land	
तिळाची फूले/Seasum flowers	
झेंडूची फूले/Flowers	
टाकळीचा ओढा/Takalicha oodha	
पूल/Bridge	
मोठी नदी/River	
कच्चा रस्ता/Kaccha road	
सीमेंट बंधारा/Cement bandhara	

Figure 5.2 Transect walk with the villagers and drawn by villagers of the village Mouje-Ghote, block Pen, district Raigad, Maharashtra. *Courtesy:* Rural Communes.

The time line exercise can be used to find out the background of a village. It can also be useful to know the evolution of specific programmes, practices in the areas of health, education, and other social activities related to transport, water, housing pattern, economic activities, etc.

The community worker can find historical events from as far as one can remember up to the present, in the life of a person, community, village, area or institution, depending on what history one wishes to reconstruct. Such a calendar can form the basis of helping us trace trends through history and study the nature of change. Since these events are reconstructed from the memories of people, the best informants are the old people of the village. Giving dates to events can pose some problems but can be overcome by asking questions such as, 'how old do you think you were when this happened?' or 'do you remember if the collector was British or Indian at that time?' and so on. To understand the agricultural pattern, occurrences of droughts, floods, adoption of new crops and varieties and fertilizer usages, years in which major crop failures took place, etc. this method is useful.

8. **Historical profile:** To understand how the social structure and culture is evolved, this method is very useful. Before starting working in a particular village, one needs to know the historical perspective of that village. This can be done by collecting and studying folklores, folk-tales, proverbs and poetry available in that area. By talking to the religious leaders, one can understand the cultural practices and belief system of the community. Traditional management system and farming practices tell us about the power structure existing in that particular village at a particular period of time. This information could be collected through elderly people, key informants of that particular village/community. Figure 5.3 shows historical profile prepared by local people of Mouje-Ghote village, Raigad district of Maharashtra.

This is based on the discussion with senior citizens of the village, *sarpanch* and other villagers residing in the village since last three generations.

This information tells us the trends that have taken place over a period of time, changes that have taken place in terms of resource utilization, cropping patterns, livestock, population, status of women, etc.

9. **Diagrams:** It is a visual representation of features as perceived by the local people. Following are the two types of diagrams most commonly used in PRA:

Venn (chapatti) diagram: This is used to identify and understand the relationships of various institutions, organizations, programmes and their importance in and for community. The perception of local people about these organizations gives an idea whether development has reached to downtrodden

सन/Year	मजुरी/Wages	अन्न/Food	झाड झुडपे/Trees	पिण्याचे पाणी Drinking water	पाऊस/Rainfall	दळणवळण/Transport	राहणी मान Standard of living	आर्थिक व्यवहार/Economy	साथीचे रोग/Epidemics	आरोग्य/Health	शिक्षणाचे प्रमाण Educational status	पोषाख Clothing style	आर्थिक परिस्थिती Economic condition	घराचे प्रकार Types of houses	घर संख्या/No.of houses	लोकसंख्या/Population
१९४०	९ आणे	नाचणी, वरई, साबुळ, काडजानी	धनदाट		भरपूर	पायवाट		धान्य रूपाल	कॉलरा		शाळा नाही		बाईट हाला कीची	गवती झोपडी	४०	१४०
१९५०	१० आणे	मिष प्राण्याचे मांस भात	धनदाट		भरपूर	पायवाट		धान्य पैसा	नारू गोवर		शाळा नाही		बाईट हाला कीची	गवती झोपडी	४५	१६०
१९६०	₹ ३	जंगलातील भाजीपाला			भरपूर	पायवाट		धान्य पैसे	नारू देवी		शाळा		बाईट हाला कीची	कारवीच्या कुडाची	६०	२२०
१९७०	₹ १५	जंगलातील भाजीपाला				पायवाट		धान्य पैसे	नारू, देवी, प्लेग, गोवर	मध्यम	शाळा बंद		थोडी सुधारली		६०	२४०
१९८०	₹ २०	जंगलातील भाजीपाला	विरळ			पायवाट	मध्यम	धान्य पैसे रुपया	कॉलरा, देवी गोवर	मध्यम	–		मध्यम		६५	२००
१९९०	₹ २५	भात डाळ भाजी, मासे		मध्यम		कच्चा रस्ता सायकल बैलगाडी	मध्यम	पैसे रुपया	नाही	मध्यम	शाळा सुरू		मध्यम	कारवी कोलाख	७०	३००
२०००	₹ ४०	डाळ, भात, भाजी, मासे	विरळ	अल्प		सायकल बैलगाडी एस.टी. रिक्षा	बरे	रुपया	कॉलरा	मध्यम	३५ मुले		बरी	विटाची घरे	७५	३२०
२००४	₹ ८०	डाळ, भात, भाजी, मासे		पाणी टंचाई		बैलगाडी सायकल टेम्पो मोटर	बरे	रुपया	नाही	मध्यम	अंगणवाडी व शाळा		बरी		८०	३४०

Figure 5.3 Historical profile of the village Mouje-Ghote, block Pen, district Raigad, Maharashtra. *Courtesy:* Rural Communes.

people or not. To carry out this activity, different sizes of circles of papers are used. The smaller the size of the circle, the lesser is its importance. In other words, this activity can be used to know how many organizations are working in a particular area and their relationship with the people. For example, cooperative banks, dairies, veterinary dispensaries, sub-centre of PHC, *panchayat*, agricultural cooperatives and their access to people can be studied by using this tool. The following Venn diagram (Figure 5.4) is drawn by local women of Mouje-Ghote village of Raigad district, Maharashtra.

A *problem tree:* This is a diagram that shows relation between the cause and effect of different phenomena. For example, Figure 5.5 shows the bad harvest (phenomenon), its causes and effects.

10. **Seasonal calendars:** This is an extremely important and useful exercise used to determine seasonal patterns in rural areas. For example, rainfalls, farming practices, employment, disease pattern, availability of fodder, credit and debt pattern, grazing pattern, breeding season, milk yields, etc. can be studied.

In a seasonal calendar, an attempt is made to determine the seasonal calendar as understood and practiced by villagers. It is a visual representation of activities that take place over a year. One can have calendars of:

मौजे घोटे **सामाजिक समायोजन नकाशा**

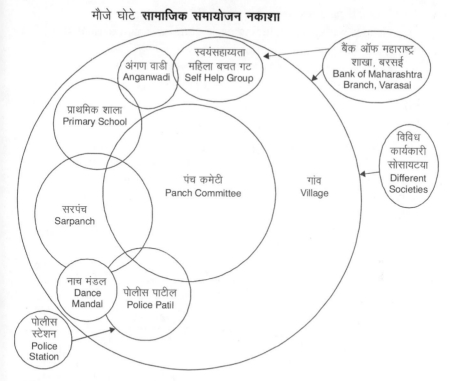

Figure 5.4 Venn diagram drawn by villagers of the village Mouje-Ghote, block Pen, district Raigad, Maharashtra. *Courtesy:* Rural Communes.

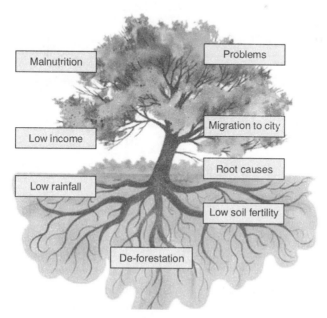

Figure 5.5 Problem tree of bad harvesting in a village.

  (i) Rainfall patterns over last ten to fifteen years

  (ii) Gender workload including agricultural and non-agricultural labour

  (iii) Diet and food consumption

  (iv) Disease pattern over last five to ten years

  (v) Sources of income, expenditure and debt pattern

  (vi) Crop cycles

  (vii) Migration and its effects.

This tool helps in collecting information based on the activities of population throughout the year in order to get a precise idea of the problems faced by them. It informs us about how their time is locally divided and helps to visualize the activities of population during different periods of the year. This helps in meticulous planning of the activities during the leisure period of people, when they are comparatively less busy. Figure 5.6 is self-explanatory.

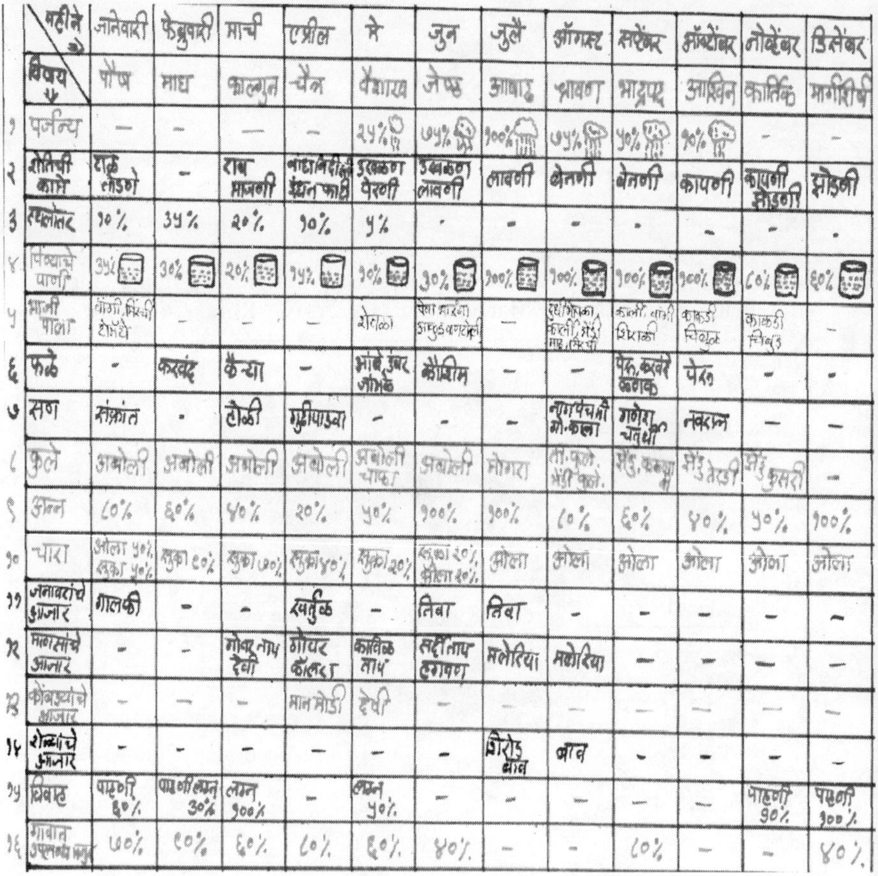

Figure 5.6 Seasonal calendar drawn by villagers of the village Mouje-Ghote, block Pen, district Raigad, Maharashtra.

Courtesy: Rural Communes.

11. **Matrix ranking:** A matrix is a tabular representation that helps to compare one selected feature with another. Examples of matrices are:

(i) *Crop matrix:* Crops grown are analyzed.

(ii) *Health matrix:* Participants describe the curative methods they use for different illnesses.

(iii) *Wealth ranking matrix:* Participants discuss the social status in the village.

This exercise is useful when we need to compare and study the merits and demerits of a variety of items such as different types of crops, animal breeds, trees, etc. In this exercise, a visual chart is prepared, where the items are put on one side and the criteria for comparing these items on the other side. These criteria are to be listed by the villagers themselves. Let us take the example of purchase of a cow. Table 5.4 is self-explanatory.

Table 5.4   Matrix ranking

Variety of cows/criteria	Ordinary/local/deshi	Jersy	Holstin frigin	Geer
Price				
Milk yield				
Fat percentage				
Disease resistance				
Fodder requirement				

Once the chart is ready, ask the villagers to give score. Scoring can be done by placing seeds or stones. In the above case, people will first rank and then take their decision, which variety of cow to be purchased. Another example is ranking of livestock, as shown in Figure 5.7.

Livestock	As helper	Market value	Provide manure	Good taste for food	Low cost (labour and fodder)	Disease resistance	Easy breeding and growth	Total
Goat		*****	*****		*****	*****	*****	25
Cattle	*****	****	***		****	****		20
Buffalo	*****	****	***		***	****		19
Pig		****	****	*****		**	***	18
Horse	*****	****	**		***			14
Poultry		****		*****	**		***	14
Dog	*****							5

Figure 5.7   Results of matrix scoring and ranking of livestock with four households in Damaide village.
(*Source:* Adapted from www.PRAMaps.Matrix ranking.com)

12. **Mapping:**   This refers to the construction of a map of the village living area using *rangoli* powders or chalk on the ground or a cement floor or on a large paper sheet. Following features can be studied through mapping:

   (i)   Natural resources
   (ii) Housing pattern(s)
   (iii) Poverty pattern(s)
   (iv) Location of the marginalized groups
   (v)   Cropping pattern(s)
   (vi) Territory of the village.

It makes our observation more accurate. Through maps we get a clear picture of the village. It is possible that we may overlook certain things, which emerge clearly through the maps. Following are some of the most common mappings practiced in PRA:

Social mapping: These maps give information about the social structure, availability of resources at a glance. One can understand the village layout, housing pattern, location of shops, *mandirs*, bank, schools, wells, hand pumps, *kaccha* and *pakka* roads, etc. Once the base map is ready, it is possible to provide/mark different types of information on it. This includes information related to the number of family members in each family, number of families having animals, number of families with illiterate members, their health status, land holding, economic status, etc. Through this map, one can also locate the free land available in the village. Social maps can be used to identify distribution of population according to religion, caste, class, status, etc. This information helps in planning different programmes in future. Social mapping of Mouje-Ghote village drawn by the villagers is given in Figure 5.8.

Following are some of the useful tips for social mapping method:

   (i)   Choose common place for drawing social maps, such as open ground in front of gram *panchayat*, school, *anganwadi*, etc. Try to avoid exercising this activity in front of somebody's house.

   (ii) Involve people from all categories—men, women, children, socially backward class people. One can have separate groups for men and women and compare how both the groups perceive the same village in a different manner.

   (iii) Make use of local resources to draw the map such as *rangoli* powder, chalk or directly drawing on the ground with the help of a stick.

   (iv) Try to avoid the temptation of giving suggestions. Allow them freedom to draw.

   (v)   Once the map is ready, you can copy it on a paper or take a photograph.

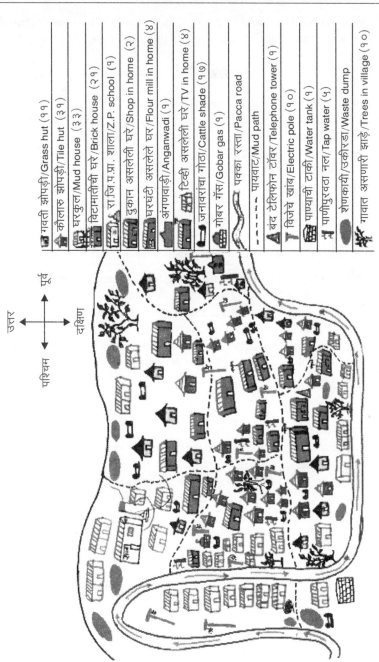

सामाजिक नकाशा मौजे घोटे, ता.पेण, जिला रायगड

उत्तर

पूर्व

पश्चिम

दक्षिण

गवती झोपडी/Grass hut (९९)	
कोलाळ झोपडी/Tile hut (३९)	
घरकुल/Mud house (३३)	
विटामातीची घरे/Brick house (२९)	
रा.जि.प.शा. शाळा/Z.P. school (१)	
दुकान असलेली घरे/Shop in home (२)	
घरघंटी असलेले घर/Flour mill in home (८)	
अंगणवाडी/Anganwadi (१)	
टिव्ही असलेली घरे/TV in home (८)	
जनावरांचा गोठा/Cattle shade (९७)	
गोबर गॅस/Gobar gas (१)	
पक्का रस्ता/Pacca road	
पायवाट/Mud path	
बंद टेलिफोन टॉवर/Telephone tower (१)	
विजेचे खांब/Electric pole (९०)	
पाण्याची टाकी/Water tank (१)	
पाणीपुरवठा नळ/Tap water (१)	
शेणकाठी/उकिरडा/Waste dump	
गावात असणारी झाडे/Trees in village (९०)	

Figure 5.8 Social mapping drawn by villagers of the village Mouje-Ghote, block Pen, district Raigad, Maharashtra.
Courtesy: Rural Communes.

(vi) Note down the names of all villagers who have participated in drawing the map. This motivates them to participate in following activities.

(vii) Propose vote of thanks to all the villagers at the end of the activity.

Resource mapping: This map helps to understand the different natural resources available in a particular village. Through this map, one can explain the people the optimum utilization of natural resources for the development of a village. Resource mapping includes availability of forest, location of a river, wells, potable drinking water, grazing land, water sheds, type of soil, variety of trees and their locations, etc. Figure 5.9 is self-explanatory.

While drawing resource map, ask the villagers first to draw the boundaries of a village. Ask them to show locations of wells, bore wells, lakes, dry land, grazing land, farms, and medicinal plants. Once the map is ready, one can have discussion on how to save the natural resources.

13. **Daily activity profile:** This exercise gives an idea about the local people's daily working schedule. It informs about the time slots when they are busy or free, the amount of time they spend on each activity, etc. It gives a clear picture of their time schedule to plan activities ensuring better attendance of people. Figure 5.10 shows daily routine of a man and woman.

Empowerment

PRA can help to empower the weaker section of the society, especially women. It can create collective awareness and develop confidence in people to confront others and argue their case/side. Our major concern here should be on the people, who are really empowered in the process and how do they use their new power. This also happens that the outsiders get empowered and exploit the people. If local elite and dominant class become more empowered, then the condition of the poor and disadvantaged worsens. In other words, the effectiveness of PRA depends on the type of people involved in it. Hence, the challenge is to introduce and use PRA for weaker sections and empower them. The current tools of PRA, if used properly, can serve this purpose. Sequences such as participatory mapping—household listing—well-being ranking-livelihood analysis can identify local people and bring them together. Focus group discussions can be used to identify the priorities and interests of different people from various categories for maximum results.

PRA helps the people to express and share their knowledge with others. Through diagramming, mapping, investigating and observing, they can enrich their knowledge. This helps to improve their understanding which leads to take desired action. The whole process helps people to gain skills and confidence. They realize their own hidden potential.

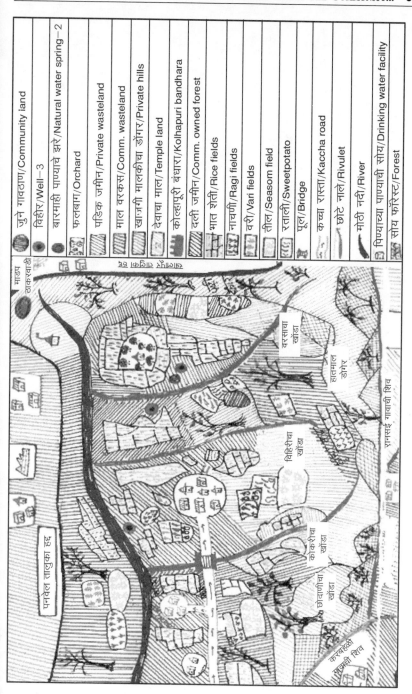

Figure 5.9   Resource mapping drawn by villagers of the village Mouje-Ghote, Block Pen, district Raigad, Maharashtra.
Courtesy: Rural Communes.

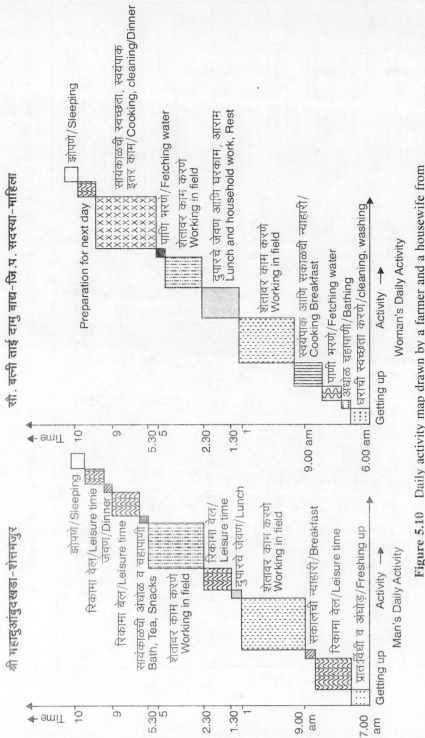

Figure 5.10 Daily activity map drawn by a farmer and a housewife from the village Mouje-Ghote, block Pen, district Raigad, Maharashtra. *Courtesy:* Rural Communes.

It is proved that empowerment serves equity and well-being. It is not a static condition, but a continuous process. It is not a product but a lifelong process. Nobody can say that empowerment is complete. It enhances capabilities and gives a wider scope for choice and action. It is an interactive process. It brings changes in power relations and behaviour.

Change in attitude: The approaches and methods of PRA have helped to change the attitudes of dominant groups. This can be reflected in social mapping by men and women. In the same village, when asked the men and women to draw the social map of their own village, the final product usually differs in many ways. Men are surprised that they did not know the women could do it. The map prepared by women is much more vivid and detailed. Many times, it turns out to be more accurate than the one drawn by men. At many places, PRA approaches have been used to enable men to appreciate the hard life and conditions of women.

To summarize, we can say that by using PRA, one can understand the power relationships, motivation of the people, values and taboos of the community. The community worker must gather this information before starting any programme/activity in the community. The community worker must understand the power centres in the community and their influence in taking decisions. Planning and implementing development programmes with people's participation is considered to be one of the keys to sustainable development.

If local people are involved in planning and implementing of the development policies, projects, programmes, the outcome would be naturally very different. Usually, the powerful few dominate the scene and marginalize the underprivileged people. Power is usually seen as an asset in development. It is a means of getting things done. PRA gives power to all people, who can decide their priorities, find resources and utilize them optimally. It results in the development of all people and not only of the selected few. It is true that PRA cannot solve all the problems, but it guides to tackle and deal with these challenges. PRA's basic principle—'use your own best judgment at all times' permits and encourages creativity.

As mentioned earlier, PRA methods and approaches continue to unfold. PRA is both popular and powerful. It has spread with alarming speed. This is one of the best methods to empower not only the local people but also the vulnerable and the marginalized. It allows them to express, share and analyze the complex and diverse realities of their life. It encourages them to plan and act on it.

For successful implementation of development programmes/activities, the community worker needs to involve all people, especially the decision makers as often as possible. Hence, it is necessary to understand the various participatory methods of collecting information. A few of them are mentioned above. The community worker can invent new methods and add to this collection. After understanding the community, the community worker needs to conduct meeting and plan activities. This requires skills in conducting meetings. The next chapter deals with this aspect.

Review Questions

1. Give rationale of participatory approach.
2. Illustrate different barriers to people's participation in community development process.
3. Briefly describe the evolution of PRA.
4. Explain the pillars of PRA.
5. 'PRA is different from other methods of research.' Illustrate with suitable examples.
6. Compare RRA and PRA.
7. Explain different steps to be followed in PRA.
8. What preparatory work should one do before conducting PRA?
9. What precautions should the community worker take while doing PRA?
10. Explain different types of PRA.
11. Illustrate different principles of PRA.
12. Give a list of approaches followed in PRA. Illustrate any two of them.
13. How will you conduct a transect walk in a tribal village?
14. 'Venn (*Chapati*) diagram is used to identify and understand the relationships of various institutions, organizations, programmes and their importance in and for community.' Explain with suitable examples.
15. 'Social mapping gives information about the social structure, availability of resources at a glance.' Comment.
16. 'The daily activity profile helps the community worker in deciding the timings of programmes to be conducted in the community.' Explain with examples.
17. Conduct social mapping of any nearby area and write your experiences.
18. Which tool will you use to finalize the venue and time for organizing skill development programme in a community? Justify your answer.

6
Holding Meetings in the Community

The organizations working with the communities must establish trust and honesty with the community people. Community people should participate in community mobilization process so that they feel a sense of belongingness and ownership. This can happen when the community workers listen to their views and opinions. In the initial stage, the community people may not participate fully. It takes time especially if the organization is from outside and new to the community. The community worker should always listen to the people and understand them.

The mobilization process starts with establishing contacts with the community. This can be done through a number of ways. One of the ways is conducting meeting. Meetings help in building relationships. It is necessary to organize a meeting as early as possible. Once the organization gets acquainted with the community, it builds the trust with the people. Meetings also give an opportunity to learn about the strengths and resources of the community.

Community meetings play a vital role in community organization. Convening a community meeting is an important way to facilitate the process of community organization. It helps to establish a rapport with the people. Still, many people do not realize the necessity of organizing meetings in the community.

The community worker should understand the importance of meetings. As these meetings play a crucial role in community work, the community worker should make these meetings run effectively. The community worker must remember that most people do not like to attend meetings. They feel it is just time pass, especially when they are not aware of the purpose of the meeting. It is possible that their opinion may be based on their past experiences. Hence, the purpose of meeting must be clearly explained to the people concerned. The community worker should also make sure that the meetings are not held very frequently or for very trivial issues. Unless it is necessary, meetings should not be called.

PURPOSES OF MEETINGS

Following are some of the purposes of organizing meetings in the communities:

1. To build a rapport with the people.
2. To interact with the people about their issues and ideas.
3. To understand the current status of the people.
4. To find out the key informants and resources available in the community.
5. To build a team for further planning and action to be taken based on the needs of people.
6. To find local leaderships.
7. To discuss the purpose and role of the community worker and his/her organization.
8. To discuss the role of the community.

The above list is not totally exhaustive. The purpose of conducting meetings depends on the type of community and its needs. Generally, there are two types of meetings, namely:

◆ Open meeting
◆ Closed meeting.

Open meeting is one which can be attended by any person. Public meetings on the issues such as Right to Information, discussion on Annual Budget of India, health awareness lectures, etc. are examples of open meeting. For closed meeting, a few people are invited. Anybody cannot walk in. The members are invited to participate in it. For example, meetings of staff members in an organization, monthly review meetings, distribution of medicine to HIV infected people, etc. come under this type of meeting. There are varieties of meetings based on time intervals, issue based, etc. Some of the meetings are organized at particular time interval like monthly, quarterly or annual meetings. They are well planned and venue, date and time are pre-decided.

There are certain meetings which are issue based. For example, a meeting of people who want ration card, have drinking water problem, getting a voting card, etc. is called an issue-based meeting.

The status of people who attend meeting depends on the type of meeting. For example, in regular meetings, most of the participants/members know each other, whereas in issue-based meetings, participants/members not necessarily know each other. They come together because of a common problem/issue. Hence, the community worker should handle such meetings very carefully.

HOW TO PLAN A MEETING

Conducting meetings is an art as well as a skill. The community worker should be clear about the objectives of the meeting. Accordingly, s/he should plan the meeting. Meticulous planning ensures participation. The community worker should ensure that the participants are well prepared for the meeting. Whether it is a regular meeting or an issue-based meeting, the community worker should ask himself/herself the following questions:

1. What is the main issue to be addressed in the meeting?
2. Who is affected by it?
3. Are people aware of its causes and effects?
4. Is there any organization which is working on the same issue?
5. Has anyone individually or in groups taken any action? If yes, what action? What was its result? If no, why did people not take any action?
6. Are there resources locally available to address these issues?
7. Does it fit with the organization's goals and objectives where the community worker is working? Does it come in the purview of the organization for which the community worker is working?
8. What kind of help the organization represented by the community worker can offer?
9. What action the community workers expect from the people?
10. What methods are going to be used to address the issues? (Brainstorming, audio-visuals, charts, statistical data, references of laws, etc.)

It is the responsibility of the community worker to ensure that everyone has been informed about the date, time and venue of the meeting, along with the agenda (wherever necessary) of the issues to be discussed. Whenever a meeting is organized, the community worker should make an attempt to conduct it in a friendly and comfortable atmosphere. Members should feel welcomed and encouraged to participate. Nobody should dominate others. Each participant should be given an opportunity to express his/her opinion, feelings, and discontent. The community worker should see that conflicting situation does not arise. If such a situation arises, s/he should handle it in such a way that both parties feel to be in a win-win situation. The agenda should be explained at the beginning of the meeting. The community worker's role is to see that the agenda is followed. All the participants should understand what is going on. Decisions should be taken with mutual consensus. Meetings should end with certain decisions and actions, which should lead to solving the issues.

Sometimes meetings are conducted without any obvious output. For hours, the discussion goes on without any conclusion. Why does this happen? If you go to the root cause, you will find many reasons for ineffective meetings. Following are some of the reasons for failure of meetings. The community worker can add to this list, as per his/her experiences.

1. There are certain issues which need not be discussed in meetings.
2. The purpose of the meeting is not clear.
3. Participation of wrong people as the issue does not concern them.
4. Discussion, if goes out of track and not controlled/guided properly.

HOW TO HOLD A SUCCESSFUL MEETING

To make the meeting successful, the community worker should pay attention to the following points:

1. Selection of a convenient venue for the meeting
2. Appropriate timing
3. Participants' selection
4. Timely intimation/invitation of meeting
5. Preparation of an agenda
6. Circulation of resource material/handouts in the meeting, if required.

Organizing a meeting in the community plays a vital role in facilitating the community organization process. This is an entry point to establish rapport with people. This allows the community worker to understand the current situation of the community, its issues and their background. At the beginning, the community worker should invite a wide range of people for the meeting, who, with their experiences, can contribute towards giving broader perspectives to the discussion. A community meeting can be beneficial, if conducted properly.

Before calling a meeting, identify the issue/s to be discussed at the meeting. For example, there may be a variety of issues like unemployment, starting an income generating programme, malnutrition, health issues, draught, scarcity of drinking water, etc. Once you select the issue, follow the steps given below.

1. **Decide objectives:** It is very important to decide the objective/s of the meeting, before you conduct the meeting. These objectives will affect the way the meeting is planned and facilitated. Even though the issue might be clear, there can be a number of possible objectives, and you should plan the agenda accordingly.

2. **Selection of a venue:** The venue should be accessible and familiar to all the people who are going to attend/participate in it. It should be centrally located. The room, where the meeting is going to be held, should have enough space to accommodate all the people. It should also provide enough space to small groups, if they want to discuss different issues. It should be properly ventilated (airy, enough light arrangement, etc.). The seating arrangement should be comfortable. If women are participating in the meeting, make some space available for children, as mostly women carry their children. Some open space for their children to play will help women to participate wholeheartedly. The venue must have drinking water and toilet facilities. Even though the meeting is for an hour, these facilities are necessary. The community worker can choose familiar places as a venue for the meeting such as school, *anganwadi*, *samaj mandir*, etc. The advantage of these places is any person, irrespective of caste or religion, can enter these places. If the meeting is to be conducted in an open area, the community worker should make an arrangement of *Dari*/mat for seating on the ground. If many people are going to attend, then s/he has to make an arrange-ment of sound system (mike) as well.

3. **Convenient timings:** To increase attendance and participation of more people in the meeting, timings should be decided in consultation with the participants. For example, if the meeting is for farmers and if it is the peak season of farming, the best way of calling a meeting is in the evening or at night (may be after 7.00 pm). If a meeting is to discuss the issues related to women and if they are housewives, the convenient time for meeting is in the afternoon (may be 2.00 pm to 4.00 pm). If all of them also do agriculture work, then the best way to conduct meeting is in night.

If meetings are organized in the night, select the venue which is safe, especially for women and girls. Make sure electricity is available. If not, at least *petromax* should be available.

The community worker should take into consideration that the meeting does not clash with other organization/group meetings. For example, some other agency working in that area has planned its meeting on the same day, may or may not be at the same time. People will get confused which meeting they should attend. Hence, the community worker should see that his/her meeting does not clash with others'.

While deciding the date and time for a meeting, the community worker should consult the key persons. Avoid calling meetings on a day of festival, local ceremonies, marriages, ration distribution day, water timings, etc. Start and end the meeting on time without waiting for the habitual late comers.

4. **Agenda:** Agenda refers to the list of most important items/issues to be discussed in the meeting. Based on the objectives of the meeting, an agenda should be prepared. Involve some key participants/leaders, if possible, in preparation of the agenda. The agenda should be clear, understandable to every participant. Do not keep too many items at a time to discuss in one meeting. If there are many issues to be discussed, the community worker should prioritize them and plan the meeting accordingly. The agenda should have a last item known as 'any other matter'. With the permission of chair, one can discuss the subjects which come at the last moment. This allows individuals to raise those issues which are not included in the agenda.

Once the agenda is ready, try to intimate the participants about the date, time and venue along with agenda of the meeting. The community worker can use different ways to intimate the participants about the meeting such as by sending letter, meeting personally (if the number is less), writing on a notice board kept at prominent places in the community, *davandi*, announcement, etc. If the agenda is not sent well in advance, the community worker should make sure that it should be explained at the beginning of the meeting. Agenda helps the participants to know the issues to be discussed. It also helps them realize the importance of attending the meeting.

5. **Identifying participants:** The selection of the people to attend the meeting depends on the issues to be discussed there. Sometimes the issue is related to a specific group of people; in such a case invite only that group of people. If the whole community is affected by the problem, then it is necessary to involve the whole community in planning an action. Make sure that the decision makers are involved in meetings. It is better to involve local leaders, religious leaders, heads of educational institutes, cooperatives, representatives of *mahila mandals*, youth *mandals*, etc. If possible and necessary, involve representatives of government departments as well. Take down names and signatures/thumb impressions of the participants. Keep a separate attendance register for this. In future, one can know who attended the meeting.

6. **During meeting:** At the outset, welcome all the participants. Select one chairperson or a facilitator, who can conduct the meeting. Any organized meeting will not happen spontaneously. It will be necessary to have a chairperson/facilitator, who will facilitate and direct the discussion. The community worker himself/herself can play this role. The facilitator should see that nobody monopolizes the discussion. S/he should see that everyone expresses her/his feelings or opinions frankly. Those who are shy and do not speak should be encouraged to speak. It is the role of the facilitator to use

proper skills and techniques to seek participation of all participants. The facilitator will lead the discussion to achieve the objectives of meeting and guide the participants to come to a consensus or unanimous decision. Accordingly, they can decide a plan of action to overcome the problems. Throughout the meeting, the community worker should keep on eye contact with the participants.

In the beginning of the meeting, the facilitator should read the agenda, followed by reading of minutes of previous meeting (wherever necessary). Then the participants should be given a chance to express themselves. They may add a point, which might have been left out. Then, the minutes should be finally approved in the meeting.

Minutes are actual records of what is discussed and decided in meetings. It is necessary to note down the proceedings of meetings every time. Writing minutes of each meeting helps to know what issues were handled, what actions were taken, who were involved in solving problem, what resources were used, etc. It also suggests the need of the outside resources and expertise. It also reflects the difficulties faced by people. This information helps in planning the future actions.

While facilitating the meeting, the community worker should ask 'open ended' questions. For example, what will you do in this situation? Questions starting with why, how, when, where, who, what, which should be asked. By asking open-ended questions, you seek their active participation. After asking question, give them some time to think. Their silence or pause should be understood. Even after prolonged silence, if they do not respond, rephrase your question. Do not change your question. Try to get answers by rephrasing it.

Be cautious that the questions do not mislead or confuse or put people on the defensive side. Questions should be well-phrased, and clarify the areas of discussion and make them feel free and open to respond. If the group does not respond, do not impose your ideas or decisions on them. Always avoid calling them by their first name. For example, *Kamala, Rama, Hari,* etc. Address them respectfully. For example, *Kamalatai, Rambhau, Haridada,* etc. (as per the local cultural norms)

Sometimes the facilitator can ask direct questions to the participants attending the meeting. Such questions help seek more participation and attention of people. For example, what is your opinion? Would you like to comment? Also try to analyze why a few people are silent. What could be the reason for their non-participation? Try to explain how this meeting is going to affect their lives directly or indirectly.

If a meeting is called to present a report of activities carried out, then it should include the list of tasks conducted, and the problems (if any) faced in carrying out the task. It must mention whether the task is completed or still needs more time to complete. It must suggest if any help is needed from outside to finish it. If the task is not completed, seek help of the people and assign responsibilities to them, ensure some follow-up mechanism to complete the task. Ask people to give their ideas, viewpoints, which will enable to finish the task in stipulated time.

The two most important strategies used in taking decisions are consensus and voting.

In consensus, the issue is discussed at length with focus on each cause and effect side and then come to a conclusion, which is accepted by all the participants or majority of the participants.

Voting is done when there is a difference of opinion among the participants. The community worker or the chairperson of the meeting puts forward one decision (raised through discussion in the meeting) and asks the participants to raise hands, if they agree with it. If the majority of the participants accept it, then it becomes the decision and other participants have to accept it.

At the end, the community worker must thank all the participants and others involved in the meeting. They can also announce the date of next meeting.

FACTORS AFFECTING THE SUCCESS OF MEETING

There are many factors which affect the success of the meeting. For example:

1. The seating arrangement is not proper.
2. The place is congested, not airy but suffocated.
3. It is very far/not easily accessible.
4. No proper light arrangement is made.
5. It is too noisy and discussion cannot be heard properly.
6. No arrangement of sound system and/or failure of sound system.
7. Domination of certain people or group which denies others to express their opinions, feelings.
8. Inconvenient timings.
9. Meeting stretched for too long.
10. Disturbance from children.
11. Lack of proper publicity of the meeting due to which people did not receive information about the meeting.
12. No communication or communication gap.
13. Lack of appropriate resources (such as black or white board, audio-visuals, posters, etc).
14. Non-availability of facilities like drinking water, toilets, child care, etc.
15. Negligence towards people who need special arrangement such as handicapped and old people.

Figure 6.1 explains resources required for a successful meeting.

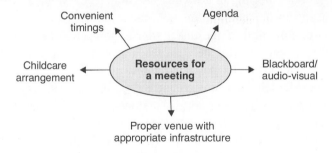

Figure 6.1   Resources for a meeting.

There are different styles used to facilitate the meeting. Following are some of them. The community worker should use either one out of it or use a combination of them as per the demands of the issue and the local situation.

1. **Autocratic style:**   In this style, the community worker himself/ herself is the decision maker. S/he just dictates the participants (local people) about what, when and how to do certain things. The limitation of this style is that it does not allow people to participate in decision-making. Limited people get involved. So, it may not represent the whole community. Ideas of all people are not considered here. This method increases dependency on outsiders.

2. **Democratic style:**   Such style allows the community worker to play the role of a facilitator. By establishing a good rapport with people, s/he just guides them about the different aspects of a task for better results. Here, the community worker seeks full participation of people. People themselves take decisions. They decide issues, prioritize them, and are involved in action to solve the problems and also in evaluation process. This method helps to build local leadership. It also develops skills and abilities of the people. Capacity building of local people takes place by using this style, which is the ultimate goal of community organization.

The good community worker makes use of both styles, depending on the local situation/s. S/he encourages people's participation, and facilitates them to make decisions. If they are not able to take the right decision, or go in the wrong direction, at times, s/he takes decisions on their behalf with their consensus.

TIPS FOR CONDUCTING MEETINGS

To facilitate any meeting in the community, the community worker should keep in mind the following points:

1. Establish rapport by using different skills and techniques.
2. Start the meeting in a friendly environment and make it interesting.
3. Maintain the tempo throughout the meeting.
4. Give direction, if the discussion is going off the track and bring discussion towards the right track to achieve aims and objectives, without hurting anyone's emotions.
5. Seek participation of each and every participant.
6. Handle carefully the hot discussion/s, aggressive behaviour, dominant people, conflicts, attention seekers, etc. S/he should control the over articulate people as it may disturb the time schedule and may result in the departure from the discussion of the main issue.
7. Summarize the meeting.
8. Bring discussion towards decision-making and prepare an action plan and distribute the responsibilities.

Let us deal with a real-life situation. Read it carefully and anticipate and analyze your handling of a similar situation.

'The community worker calls a meeting of the community people to start a primary school in that locality. For this purpose, s/he has invited a Block Education Officer, Education Inspector, the *Sarpanch* and representatives of *Panchayat Rajya* Institution. The meeting was called in an open ground outside the *Gram Panchayat* office. At the venue, a small stage was built where seating arrangement for guest speakers was made. As it was a public meeting, mike was also made available. One of the elected members was asked to facilitate the meeting and introduce the guests at the last moment. The Block Education Officer explained in detail the Right to Education Act. It was too technical and very lengthy. The Education Inspector also took a lot of time and gave a lengthy lecture on education system. There was no time left for discussion and question-answer session. At the end, the facilitator formed a group of interested people to take further action.

Many parents and women left the meeting half way as it went on for a long time. A few parents raised their problems, but nobody paid any attention to their issues. They felt left out and neglected.'

Let us analyze the above situation in the light of the following questions:

1. What was the objective of the meeting?
2. Was it realized?
3. Whether people's issues were discussed or not?
4. Were the facilities at the venue adequate?
5. How was the facilitator chosen? Was the method of choosing correct?
6. Did the facilitator perform his role properly/as expected?
7. What went wrong?
8. How would you have handled this situation?

To make the meeting successful, the community worker should use the following skills and techniques:

1. Good listening skills
2. Good planning skills
3. Thinking skills (what to say, when to say (appropriate time), and how to say (manner which will not hurt or insult anyone, without dominating people)
4. Never be partial to anyone, be balanced and neutral
5. Encouraging every one's participation
6. Helping participants to take decisions (encouraging them to take action)
7. Appreciating people's contribution
8. Negotiation skills
9. Conflict management skills
10. Communication skills, especially in cosmopolitan culture
11. Public speaking and presentation skills
12. Networking, wherever necessary
13. Neat record keeping.

WRITING MINUTES AFTER MEETING

Once the meeting gets over, the community worker should write minutes of it. It is a document, a record, which may be useful in future actions. The minute should have the following details:

1. Date, time and venue of the meeting.
2. Names of the participants who attended the meeting (if it is a small group, write their names. If more than 20 participants have attended, attach the list of their names along with their signatures/or thumb impressions).
3. Agenda (copy of the agenda can be attached separately if the number of items discussed is longer).
4. Summary of the discussions taken in the meeting.
5. Decisions taken (agenda itemwise).
6. Details of actions to be taken, shortlisting of the people to be involved, and mention the time limit required to complete the action.
7. Follow-up action to be taken.
8. Time, date and venue for the next meeting.

A separate register can be maintained for writing minutes. If required, these minutes can be circulated to participants. Minutes should always be read in next meetings so that transparency could be maintained. People remain aware of the happenings. Details of how to write minutes are given in Chapter 11.

Before organizing any meeting for any purpose, the community worker should remember the following points:

1. Be aware of the diversity of the community.
2. Get acquainted and respect cultural and spiritual differences.
3. Respect the knowledge and experiences of the elderly people and leaders.
4. Understand and respect the local protocols and codes of ethics of each community.
5. Understand and learn the way the community communicates with each other.
6. Give sufficient time to people to communicate to you.
7. Provide adequate opportunities for giving feedback about strengths and shortcomings of the actions taken.
8. Understand and learn local people's language and respond to them in their language.
9. Ensure that the work does not clash with any social or cultural activity.
10. Do not get involved with any political party.
11. Promote two-way communication across cultures.
12. Do not enter in any community with a biased mind.
13. Be ready to learn from people.
14. Never keep any personal agenda.
15. Do not enter the community in an inebriated state or under the influence of any drug.

To summarize, the role of the community worker in organizing meetings in the community is very crucial. It depends on the type of the community and the nature of the issues to be dealt with. The community worker has to adopt or adapt certain strategies. S/he has to remember that the ultimate aim of her/his work is to improve the quality of life of people. S/he should always try to build up local leadership, which will take action to materialize their unattended needs and solve problems.

Remember, meetings play a significant role if the organization wants to work with the communities. Meetings, if conducted properly, help in collective decision-making, planning and follow-up actions. They result in accountability of the decisions and the actions taken. They help to build a good organization. If meetings are used in the right way, organizations can work efficiently and effectively. If meetings are not used properly, they end up without any results. Hence, they defeat the purpose that they are supposed to serve. Sometimes we see that meetings go endlessly long, without resulting in any concrete decisions or outcome. Such meetings create bad impression on participants and demotivate them. It is essential that some concrete decisions are taken whenever you conduct a meeting.

Try to utilize meeting places for democratic and constructive discussions which will automatically lead to the total participation of the community people. The platform of meeting can also be used for conflict resolution. The same is discussed in detail in the next chapter.

Review Questions

1. Illustrate the purpose of organizing meetings in the community.
2. What different factors should be kept in mind while organizing a successful meeting?
3. What important factors should be kept in mind during a meeting?
4. Explain the factors affecting a meeting.
5. What skills a community worker should have for conducting a successful meeting?
6. Explain the importance of meetings in community mobilization process.
7. How will you conduct a meeting of rural people for an awareness programme on health?

7

Conflict Management in Community Organization

Conflict situations arise frequently in our daily life—both in public and in private. Conflict is an inevitable part of human relationships. It arises when people disagree over anything perceived as important. One sees things in a particular manner, but other may have a different perception, different attitude, which may not match with us. Differences of opinions cause conflict. Conflict may arise on a small or large scale. It may occur within and among groups or communities. It may be triggered by ethnic, racial, religious or economic differences. Sometimes, conflict may arise due to differences in values, beliefs, attitudes and cultural background towards the issues.

Generally, it is found that the larger and more diverse a group or community, the greater the chances for conflict. Each group may have different beliefs, goals and perceptions, which pose many challenges. The community worker should prepare himself mentally to resolve the conflict by using different skills and techniques. He should be aware of the issues and value differences that may cause conflict within groups or community. Conflict can be either constructive or destructive, depending on how it is approached and managed. Conflicts arise on a daily basis, sometimes as a small dispute, sometimes as a violent battle/situation. Based on our personality and peculiar cultural background, each one of us responds to conflict differently. Two persons can perceive and interpret the same situation very differently. Misperceiving what others say and do, can lead to confusion and conflict. Unmanaged conflict is a threat to development.

Usually, conflict reflects a negative connotation. It is always viewed as a bad thing which becomes a hurdle in the smooth functioning of the programme. But one should remember that conflicts are bound to result while working with people. It is important to find the right way to overcome them and continue working productively. Hence, the community worker should know his/her role in conflict situation. It is necessary for a community worker to understand the causes of conflict, and how to minimize or deal with them, or resolve them. Conflict can be used as a strategy to bring a desired change. We need to understand the steps and techniques required to resolve the conflict so that both sides have a win-win situation. This chapter addresses these questions. It provides information to community workers to understand conflict and to deal with it within and among groups and communities.

Each conflict has a relative significance. People react in their own way to a particular situation. Conflict is not necessarily negative. Actually conflict in itself is not a problem, but the way it is handled determines a positive or negative outcome. Conflicts could be productive. Anna Hazare's campaign to curb corruption is an example of this. Such conflicts can create positive effects. They can strengthen relationships, improve the decision-making process, generate discussions and result in more participation of people. The involvement of people helps to clarify goals, brings the groups together and hence, results in development. Remember, once the conflict arises, do not ignore it, handle it. Conflicts will not disappear on its own. Conflict, if handled tactfully, releases tensions, provides scope for discussion and results in creative work. It may lead to positive changes. The most common forms of conflict resolution are negotiation, mediation, community conferencing and conflict transformation. The community worker may use one or a combination of these forms depending on the nature of the conflict and the people involved in it. Let us understand the concept of conflict.

The word 'conflict' is mostly associated with negative connotations. It is often viewed as the opposite of cooperation and peace. Hence, it is generally related with the threat of violence or disruptive (non-violent) disputes. But this view is not always correct. In certain situations, conflict has acted as a positive force to bring the desired social change. The latest example of this is *Narmada Bachao Andolan*.

The possibility of conflict exists whenever and wherever more than one person comes in contact. Conflict can arise within groups, among groups, within communities, between community and organization/s. In community organization, people with diverse interests, goals come together, which incre-ase the possibility of conflict. All conflicts are not the same. We face conflicts at all levels such as within family, with friends, colleagues, neighbours, political leaders, teachers, etc. It is better to resolve them before they explode.

COMPETITION AND CONFLICT

Competition and conflict have common root of striving towards goals. The major difference between the two exists in the manner of attaining the goals. Competition occurs when persons or groups have incompatible or opposing goals but do not interfere with each other as they try to attain their respective goals. On the other hand, conflict takes place when persons or groups have incompatible or opposing goals and they try to interfere with each other as they try to achieve their respective goals (Gray and Starke, 1988). In other words, in competition, one does not try to trouble the other person/party whereas in conflict, one person tries to trouble, hurt the other person/party and sees that others efforts and actions go futile.

There can be healthy competition between two groups or two communities towards the same goal. Making more number of people literate, reaching health facilities to maximum people are some of the examples of this. In competition, there are certain rules, may be written or unwritten. As long as the groups or organizations are working without interfering with each other, competition exists. If one of the groups or organizations interferes or disturbs other party's programme, conflict starts.

Competition can be used as a technique to stimulate community groups to action. Healthy competitions always lead to desired social changes. One can offer incentives while organizing competitions. For example, to stop dumping garbage on the roads, one can organize beautification competitions among different societies. This will improve cleanliness and lead to healthy environment. Competitions often lead to new achievements, inventions, and outstanding efforts in solving problems.

When competitions become unhealthy and unfriendly, conflicts arise. The organizations working with the communities should be sensitive to potential conflict. This is important throughout the community organization process. This ensures that our work does not create tension between groups or communities. The organizations should keep the 'do not harm' policy.

Conflicts can be resolved and transformed through building capacities of the people. This brings individuals, groups and teams closer. It also empowers them to find solutions to their own problems and needs.

CONCEPT OF CONFLICT

All of us wish not to have conflict. Many of us try to escape conflict as well. Sometimes we get surprised when conflict arises. According to Allport (1955), the way a person defines his/her situation constitutes for him/her its reality. Conflict, therefore, is real but a subjective and an intangible entity. Conflict, whether it is healthy or destructive, depends on how the person/s involved in it interpret it. All types of conflicts create anger, fear, sorrow and frustration. Sometimes it leads to some creativity, planning, establishing new relationships. Conflict influences a person's behaviour, performance and outcomes as well.

DEFINITIONS OF CONFLICT

Following are some of the definitions given by different people at different points of time:

Conflict is defined as 'an interactive state manifested in incompatibility, disagreement or difference within or between social entities'. (Rahim, 1986)

Conflict is 'a process that begins when one party perceives that another party has negatively affected, or is about to negatively affect, something that the first party cares about'. (Thomas, 1992)

Chung and Megginson (1981) define conflict as 'the struggle between incompatible or opposing needs, wishes, ideas, interests or people. Conflict arises when individuals or groups encounter goals that both parties cannot obtain satisfactorily'.

SOURCES OF CONFLICT

The sources of conflict may be various, depending on the type of community, people and situations. Following are some of the common ones:

1. Scarcity of resources is one of the root causes for conflict. These resources could be in the form of livelihood, water, housing, employment, space or even funds.
2. Conflict may arise due to anticipation of trouble. If a person has antagonized another person, s/he may expect obstacles to goal accomplishment.
3. Conflicts may arise due to difference in perceptions.
4. When people with different values, ideologies try to work together, there are chances of conflict. Values build our belief system, which controls our behaviour.
5. Power, authority and status also create conflicts.

TYPES OF CONFLICT

There are different types of conflicts, which can be categorised as follows:

1. **Conflict between organizations:** Conflicts can often arise between organizations working for the same cause, especially if they are working within the same area. Sometimes, in a defined area, more than one organizations work. All of them may be addressing to the needs of the local people. There may be tension over target group and available resources. But, there may be difference in approaches. If these approaches clash, there is a potential for conflict. When the time for taking credit for good work comes, all the organizations may want to take whole credit, which may lead to a conflict situation. This can be resolved through mutual communication, demarcation of geographical areas, etc. Transparency in their work should be maintained. But this is not easy. For example, two organizations are working in the same community for economic

empowerment of women. Both have started Self Help Groups (SHGs). After two years of running SHGs successfully, both organizations might claim that it is because of their efforts, women are economically empowered. None of them would like to share success with anybody else. Such situations lead to creation of tensions resulting into conflicts.

2. **Conflict within community:** When social change takes place, there is a challenge to existing power structure. It affects the decision-making process, especially if it is related to distribution of resources. It generates questions such as who should receive resources. What should be the order? To what extent the resources should be distributed? In such a situation, possession can confer power. Those who have power dominate over those who do not have it. Sometimes these conflicts develop into fights/violence. Power is a vital ingredient in any human problem. Conflict always centres around power. Those who have power, have a fear of losing it or those who do not have, are in search of power. Power influences our lives continuously. In such situations, the community worker has to resolve the disputes peacefully. It should be done so carefully that both the parties feel happy and accept the decision.

Always remember that each conflict is different. It is also important to note here that people have their own way of reacting to it. The community worker must have a deep understanding about both the parties involved in conflict and the underlying causes of the disputes.

3. **Conflict among stakeholders/beneficiaries:** Marginalized people mostly lack basic amenities. They do not have access to resources. Situations may arise, especially during distribution of resources, that people express their anger, fear, frustration through socially destructive behaviour. Open fights, riots, etc. are examples of this. For example, in flood relief or earthquake relief programme, if the distributing agencies are careless and do not ensure that the affected people are being served, this may result in a conflict. One must ensure that aid is not manipulated by a few people only.

4. **Task related conflict:** It stresses upon the content and goals of the work to be done. In any organization, a conflict may arise between authorities and the staff on any issue. This can even happen in groups as well. Basically, the members disagree with the opinions of authorities and the way they distribute responsibilities. It may be seen in decision-making process. Task conflict can be productive, as this includes critical thinking. It also improves the quality of the decisions. Constructive criticism, careful evaluation of alternatives suggested by members, realistic questioning to ideas and opinions of members are beneficial in task conflict. This increases effective

functioning of a group. This approach enables members to see different perspectives. It allows a chance to discuss on its implications before making a final decision. Unequal distribution of tasks often results in conflict, mostly the negative one. At times, only the powerful people in the hierarchy get the cream projects, which frustrate others. Sometimes, only one person is burdened with all the responsibilities, the seniors take all credit for the hard work done by the juniors. This demotivates people to work. Such situations result in negative conflict and, as a result, the work of the organization suffers.

5. **Interpersonal conflict:** It is also known as relationship conflict. Interpersonal conflicts can take place within the organization or groups or teams. This indicates disagreement with colleagues/ members. Sometimes it is referred to as 'personality clash'. At times, this may take the form of antagonistic remarks that refer to the personal characteristics of a group member. This type of conflict is usually expressed through subtle and non-verbal behaviour. The members do not see eye to eye. They try to avoid each other. Interpersonal conflicts interfere in tasks, as members focus on anger, frustration and show their power. Due to emotional interference, they stop thinking rationally. This affects their efficiency to work. This results in slowing down the speed of the work and at times stops the work completely.

Before the conflict explodes, we should try to seek solutions. Some guidelines include—do not wait for the other person to take the first step. You take initiative to solve it. If you cannot, just take the help of someone (mediator) who can guide you. Always remember that not all conflicts are negative. Sometimes, conflict is necessary to air one's opinion, frustration and fear. This helps to move forward in a relationship. Conflict, if managed correctly, can bring people together and develop trust between them.

Interpersonal conflict may be inevitable, but should be handled properly.

6. **Procedural conflict:** This is also known as process conflict. It focuses on how the work gets done. The community worker has to follow certain pre-designed procedures to start and complete a task in a particular manner and time-bound frame. The local people may not be aware of these procedural constraints, which may result in conflict. While working in the organization/ community, a few members disagree with the procedures followed in assigning responsibilities to the people, who are involved in the implement-ation of activities or programmes to achieve the goals of develop-ment. In such situations, roles can be reassigned; new methodologies can be used in the implementation of strategies. This increases the participation of people as well. People's knowledge, experiences can

be utilized. Like task conflict, this procedural conflict, too, can prove productive.

NEED TO RESOLVE CONFLICT

Conflict, when not resolved, has adverse effects on the process of community organization. It can lead to the reduction in people's participation (on a temporary basis) or result in complete collapse of the programme. In extreme cases, it may take the form of physical violence. For the following reasons, we should try to resolve the conflict. The list is not exhaustive. One can add more points to it.

1. Conflict is harmful to the progress of the development programmes.
2. It is harmful to individuals and/or groups.
3. It affects decision-making process.
4. It increases bitterness, alienation and divisiveness.
5. It decreases participation, especially of exclusive people.
6. It weakens the capacity of people.
7. It disempowers local people.
8. It increases tensions, frustration between people, among groups.
9. It reduces cooperation.
10. It results in inequality.

POSITIVE ASPECTS OF CONFLICT

As stated earlier, conflict brings arguments. This helps to clarify the issues in detail. In conflict, sometimes people challenge the authority. It helps to clarify the roles and responsibilities of the people involved in a programme. People also understand the power of people involved in the programme.

Conflict situations bring more transparency in the whole process. For example, let us see Case I.

CASE I: A meeting is called to discuss the issue of absenteeism in adult literacy class. If you tell the people that the adult learners do not attend the class regularly. You are not sure whether to continue the class or to close it down. All people may not agree to closing down the class. Those who attend the class will disagree. Those who remain absent for a few days may also disapprove this idea. They will blame it on those who do not attend the class. They may say that it is injustice to those who attend classes regularly and demand to fine those who remain absent. The people, who remain absent, try to clarify their position. But nobody listens.

In such a situation, what would you do? It is better to announce the names (from the register) of frequent absentees. Give them a chance to explain their side. Check if there is any possibility to change the venue or time, so that these people can also attend the classes. Think of any method, which can increase their interest in the class.

So, such conflicts lead to more discussions and may result in change of decisions. Thus, it may increase unity and cohesiveness among group members. So, the conflict brings out the positive implications of the programme.

Conflicts increase excitement. Sometimes they generate negative feelings. But remember, they are proof of people's involvement. In conflict, even the anger of the group members shows their involvement in discussion. Their arguments may result in rethinking and revamping the whole process. Sometimes the issues are viewed from only one angle. Arguments help to discuss in detail and take a holistic approach. Conflict can serve as a catalyst for healthy development. It brings issues on the surface, forces for discussion, which helps in clarifying and realizing the goals and objectives.

To summarize the positive effects of conflict, we realize that they:

1. Have positive results.
2. Define, redefine and help to identify the real issues in the community.
3. Improve quality of the decisions taken.
4. Give recognition to individuals and groups.
5. Increase unity, cohesiveness and cooperation among group members.
6. Strengthen group boundaries.

One can add to the above list of the positive effects of conflict, which they come across while working with communities. As a successful community worker, s/he should have an ability to recognize the emergence of conflict. Following are some guidelines for the same.

IDENTIFICATION OF CONFLICT EMERGENCE

Usually, the chances of conflict are there if there is a scarcity of resources, differences over goals, purposeful exclusion, unequal power sharing, etc. The process leading to conflict is dynamic. There are several factors which cause conflict. For example, if the aspects are directly related to people's lives such as struggle for livelihood, scarcity of water, unequal distribution or non-availability of ration, closing down of factories, the geographical area (encroachment, illegal construction), religious (inter-religious marriage), cultural value and beliefs (education of a girl child, female infanticide), etc.

The community worker should remember that all the communities have potential for conflict, regardless of their socio-economic conditions. Intensity of conflict has no limitations in any community. If the size of the population is very large, there are more chances for conflict. The resources are unequally distributed among them. Industrialization and now globalization also increase potential for conflict.

The leaders and members of the organization, group, and teams should be alert to the signs of conflict among colleagues and members, so that steps can be immediately taken to solve them, before they explode. It is better to go to the root cause to solve them. One can easily notice the conflicts if one finds the members ignoring each other, not paying attention to other's opinions, feelings or always contradicting with the other person, insulting other person, deliberately undermining, not extending cooperation, backbiting and gossiping about others.

If there is a conflict between groups, they usually do not share resources with others, try to dominate other groups, try to disturb in their work, etc.

The most common causes resulting in conflict are:

1. Scarcity of resources
2. Different attitudes, values, cultures and/or perceptions
3. Disagreements in prioritizing needs, goals, problems
4. Poor or lack of communication
5. Poor or no access to authorities/decision-makers
6. Lack of clarity in roles and responsibilities.

Following situations show potential conflict within the group:

1. The members of a group attack each other.
2. Tense and uncomfortable environment in the meetings.
3. Discussion on issues goes on, without reaching any consensus.
4. Gradual withdrawal of group members from participation.
5. More preference to personal agenda rather than group welfare.

The conflict must be handled timely and properly, otherwise like weeds in a garden, it can overgrow and destroy the whole programme. The process of community development may be hampered due to this. Once the community worker understands the dynamics, s/he realizes the phases of conflict as well. Some of the different phases of conflicts are as follows.

PHASES OF CONFLICT

The nature of conflict is progressive if not attended immediately. It should be nipped in the bud, otherwise it may explode and become difficult to handle. Usually it is associated with more than one factor. In the initial stage, it is hidden. Slowly it comes to the surface. Then, it can be seen in the form of confrontation. This may be violent or non-violent or both. If there is a better understanding and readiness to share power, it results in negotiation phase. The last phase is of reconciliation where the parties get ready to work together in cooperation. It is very important that people negotiate, resolve their conflict and restructure their relationship. Reconciliation is a necessary factor in community mobilization.

Conflicts occur due to various reasons. Conflicts within community groups can be very harmful. They create tensions and unhealthy working environment. This hampers the programme implementation process. It becomes a hurdle in the development of a community. The community worker must play the role of a mediator. If needed, the can get help from an outsider in understanding the motivation of people and reasons behind the other's peculiar behaviour. Such mediation mostly proves to be productive and beneficial for the process of development.

The community worker must understand thoroughly the existing power structure in the community as well as in the organization, where s/he works. Remember, power does not exist in a vacuum. It springs from relationship such as parent to child, teacher to student, landlord to labour, government to voters, boss to subordinate, employer to employee, etc. One has to understand this dynamics of power structure.

All of us know that conflict is inseparable from human's life. So, it is better to be aware of potential conflicts—both as a community member and as an outsider. Remember, all conflicts are not negative or harmful. If handled properly, they can turn into advantages required for the development of individuals or the group as a whole. They may even strengthen the group and increase unity among members.

Many times, we see conflict arising due to disagreement over an issue. The issue may be trivial. Take the example of selection of a venue for a meeting. There may be different opinions—a few may want to have it in a closed atmosphere, and others may suggest an open ground, some prefer a temple, others prefer a school, etc. This discussion could be never ending and may lead to grumbling, loss of temper (if their opinions are not considered), verbal fights, use of abusive language, ultimately walking out from the meeting and may not turn up for the meeting. Such situations create hurdles in programme implementation.

Sometimes, the community worker is also responsible for conflict, unknowingly or due to the stress of getting the work done. Whatever the reason may be, the community worker should also check his/her own behaviour. S/he should ask the following questions to self and try to answer them:

Am I short tempered/tired/impatient/at times rude to people? Am I frustrated? etc. If the answer is yes, s/he should introspect and find answers to these questions.

In conflict situation, always remember to listen attentively and empathetically to the 'others' and apply analytical thinking skills. Ask the following questions:

1. Is there a misunderstanding?
2. Is it due to difference in style of communication or method of working?

3. Are both the parties respectful to each other?
4. Is there a difference in priorities?
5. Is the help of a mediator required?

As stated earlier, conflicts can even help the groups or teams to improve their work. It increases mutual understanding and respect for each other. Members become aware of each other's potential which helps them to work together to cope with challenges. It helps to break the wall of silence.

Conflicts should not be overlooked, neglected or treated lightly. The unresolved conflict creates lots of misunderstanding and stress. It wastes a lot of time, which can be used constructively. Many times, the team/group members leave the team/group or do not participate in any of the organization's activity. The suppressed conflicts can cause more harm afterwards.

If you cannot handle the situation, take the help of a mediator. While selecting a mediator, select such a person who has some say in the community or who is respected by people. They listen to him/her. Usually an elderly person is selected either from the community or an outside. S/he should be a good communicator with better understanding of human psyche. S/he should speak on the issues using interactive and participatory methods. S/he should encourage both the parties to discuss their problems, speak about difference of opinions fearlessly. Equal opportunities should be provided to members of a group/team to vent out their problems, fears, opinions, etc.

STRATEGIES TO MANAGE CONFLICTS

Each community is unique in itself. The nature of conflict varies from time to time, community to community, people to people and from issue to issue. In spite of these differences, each conflict is definitely unique. It exists in a particular context. No one can give a perfect solution or strategy to solve it. Still, we can streamline the following strategies to resolve conflict:

1. **Time:** Give enough time to conflicting parties to vent out their emotions, feelings, hurts, frustrations, disappointments, misunderstandings, etc. This should be done with all the parties involved in conflict. Do not use any force. Let it be resolved with a mutual understanding.

2. **Force:** Sometimes, people use force to manage the conflict. When one party has the means and inclination to win, this strategy is used. Here, the party which has power is not bothered about the other party. They are not concerned with loss or damage caused by them to relationships. This strategy cannot be used everywhere by every party, as all parties do not have power. This includes physical violence, threat of physical violence, and exertion of economic

dominance, corruption, and blackmail. In extreme cases, it can be a manipulation of the electoral system, use of media to rally public support, public protest, threat of withdrawal, etc.

3. **Adjudication:** This process does not encourage much participation. Most of the time, the decisions are one sided. There are more chances of doing injustice to one of the parties involved in conflict.

4. **Arbitration:** Traditionally, this method was used very frequently. Mostly this was used to solve family conflicts, conflicts within groups, etc. Here, an experienced and elderly person is appointed as an arbitrator (adjudicator/judge). Parties involved in conflict accept the decision given by the arbitrator, even if it is not correct. The decision will be binding on them. Usually, they do not protest against the decision. The main disadvantage of this strategy is that the younger/weaker person is usually asked to apologize to the older/dominant person, regardless of the merits of the dispute. This is different from mediation and negotiation. It does not promote collective bargaining. The arbitrator listens to and investigates the demands. Based on this, s/he takes decision. His/her decision is final. People or organizations can have one or a panel of arbitrators whom they respect, whose decision they will accept and resolve conflict.

5. **Withdrawal:** Those who desire to avoid confrontation use withdrawal approach. The power (either positive or negative) of withdrawal should not be neglected and underestimated. Sometimes, they can become more powerful parties by using following strategies—for example temporary boycotts, strikes, postponing decisions, delay tactics, leaving the programme/activity in between, etc. This may harm the process of community mobilization and development, as these parties will always disturb the ongoing activities.

6. **Negotiation:** This gives both the parties an opportunity to participate in discussion and express their feelings and views. Both the parties compromise on certain issues and find out a via-media. This gives a win-win situation to both parties involved in the conflict. Negotiation also helps to continue relationships and carry on activities smoothly.

7. **Mediation:** When negotiation fails, one can take the help of a mediator. The mediator should be neutral and should not be partial. S/he facilitates to settle conflict. S/he advises the members involved in the conflict and suggests possible solutions. Remember, the mediator plays the role of advisor and not of a decision-maker (just like as an arbitrator). S/he cannot impose his/her ideas on people. The mediator has to gain trust and confidence of groups/ people involved in conflict.

8. **Collective bargaining:** This is a democratic process used to resolve conflict. Representatives of each group are interested in resolving conflict. They come together to discuss the differences and try to work out collective solution/s. This is better than withdrawal strategy, as people resolve the conflict and cooperate in the process of development. Once the conflict is resolved, people extend their cooperation and work productively. The functioning of a union is an example of this.

To resolve conflicts, one should have:

1. Conflict analysis skills
2. Communication skills
3. Negotiation skills
4. Facilitation skills
5. Mediation skills.

The organizations working with communities and the community workers can use one or a combination of more strategies discussed above, depending on the nature of issue and type of community. Remember, the attitude and perception of people involved with conflict is very important. Whatever may be the situation, the community worker should:

1. Respect the people.
2. Respect the culture and customs of people.
3. Understand the people rather than judge them.
4. Have patience with the process.

It is the nature of human beings to blame others, especially when facing a conflict situation. People easily misinterpret or mis-perceive other person's behaviour. They try to justify their stand. This self-justifying viewpoint results in blaming other party. People never reflect on their own behaviour or action.

As a community worker, it is important to view the situation from the third party's point of view or objectively. In many conflict situations, there is no one at fault. Simply there is a difference in perception of both the parties. In such a situation, people should be encouraged to talk and resolve the problem.

While resolving conflicts, one has to pay attention to the motivation and cultural background of the people. Some communities pay more importance to their culture. For example, in certain communities, women and men both cannot attend the meeting together, even though the issues are common to both the groups. In handling such situation, one has to get attuned to the cultural values and motivations of both the parties.

It is essential to get the cooperation of local people for effective and successful implementation of programmes. The community worker should see that people do not get divided by conflict factors. It is better to work in small teams and groups where they can share their experiences and knowledge. All the members of the community should work towards common goals and objectives. To minimize the conflicts, there should be:

1. Sharing of information within and across the teams/groups. This will help the people in updating the happenings.
2. Expressing clearly the expectations from each other and from the organization. It should not leave any chance for confusion, mis-understandings.
3. Always publicly praise and appreciate the work done by people. Giving due credit to people, groups, teams who have performed better, helps to motivate people and increase their participation. This boosts their self-esteem and people cooperate more. They work hard.
4. Try to resolve conflicts at the initial stages. Allow people to express their differences.

USING CONFLICT AS A STRATEGY TO BRING SOCIAL CHANGE

We have seen the positive and negative aspects of conflict and different strategies to manage conflict. The community worker should learn to use conflict as a strategy to bring social change. Saul Alinsky is in favour of using conflict to achieve the goals of development. There are contradictory opinions about using conflict for social change. Those who favour this, think that conflict gives a chance for argument and stimulates participatory decision-making process. To bring social change, they use conflict as a strategy along with the tactics of protests, boycotts, demonstrations, etc. Sometimes they make use of violent action as well.

Others feel that decisions taken through consensus and cooperation of the community people are the best methods to bring social change. There are risks involved in using conflict as a strategy to bring social change. The non-violent tactics may turn violent. It may result in uncontrollable situation. We have a number of examples where a peaceful protest/rally results in a mob fury because of some actions like stone pelting, hurling abuses on the people. This may result in riot also. It may harm the community instead of benefiting it. It is up to the organizations working with communities and community workers to decide whether to use the conflict for bringing change or not.

ROLE OF THE COMMUNITY WORKER IN CONFLICT MANAGEMENT

The community worker has to work as a mediator in resolving conflicts in the community. Converting conflict in a constructive action requires special skills.

The community worker should see that conflict turns into a positive force and not a negative force, which can be a threat to the programme or a group or to the whole community.

As stated earlier, conflicts, if not managed properly and on time, results in delays, disinterest in people, lack of action and sometimes in extreme cases can breakdown the process of development.

Never avoid conflicts as they lead to hostility and may later cause greater problems. Do not ignore and think that it will disappear on its own. Remember, as a mediator, the community worker should listen to both the parties and advice them. S/he cannot take or suggest any decisions. To be a mediator, one should:

1. Listen to both the parties attentively. Raise questions, if required to understand correctly.
2. Observe carefully their body language.
3. Build trust, acceptance, confidence and a sense of cooperation in both parties involved in conflict.
4. Talk less and allow others to talk. Enhance communication. Promote free and fearless discussion.
5. Have good analytical thinking skills to identify the exact root problem and offer practical, workable solutions.
6. Focus on problems rather than emotions and feelings.
7. Be compassionate and empathize with people without taking sides. Avoid favours and priority treatment for either party. Try to be neutral.
8. Have good verbal and non-verbal communication skills to convince people confidently. Give them proper and just advice.
9. Know the community, especially power structure and attitudes of people.
10. Be tactful and diplomatic to pursue people towards an agreement. People should feel that he is interested in resolving conflict and does not have a personal agenda behind it.

While playing the role of a mediator, the community worker has to maintain confidentiality, respect for each others. Be honest and give practical/ achievable solutions. S/he should ask probing questions and try to point out the areas of commonality, goals and positive intentions. Make sure that parties come to a common agreement. He should also remember that all conflicts cannot be resolved. Sometimes, individuals or groups are not interested in resolving a conflict. Unfortunately, they are ready to pay heavy price, but do not want to compromise or negotiate. The recurrent Hindu-Muslim riots are an example of this. In such situation, the conflict is likely to continue. The community worker should ensure that it affects the programme to a minimum extent.

TIPS TO BE A SUCCESSFUL COMMUNITY WORKER

Cooperation of all the colleagues from his/her organization and from local community members is the key to the success of a community worker. S/he cannot be successful without cooperation. Hence, cooperation should be nurtured at all the levels. There are many chances of conflict—both within the organization and in the community. Conflict can be avoided by ensuring good relationships. Cooperation and transparency can greatly help to reduce conflicts. Therefore, the community worker should:

1. Take lead to talk to the people, if conflict arises. Try to explain your side and listen to their perceptions. Make an attempt to resolve the disputes when it has just begun. Do not wait for others to initiate a talk. The delay in starting dialogues nurtures conflict and like weed, it grows very fast.

2. Participate in local events, festivals, spiritual activities, whenever possible. Introduce yourself and the organization, its goals and objectives, type of work, etc.

3. Understand the community's power structure and its functioning; identify leaders and their role in decision-making process. Make a list of people who can be helpful in development process.

4. Establish a good rapport with local authorities who may be helpful in implementation of different activities, programmes.

5. Develop local leadership, which will help to build ownership feeling among the local people. This empowers them.

6. Understand the potential conflict situations and available conflict resolution tools that work in respective community.

7. Take into consideration the experiences and knowledge of local people and utilize them at appropriate time.

To summarize, we see that each community and organization has a conflict-prone situation. The community worker should try to resolve conflicts peacefully in such a way that both sides find the solution acceptable. Each conflict is unique and should be handled differently. The community worker should have a deep understanding of the people, their perceptions, culture and underlying causes of the dispute. By using different strategies, if required, seek help from outside, try to resolve conflicts before they become violent. Always try to use 'do not harm' policy in conflict-prone, active conflict and post-conflict situations. 'Do not harm' policy includes participation of people, transparency in decision-making, where and with whom to work, criteria of selecting people to form teams to take actions, cooperation of local authorities, etc. This brings cohesiveness to people's interaction and encourages them to take actions to improve the quality of life.

Conflict is neutral. It depends on how you handle it. Conflict, if dealt proactively, may lead to positive changes. Honesty and trust help to reduce unnecessary conflict. Disputes, if viewed as an opportunity, help to understand other people's perspective. It helps to clarify the real issues, problems, needs and values. Conflict brings out the hidden abilities and skills of people. It also improves self-confidence and develops critical thinking skills.

In conflict situation, the community worker should create a secure, open and friendly environment and encourage members to interact with each other. This helps to vent their feelings and understand others' point of views. We should promote interpersonal communication. Effective communication is a key to resolve conflict and to build a healthy relationship. This is an important prerequisite in the development process. As stated earlier, to avoid conflict, one has to understand the power structure in a particular community. The next chapter deals with this aspect.

Review Questions

1. Define conflict. Explain the difference between conflict and competition.

2. Illustrate different types of conflicts.

3. 'Conflict among beneficiaries affects the process of community development.' Illustrate this statement based on your field work experience.

4. 'Conflict, if not resolved, affects the process of community organization.' Comment critically on this.

5. Illustrate the necessity/need to resolve conflict.

6. What are the positive aspects of conflict?

7. How will you identify the emergence of a conflict?

8. Explain the different phases of conflict.

9. What are the different strategies used to resolve a conflict?

10. What skills are required to resolve a conflict situation or cases?

11. Explain the role of a community worker in community management.

8

Power Structure and Leadership

Every community has one or more power structures and leaders. As stated in earlier chapters, the community worker has to understand the power structure before starting the actual programmes/activities. Understanding this helps to work smoothly, helps in decision making, planning and executing the plan of action. Usually, the words 'power' and 'leadership' are used synonymously. In this chapter, we will analyze and understand the meaning of power and leadership, and different styles of leadership. We will see how power creates inequalities and also understand the role of a community worker in handling the power structures.

MEANING OF POWER

Power means an ability to influence other people. It may refer to an action, belief, thought process or behaviour pattern. Power compels others to behave in the desired manner. In other words, those who hold power will generally control the happenings in the community. They are the ones who determine the course of action. For example, the *Sarpanch* decides the location of digging of a well to solve the problem of drinking water in a particular village. In a family, generally, the head of the family (who has the power) takes all the decisions and others are forced to follow them.

Power has various forms and it appears in a variety of combinations. For instance, the ability to influence may be through one's position (head of the family, institution, chief minister as a head of state), access to knowledge or resources (money or skills or education). In other words, power flows from many sources such as money, position, education, ability and skills, religion, caste, intelligence, media, etc. It is interesting to know and understand the different ways in which power is exercised and what happens when individuals exert power over others. Almost in all the relationships—personal or social—power always exists. The manner of executing the power is very crucial as it may or may not result in problems.

The accumulation of power in a specific area is known as 'power centre'. Institutions, laws and ideologies are structures or mechanisms through which power is exercised. Power can be distributed too. Every person has power. One has to understand, realize and execute it in the right manner. This should be done without violating other person's rights. You cannot see power unless it is executed. So, one has to put power in action and exercise it on someone. The relationship between a landlord and a labour is a good example of this. The landlord has the power of money, land and social status. He can exploit the labour by paying paltry wages, by giving irregular work, make him work extra time, etc. As stated earlier, everyone has power. In this particular case, the labour cannot raise his voice due to his position, or even if he raises his voice/complaints, the landlord will not pay any attention. But, all the labours working for the landlord may unite, raise voice and fight for their rights. Collectively, they can show their power.

Thus, power can be used for constructive purpose as well as destructive purpose. In the above example, the landlord is abusing the power. While working with communities, the community worker has to understand these unequal power equations. S/he should try to promote resistance against all forms of domination and oppression. It is also necessary to understand the direction in which the frustrated power relations are moving. This will always end into coercion. One of the reasons of conflicts in the community is misuse of power. Power dynamics is the root cause of many social problems, which a community worker has to address. From this point of view, understanding power and power structures is very crucial for the community worker. S/he should understand it and harness the power to promote social justice.

One can achieve power by acquiring/improving knowledge, ability and skills, by participating in socio-economic, political activities, helping other people to solve their problems, etc. The community worker should try to intervene in the current power structure to bring social change and give social justice. S/he has to use different intervention approaches and strategies for collection, mobilization of different forms of power to bring social change. The community worker has to use different strategies which include:

1. Consciousness raising
2. Social action
3. Community development
4. Community coalitions
5. Organizational consultation

6. Alternative settings
7. Policy research and advocacy.

Power also refers to the ability to bring about change in the behaviour of others, at times even against their own wishes. When this ability is legitimatized through legislation or through acceptance by everyone, this power becomes an authority. For example, the power of court/judge comes through legislation. But, the authority exercised by the head of the family is an example of power accepted by everyone.

DEFINITION OF POWER

The term 'power' means different things to different social scientists. For some, it is 'power' and for others it is 'influence'. But, all of them agree that it is different from the term 'authority'. According to them, 'authority' is either legitimized power or illegitimated one. They agree that power is some form of energy. Following are some of the definitions listed by Paul E. Mott (1970) in his article on 'Power, Authority and Influence'.

Goldhammer and Shils believe that a person has power "to the extent that he influences the behaviour of others in accordance with his own intentions."

According to Weber, "Power is the probability that one actor within a social relationship will be in a position to carry out his own will, despite resistances, regardless of the basis on which this probability rests."

For Bierstedt, power is latent force.

Dahl exemplifies that "**A** has power over **B** to the extent that he can get B to do something that he would not otherwise do."

Blau defines that "Power is the ability of persons or groups to impose their will on others despite resistance through deterrence either in the form of withholding regularly supplied rewards or in the form of punishment, in as much as the former as well as latter constitute, in effect, a negative sanction."

Lasswell and Kaplan believe power is "participation in the making of decisions."

In other words, power is an act in itself, which forces, persuades others to do things. Some social scientists look at power as individual or personal characteristics. Others see it as an organizational property, which individuals enjoy because of the positions they hold in their respective organizations. In most of the above-mentioned definitions, the element of coercion is shown as a part of power. People, on whom this power is exercised, are forced to behave in a certain way, mostly against their will. For example, a community worker wants to start a new project in a village. To gather the basic information of this particular village, s/he visits the village. For this s/he has to secure the cooperation and approval of the *Sarpanch* (head of the village) before s/he interviews the members of the village. The *Sarpanch* uses his/her position as a device for social control. S/he makes it sure that the community worker does not get any wrong impression, which may go against his/her interest.

The person, who has power, usually keeps resources under his/her control. This results in unequal distribution of resources. The privileged one, who controls resources, can control the behaviour of others—intentionally or unintentionally. In other words, this powerful person can utilize/exploit others for his/her own vested interest. His/her monopoly further increases his power of exploiting people. According to Blau (quoted by Mott, *op. cit.*), this ability to control others can be reduced by:

◆ Devaluing the resources or finding a substitute for it

◆ Finding a less adequately controlled source, or

◆ Increasing control over another resource needed by the controller.

In today's social context, the use of the above alternatives is not feasible. The power holders are economically, socially and politically so well connected that the common person, who is deprived of his/her own rights, does not dare to take any of the above steps.

Power exists in every organization/community. Whether it serves for collective purposes or not is a different thing. Remember, power is coercive whereas influence is persuasive. Instead of using power for coercing purpose, one should use it to serve for collective purposes. The amount of power varies from organization to organization, community to community, person to person too.

Power, usually, reframes decisions. In a community, one can find two types of people—the decision-makers and the decision-shapers. The decision-makers are directly involved in decision-making process. They control the whole process in such a way that they are always benefited by it. The decision-shapers do not hold any direct power, but they can influence decisions. For example, the issue—'introduction of sex education in the curriculum of schools' was discussed at all the levels in Maharashtra. But, this was changed due to pressure from some parents and a few political party members. Values, norms, customs, traditions, religion, etc. also influence decisions. Attitudes and opinions of specific people can also shape the decisions. For example, in case of Shahabanoo, Rajiv Gandhi, the then Prime Minister, had power to implement the Supreme Court's decision, but the Muslim leaders influenced the decisions in the name of religion.

Community is made up of different groups. Each group has its own power, but some have greater power than others, depending on the number of people, nature of interpersonal relationships, organization capacity, holding of resources, etc. Each group has the potential ability to shape the actions of others.

Keeping this in mind, the community worker should try to understand the process of decision making in the respective community. Who takes the decisions? Check, if this power is illegitimate, is it rampant? The following discussion will be helpful for a community worker to understand how power is exercised and made legitimate. There are mainly three ways in which power may become authority:

1. **Charismatic leadership:** In this type of power, the superhuman characteristics are attributed to a person who becomes a powerful person. Such persons have vision, qualitatively superior intelligence, experience, problem-solving and decision-making capacity. Power and authority automatically come to them. Mahatma Gandhi, Nelson Mandela, Medha Patkar are examples of such type of leadership.

2. **Tradition:** In many communities, power is assigned on the basis of tradition. Traditional power may be assigned to a family where the successive generations automatically inherit it such as landlords, or the priest of a *mandir*. This is true of political parties too (Congress party and Gandhi family, Shiv Sena and Thakare family).

3. **Legal enactment:** This refers to prescription of power. Government, bureaucracy, *Panchayat Raj Institute* (PRI) are examples of this. Rationally implementing policies, division of labour, etc. are the basis of power relations in the legalized power structure.

To understand the power structure and authority students can do the following activity:

Students can visit any small village. Meet the *Sarpanch* or *Mukhiya* or elected member of that particular area. Ask him/her how does s/he take decisions to implement the government's welfare schemes? How does s/he select the beneficiaries? What are the criteria followed for prioritizing the needs of people?

After collecting the above information, students can have separate dialogues and informal meetings with community people. Ask them the same questions, which you have asked the *Sarpanch/Mukhiya/*elected representatives. Visit the sites where the development work has taken place. For example, the place where the well was dug or a hand pump for drinking water purpose was installed; construction site of houses under '*Indira Aawas Yojana*' should be visited by them. After listening to both the sides and factual proof, the students can understand the functioning of power structure in a particular village.

Students can realize that the personal interests of the decision makers always reflect in this process. Sometimes conformity is expressed due to the fear of exposure. The situation of power and authority is not as simple as it appears to be. For example, the authority of a person in an organization (could be a Chairperson or Secretary) may be limited by the informal power structure. The Chairperson/Secretary may be effective or ineffective depending on his/her ability or inability to seek active cooperation from other members. It is limited by the subtle nature of the power structure. However, the community worker should be aware of possible patterns of more subtle power. If these patterns are ignored by the community worker, it may defeat the entire purpose of community development programmes.

The power centre in the community tries to expand its influence over the distribution of resources. People with power tend to join together on issues related to their gain. Of course, it depends on ideologies, personalities and need for achieving the goal/s. Power can be intellectual, political, social and psychological. To retain power, the faculty for self-awareness and self-control is required. Power helps in decision-making, executing plans and sometimes for smooth functioning as well.

Saul Alinsky was in favour of changing power structures. He believed in people's participation in decision-making and insisted for down to upward planning. Following are the few techniques for mobilization of power:

1. Appeal the person who holds the power to help/participate in achieving the common goals.
2. Develop interdependence among power centres for fulfilling the goals.
3. Establish new groups including the power holding persons and work towards achieving the goals.

Power plays a vital role in community organization. Participation of people is related to power. Power holding people can influence people's participation in order to achieve objectives. Let us take the example of awareness about female foeticide. For this, the community worker first has to approach the community leader, convince and motivate him/her. In case s/he opposes, the community worker has to find out other powerful person to implement the female foeticide campaign.

To summarize, power is an integral part in the functioning of any type of human organization. In the centralized organization, some few people have complete access to power whereas in decentralized organization, all people or group of people have almost the same amount of access to power. In decentralized organizations, the issues are discussed openly and not suppressed. This leads to less coercion. Rational arguments increase. This results in inter-group/interpersonal interactions. This also helps to create a healthy environment at work. One has to remember that there are certain social factors which operate in such a way that creates more or less centres of power. Large population, multiple social classes, ethnic and economic diversifications contribute to create multiple power centres. The community worker has to identify these factors and use different strategies to handle these power centres.

Several studies conducted in this area show that some people or groups exert either less or far greater influence than their power base would permit. The access and the use of power to an optimum level depend on position, reputation and personal traits. Those who are at higher position in an organization, usually utilize the power to an optimum level. This is because the position carries the authority/power and not the individual. Bank managers, president of a cooperative society, chairpersons of organizations are examples of this type of power. The individual may not be having any power but the position that s/he holds gives power to him/her. This can influence the decision-making. People in such positions always exert influence.

Sometimes, personal traits can also provide access to power. A person may not have any significant position (which is base for power), but still can have great access to power. This may be because of his/her intelligence, innovative ideas, knowledge, persuasive abilities. For example Medha Patkar, Anna Hazare, Steve Jobs (Apple Company), and Sam Pitroda are the people who got power without any position but because of their qualities. Remember, all those who have personal traits may not have access to power. Only those who willingly engage themselves in decision making can influence and have access to power.

A person who holds higher position (may be in hierarchy of organization or social status in community), good reputation and good personality traits has more access and controlling power than anybody else.

Thus, power is a neutral energy. It is up to the individual who holds it, to use it for coercive purpose or for welfare purpose. The person has to direct it. Decisions may be influenced by attitudes and opinions of specific person.

The community worker has to remember that the community might have one or more power centres. S/he has to study how some powerful people influence the actions of others. Who holds the power? How is it acquired? What are the issues affected by a particular power centre? Understanding the power structure helps to achieve the goals of community organization and development.

LEADERSHIP

Leadership, like power, also reflects the ability to influence others. Leadership implies the ability to help a group determine the desirable response, which they follow voluntarily. Community has its own functions. There are some tasks which need to be completed by the people themselves. Someone has to accept the responsibility for ensuring that a task is completed. Leadership is also a type of power, where there is no coercion, but persuasion. This involves distribution of duties to members, dictation of tasks to a few members and getting the work done.

Leadership can be defined as influencing people/others—by providing purpose, direction and motivation—to accomplish the objectives/tasks and directs the community/organization in a way that makes it more cohesive and coherent. Here, influence means the leader should direct the people/members to do the tasks. That does not mean ordering. The leader himself/herself sets an example of doing work.

It is said that good leaders are **made** and not born. Any person who has desire and will power can become an effective leader by developing certain skills of leadership. In other words, leadership can be learned. Good leaders continuously work and study to improve their leadership skills.

Leadership could be defined in terms of both process and property. As a property, leadership is the set of characteristics attributed to those who are perceived to use non-coercive influence successfully. As a process, leadership is the use of non-coercive influence to direct and coordinate the activities of group members to meet a goal.

Most of the definitions of leadership involve three components: influence, goal and group (Pandya, 2004). Leaders are individuals who influence the behaviour of others—usually subordinates or followers. Leadership is usually examined in the context of a group. Researches on leadership show that leaders try to accomplish group goals. Thus, leadership is the process in which an individual influences other group members towards the attainment of group goals.

LEADERSHIP STYLES

Leadership is a manner and approach which provides direction, implements plans and motivates people to participate. Following are some major styles of leadership usually seen in organizations and communities:

1. **Institutional leadership:** The person heading an institution is called institutional leader. This person may be elected, appointed or designated to carry out routine functions/activities of the institution. It is the position which carries the leadership and not the individual. Ministers, *Sarpanch,* headmaster, president of *mahila mandal*/youth *mandal,* etc. are examples of this. They are institutional leaders because of their position. The person may change but the function associated with the position will continue. For example, the headmaster may resign or retire, but the school activities continue with the appointment of a new headmaster. The main function of these leaders is to assist the institute to carry on its activities, to help to achieve its goals and objectives.

2. **Situational leadership:** Sometimes, drastic changes take place in social structure. Due to various reasons, the existing leaders may become incapable of providing the constructive guidance necessary at that particular time. In such situations, a new leadership emerges from the community without any references. They take control of situations and guide people. This is termed situational leadership. For example, during natural disasters such as earthquake and flood, some people come forward, take control of the situation and help the people in distress. Such type of leadership is temporary.

3. **Autocratic leader:** This is also known as authoritarian leadership. It is an extreme form of transactional leadership. Such type of

leaders never considers other's opinions and dictates his/her wishes. Such leaders are task oriented. The leader has absolute power over his/her employees or team. It is one way communication. They express their power in negative manner and control the whole community/organization. The members have little opportunity for making suggestions, even if they would be in the organizations' interest. Both the institutional and situational leaders may turn into dictatorial leaders. Adolf Hitler is an example of this. Such style is still seen in certain bureaucratic environments. The leader defines the roles of individuals/groups/members and provides what, how, why, when and where to do the task.

This type of leadership can be useful during crisis. When people are not sure of which actions to be taken by them, they prefer to follow orders. This could be useful only temporarily and not on a regular basis.

Remember, autocratic leaders usually are not sensitive to the feelings of others and create resentment. This type of leader tells their employees/ workers/members what to be done and how it should be accomplished without considering their opinions. There is little or no room for cooperation or colla- boration. They expect people to do what they are told without questioning.

The community worker may use this style in a rare situation, when s/he has all the information to solve the problem, has very short time and community people are well motivated. Never use this style for yelling at people by using demeaning and derogatory language. S/he should never threaten people by abusing his/her power.

4. **Creative leadership:** This is an ideal leadership. Such type of leadership has genuine vision and understanding of the potentialities of the community people. Such leaders have a desire to help others to develop their own abilities. They never exercise their own power, but allow people to exercise their power. They believe in the collective power and capacity of people and they encourage it.

5. **Self-constituted leader:** Any opportunist individual with good communication skills can project himself/herself as a leader. Such people have assertive nature. Sometimes, people mistakenly call them born leader. Their primary motive is personal growth and development. They are very much focused and determined. They have strong conviction towards achieving their personal goals, sometimes at the cost of others/group/organization or the commu- nity. They function in such a way that they make people subservient to them. Such types of leaders are found in all institutions/ organizations—business, politics, educational institutions, *mandals*, corporate sectors, etc. Initially, such type of leaders may become successful. But, once people come to know about their true motives, they are toppled from power.

6. **Group selected leader:** In this type, the group selects one person to lead them. A democratic method is followed in the selection of a leader. The group follows instructions given by the leader. S/he gets support and cooperation from the group, who has selected him/her. In turn, the leader is required to fulfil the needs of the group. S/he has to work for the betterment of the people.

7. **Democratic leadership:** This is also known as participative leadership. As the name suggests, this type of leader gives an opportunity to all members to share their ideas and suggestions. The leader consults his/her subordinates and considers their views seriously before taking a decision. S/he facilitates the group for taking and sharing decisions. Decisions are taken with mutual consent. However, ultimately the leader takes the final decision. All the members are encouraged to use their abilities and knowledge, exploit their potential and assume greater responsibilities. Such type of leader gives importance to both—the people and work. Such style boosts the morale of members, improves job/work satisfaction, and enhances group cohesiveness. In this process, all the members of the group/community/employees remain aware of the happenings in the group/community. Democratic leadership also helps to develop their skills. It motivates members leading to more productive work.

This style of leadership believes in working together and solving problems collectively. This leadership is suitable for working in teams. Whenever more importance is given to quality over productivity, this style can be useful. Remember, leader is not expected to know everything. Hence, collective information is useful for better decision making.

8. **Delegative leadership:** This style of leadership allows the members/employees to take decisions, as he has faith in people's potential for the same. However, the leader still remains responsible for the decisions that are made. This style can be used when the members/employees have the ability to analyze the situation and decide the steps to be taken and the strategies to accomplish the tasks. Remember, the leader cannot do everything. S/he has to prioritize and delegate responsibilities.

Each of these styles possesses certain strengths. When used appropriately, they can complement each other. Effective leaders should always be flexible and change their roles according to the needs and situations. A good leader uses all the styles, depending on local situations, type of community, type of issues/problems, etc.

Following are some of the factors which influence the styles. The community worker should use any one or a combination of styles of leadership by considering the following factors:

1. Availability of time
2. Relationships—good rapport, respectful and trustworthy
3. Good understanding of the exact nature of the problems/issues
4. Capacity to handle conflicts especially within different groups of community
5. Capacity to cope with stress
6. Communication skills
7. Capacity to handle different types of tasks—structured vs unstructured, simple vs complicated
8. Knowledge of different laws and judiciary
9. Knowledge of different government welfare programmes/schemes.

The leader should always be concerned about the needs of a community. S/he should build teamwork, help people to overcome their problems and provide psychological support. A good leader facilitates participation of people, and keep people consistently busy to get the desired outcome.

There are different styles of leaderships seen in the community. They are needed in different contexts and for different purposes. Usually, a leader has qualities of good communication skills, honesty, transparency, ability to organize, thoroughness, fairness, loyalty, charisma, dependability, ability to listen, patience, respect for people, etc. The general impression about a leader in the society is that of one who represents others, dictates them, and acts as the face of a group/movement. Many times, we find that the leaders are power hungry and abuse their power for their personal gains and they are not bothered about the community's welfare. In such cases, people become sceptical about the utility of leaders in the community. But, we need leadership. One of the objectives of community mobilization is to develop local leadership. Leader is necessary to provoke a community action. S/he can facilitate the thought process of people on various issues and help them find solutions for their problems.

While working with the people, the community worker may come across with self-proclaimed leaders. Many times, they prove to be worse than autocratic leaders. They disturb the routine functioning of the community. They interfere in decision-making process. Such cases should be handled very carefully.

Community has different structures based on cultural values, religion, caste, class and political groups. Sometimes these structures become the worst barriers to the community development. Hence, people always prefer to have a democratic or participatory leadership in a community.

A good leader develops 'the competence and commitment of their people so they are self-motivated rather than dependent on others for direction and guidance' (Hersey, 91).

A person, whosoever wants to become a leader, must do self assessment. S/he should have an honest understanding of self, knowledge, information, skills and qualities. One has to remember that it is the followers who decide whether to accept you as a leader or not. They should trust you and have confidence in your leadership. For this, you have to set an example.

Different communities require different styles of leaderships. For example, a person who lacks motivation requires a different approach than one with a high degree of motivation. The tribal, illiterate people will require different styles of leaderships than the highly educated people. The leader must have a good understanding of human nature, their needs, emotions and motivation levels. S/he should be a good communicator to convince people. S/he has to work in different situations—favourable and unfavourable. What works in one situation may not work in another situation. Hence, the leader must have a good judgement to assess a situation and choose the course of action accordingly. Thus, situations have a greater impact on a leader's action. People, usually, accept a person as their leader who guides them, gives a constructive direction to them, who is not selfish and who does not misuse the power.

The good leader must develop trust and confidence in people. The leader should understand the needs/problems of a community and help people to overcome problems with available resources. This is the key factor in leadership. The leader must have vision to improve the standard of living of people. Instead of working in isolation, the leader should always work in a team. This will help in achieving goals. By developing a team spirit, the leader will be able to utilize people to their fullest capabilities. For this, the leader must have certain attributes.

ATTRIBUTES OF LEADERSHIP/LEADERSHIP TRAITS

Sometimes the community worker has to play the role of a leader. There is no uniform list of leadership traits. This keeps on changing from culture to culture and context to context. What works in Europe, will not work in India. In the multilingual, multiethnic Indian scenario, there is difference in cultures. Though the umbrella culture is the same, sub cultures are different. The leader from South India may not be accepted in North India and vice versa. In every ethnic or cultural group, there are different individuals who are accepted and regarded as leaders by the members of that particular group. Every leader has his/her own place and role in that particular community. There are different types of leaders such as by areas (e.g. political, religious, social), by issues (e.g. health, education), by position/rank (president, vice-president), by place (tribal, rural, urban), by age (youth, elderly), by sex (men, women's leader), and so on. Even though there are a variety of leaders, there are certain qualities which are common in them. S/he should be a thorough professional. S/he should be loyal to his/her parent organization, perform selfless services, and should always be ready to shoulder responsibilities. The leader should be endowed with good personality traits such as honesty, competence, commitment, integrity, courage, straightforwardness, imagination etc. The leader should be aware of the situation, needs/problems of followers as well as his own strengths and weaknesses. S/he should be able to train, coach and counsel. S/he should be passionately committed to his/her responsibilities to complete tasks successfully. The leader should be ready to take calculated risks. S/he must be reflective and be able to think strategically. The leader must have a deeper sense of social justice. S/he must favour the ethical power as opposed to hierarchical power. A good leader is a good facilitator without being egoist. S/he should aim at the welfare and development of the community.

The community worker, as a leader, should create safe spaces and opportunities for people to chat and dream together. S/he should provide stimuli from other community successes with the help of pictures, videos, articles, books, speakers, community artists, activists, etc. The community worker should encourage everyone to refocus their time and commitments to the common cause. S/he should make people aware that they are part of something bigger. The community worker should try to link the different projects, whenever possible for example, through celebrations and festivals, publicising each other's projects, looking for opportunities for joint projects, sharing venues, running joint activities, social happenings/outings/excursions. S/he should constantly unleash the passion of people and channel it constructively for the project.

Leaders build their credibility not by demonstrating their superior power, authority and competence, but by exploring emerging ideas, experimenting with new ways of behaving and working for ongoing improvement in themselves and in their followers. Effective leaders express their ideas, hopes and fears and act consistently with their intensions. Many times, leaders have to work in a conflicting situation, have to complete tasks within given deadline. This involves some kind of uncertainty and ambiguity. Effective leaders cope with these with resilience.

FUNCTIONS OF LEADER

An effective leader has to perform multiple functions. Some of them are as follows:

1. Planning
2. Coordinating
3. Decision-making
4. Motivating
5. Time management
6. Mentoring
7. Negotiating
8. Confidence-building
9. Interacting.

LEADERSHIP AND COMMUNICATION

Human beings are social animals who require constant communication. It may be verbal and/or non-verbal. Communication helps to exchange ideas, emotions, information and feelings with others. Very often, misunderstandings happen if the sender and the receiver do not have similar understanding between them. Effective communication takes place only if the receiver understands exactly what the sender intended to transmit. Many of the problems occur in the organization or in the community due to the result of improper way of communication. It leads to confusion and sometimes leads to failure. Let us see in brief the process of communication.

In communication, how the message is delivered and understood by the receiver are very important factors. The context, which is also known as *paralanguage,* is a very important factor. It includes tone of voice, facial expressions, body language/postures, hand movements, state of emotions (anger, fear, sorrow and happiness). Many times, the persons to whom we are communicating misinterprets because we believe more in visual than the audio. Communication is an exchange, and not only throwing words. The receiver must decode it and understand it. In two-way communication, one can take feedback and see all parties understood it properly. One can give feedback verbally or non-verbally. The verbal response includes paraphrasing the words of the sender, restating the sender's ideas or feelings in your own words, etc. The non-verbal feedback includes nodding head, squeezing hands for agreeing, dipping eyebrows for not understanding, clapping, flying kiss or deep breathing and blowing the air.

As a community leader, non-verbal communication also matters a lot with verbal communication. The leader must be very careful about his/her own non-verbal communication and take care that it should not create any misunderstanding and confusion. Sometimes, it may lead to a conflicting situation. One should be very particular about facial expressions, gestures, proximity, postures and body orientation.

In verbal communication, one must pay attention to tone, pitch, rhythm, timbre, loudness and inflection. To be an impressive and good speaker, one must learn to vary these six elements of voice. One of the major and common criticisms of many speakers is that they speak in a **monotonous** voice. Listeners perceive such type of speakers as boring and dull. Many a time, the listeners leave the speech in between or start doing other things. Following are some of the fruitful hints to improve verbal communication:

1. Speak in a simple language. Use comfortable words.
2. In between, ask the listeners whether they are following.
3. Give a chance to the listeners/receivers to ask questions or give their comments/feedback.
4. Be empathetic and understand the receiver's feelings.

5. Be clear what you want to say. There should not be any ambiguity.
6. Keep an eye contact with the receivers.
7. Make sure your words match your tone, and body language.
8. Make sure there is variation in tone and pace be maintained.
9. Do not ignore the questions and comments of listeners.
10. Keep yourself happy while talking to people.

ROLE OF A COMMUNITY WORKER

As a part of community mobilization process, the community worker needs to identify community leaders and potential leaders as leadership is a vital element of the whole process. This is essential as the community worker will leave the community after some time and it is necessary the local people should carry forward the work. The community worker can tap the potential leaders and train them.

To summarize, each community may have more than one leader. They may have different ideologies, which can directly affect the community development process. It is the role of the community worker to establish a rapport with local leaders and involve them in development work. Simultaneously, s/he has to tap the youth with potential leadership qualities and involve them in all social activities, orient them and, if required, train them for participating and leading the social action, which is an important aspect of community development. The next chapter highlights this aspect of social action in detail.

Review Questions

1. Define power. How does power affect community development process?
2. What are the different power centres work in the community?
3. What do you mean by leadership? Explain different styles of leadership.
4. Explain the difference between the autocratic leader and the democratic leader.
5. Which style of leadership will you use as a community worker, while working with the community? Justify.
6. Explain the different functions of a leader.
7. 'A leader should be a good communicator.' Comment.

9

Social Action

Every community in this world has experienced some sort of oppression, exploitation, inequalities and injustice in one point of time. Its forms and degrees may vary. People have been divided between the two extremes of the haves and the have-nots, the powerful and the powerless, the privileged and the underprivileged. There were many social actions, social movements, which tried to fill this rift of inequality by ensuring social injustice. But the problems still exist.

Usually, social action comes with potential conflict. In social action, one of the parties challenges the existing power structure, directly or indirectly. Social action aims at bringing social change. In a democratic society, social action works as a catalyst to bring social change. The social action values people's participation for their own development. In past, social activists along with local people initiated a number of social actions, which brought positive social transformations. Social action is not a new concept for Indian people. In India, before and after independence, a number of social reformists have carried out various reform movements. Some of them were related to social evils (for example child marriage), gender discrimination (Sati, widowhood practices), environment, etc. Volunteerism was the crux of these movements. These movements were carried out with different objectives and used various methodologies, but all these actions had one definite goal of bringing 'social change'.

Social action is one of the important methods of social work practice. It is used as a powerful intervention strategy to overcome exploitation, injustices to disadvantaged and marginalized people. This method seeks to attempt change in the social systems—laws, customs and practices. In other words, social action is always concerned with social issues. The issues, which hinder social progress, create social problems and disturb the society, are usually the central themes of social action. Social action is a method which focuses on organized efforts to change the social and economic situations. Mostly, it aims to fight for the rights of the deprived and socially excluded people. The basic assumption in social action is that there is a certain power centre with vested interest, which controls the policies and administration of welfare services in each country/community. This needs to be corrected to bring equality.

Social action can be defined as an organized, collective action of people, aimed at attaining some definite goals. It involves organized efforts to influence public opinion. It also involves commitment to a social cause. Social action means social activity, social behaviour, social operation and social gesture to bring the positive change. Social change refers to size, composition and the relationship between individuals and groups. Social action can be initiated by an individual with his/her supporters or by a group of individuals. Voluntary organizations can also initiate social action. Social actions usually aim at social change through philanthropy. These aim at social change by giving social justice. Elimination of untouchability, gender inequalities, child labour, child marriage, and unfair human trade practices are the examples of this.

Social action rules out physical coercion including street fighting, mob violence, civil insurrection or any other illegal action. In every case, the effort is to bring social pressure on the opponent (may be government system or social system) to take action to change the current situation. The activists along with the people create such a situation that the system does not have any choice but to change. In social action process, various means other than physical coercion are very strongly used.

FIVE Cs

Social movement is social action for change. Kitler (quoted in Tripathi, 1988) defines social action as "the undertaking of collective action to mitigate or resolve a social problem." According to him, five Cs are important in social action and movement. These are cause, change agency, change targets, channels and change strategy.

1. **Cause:**   It is an objective. It is the base of social problem for which the change agents will work. There are three types of causes, namely helping causes, which attempt to help the victims; protest causes which attempt to discipline the offending institutions; and revolutionary causes, which attempt to destroy the offending institution.

2. **Change agency:**   It is an organization whose primary mission is to advance a social cause.

3. **Change targets:**   They are individuals, groups or institutions designated as the targets of change efforts.

4. **Channels:** Are ways in which influence and response can be transmitted between change agents and change targets.

5. **Change strategy:** It is a basic mode of influence adopted by the change agent to affect the change target.

Social action may be legal or illegal. In our present discussion, we will not go into the details of 'legality' part of social action. A particular action may be legal in one country and illegal in another, may be legal in a particular context and may be illegal in another context. Here, we will not go into nitty-gritty of civil disobedience. It is too difficult to say under what circumstances the violation of law may be justified. As we know that in past many social actions concerning social welfare have taken place, which aimed at changing legislations. Take the example of reservation policy. In this case, promoting legislation to change existing status is legal. In such cases, the question of legality does not arise. But the objective should be socially desirable. Public speaking and discussion, newspaper publicity, use of radio and television, fasting/hunger strike, demonstrations are the methods commonly used in social action, which are accepted. In social action, the social/community worker plays multiple roles such as stimulator, catalyst, encourager, organizer, spokesperson, activist, educator and facilitator. In other words, s/he can be a guide, friend and philosopher. The social workers, especially working at micro-level, organize, conscientize and educate people for a social action, which transforms their life style both quantitatively and qualitatively. These activists usually create their own place outside the political structure and also outside the institutional framework.

The historical perspective of social action groups, especially after emergency period (in India), shows many common characteristics among the activist people, which are as follows:

1. All of them have worked for the cause of human rights and democratic values.

2. They intended to work towards eradication of wrong practices that existed in social, economic and political system.

3. Most of them were non-political.

4. They have diverse ideological orientation. It ranged from Gandhian ideology to militant radicalism of the left.

5. They were successful in getting support from media, judiciary and intellectual people.

6. They have worked on a variety of issues, namely environment, rights of women, child labour, child abuse, elimination of untouch-ability, unemployment, poverty alleviation and consumer rights.

7. They succeeded in showing the power of people.

Most of the social actions that took place in India were non-violent, voluntary and humanistic. The social activists associating themselves with marginalized, oppressed and weaker sections have been contributing in their own way to the process of social transformation.

Social action has been used as a means for conscientisation, for creating awareness among exploited and oppressed people. These people are usually ignorant, especially about their rights. They believe that such oppression is their fate. The social action attempts to unmask this belief. It makes people aware of the reality that helps them to liberate from oppression and get their legitimate due in the development process. Paulo Freire and Saul Alinsky also believed in this process. Social action tries to fill the gaps and traps in the way of social transformation process. It results in taking corrective measures. Though taking corrective measures is the responsibility of the government, which is the biggest agency of the change process, it has its own limitations.

Social action is a process in which conscious, systematic and organized efforts are made to bring change in the system for the benefit of the weaker and vulnerable sections of society. Though it is conflictual in nature, most of the time it is non-violent. Social action is a process which goes through different stages. Initially, the social workers/activists have to understand the social problems/inequalities and conscientize the local people. This is followed by finding possible solutions. With the public support, these solutions are presented to the authorities, who have the power to implement it. The authorities usually do not accept and/or show reluctance to act on it. Many times, they use the delay strategy and do not take any action. The social activists then start propagating the issue/s. They try to persuade the authorities or use pressure techniques as well. To bring the desired change in the current social practices/situations, different strategies are used at different places depending on social, cultural, economic and political conditions prevailing in a particular society at a given time. These strategies include bargaining, confrontation, conflict, etc. Bargaining includes lobbying, submitting petitions, public campaigns, etc. Confrontation includes strikes, demonstrations, sit-ins, etc. The selection of strategy depends on many factors such as:

1. Goals and the extent of vested interests of the people in authority/power
2. Selection of modes to bring a change
3. The participants in social action
4. The beneficiary—women, excluded people, children, etc.
5. The target group—legal system, government, social practices, etc.

As mentioned earlier, the selection of a particular strategy depends on the nature of the problem, type of the society, and the nature of the change to be brought. One has to visualize the hurdles in the process. One should try to identify change resistant persons and forces with whom they may have to confront with. One should be able to anticipate the nature and extent of cooperation likely to be available from people who may be benefited.

Srivastava (1990) categorizes social action model into two:

1. **Elitist social action model:** Some elites who have commitment to serve the disadvantaged section of society take initiative and conduct an action for their improvement. This model has three sub-models as follows:

   (i) *Legislative action model:* In this model, the elites and other people who are going to be involved first fully study and try to understand the nature of the problem, discuss and decide certain strategic conclusions. Then, by using different means, methods, they build up favourable public opinion. Then, they do the necessary lobbying to get the policy/programme/law framed— as it is or by making necessary changes. Accordingly, they render help to potential beneficiaries.

   (ii) *Sanction model:* Due to oppressive social, economic and political situations, certain class of people cannot fulfil their needs and aspirations. A group of elites attempt to obtain control over such situations and try to help to obtain rights of oppressed one.

   (iii) *Direct physical model:* In this model, the elites directly come in conflict with perpetrators responsible for injustice and fight for the rights of the oppressed one.

2. **Popular action model:** In this model, a section of the society which suffers makes sustained efforts to bring change in their own conditions. This model also includes three sub-models, as follows:

   (i) *Conscientization model:* This is based on Paulo Freire's philosophy of conscientization. This includes realization of reason for oppression, power structure and taking action against oppressor. Awareness helps to express the social discontentment. This model insists on breaking "silence culture".

   (ii) *Dialectical model:* This model mobilizes people to overcome the contradictions. Conflict is a part of this model as people have to fight against power structure to get their rights.

   (iii) *Direct mobilization model:* This model encourages people to take up a specific issue/s causing social injustice. People organize themselves to resolve the oppressive elements. It involves direct actions such as protests, boycotts, campaigns, strikes, etc.

ROLE OF COMMUNITY WORKER

In social action model, the role of a social worker/community worker/activist is very crucial. His/her role is multifarious such as a stimulator, a catalyst, an advocate, an encourager, an organizer, a spokesperson, an educator, and a facilitator. The social worker can work to bring pressure tactics, if needed. S/he can advocate on behalf of the oppressed people.

The community worker/social worker/activist leading social action requires to have additional knowledge and skills of bringing a wide variety of people and interest groups together in order to work for the common purpose/ goal. S/he must have a thorough understanding of the goals to be achieved and probable strategies to be used.

ORIGIN OF SOCIAL ACTION IN INDIA

Social action as a practice to bring social change is not a new concept in India. Looking back to the history of India, one can see a number of examples of social action, social movements. They included socio-religious reform movements (1800–1857), nationalist movements for India's independence (1857–1920), mass based political movements for the freedom struggle (1920–1947). In the nineteenth and early twentieth century, a number of social reformists like Raja Ram Mohan Roy, Jyotiba Phule, Mahatma Gandhi, Shahu Maharaj and Ambedkar fought against social evils. They have set an example of effective advocacy methods to be practiced. There were also social actions on other issues related to environmental degradation, rights of the dalits and tribals, women's rights, child labour, etc. Different strategies were used in all these actions, depending on the then socio-political situations. Some of the common strategies used included mass mobilization, non-violent protests and persuasion, public interest litigation (PIL), legislative advocacy, lobbying the bureaucrats and media advocacy. *Narmada Bachao Andolan* used grass-roots mobilization along with other advocacy strategies including activating global pressure through international advocacy groups and development lobbies. (The details of *Narmada Bachao Andolan* are discussed in the later part of this chapter.)

ELEMENTS OF SOCIAL ACTION

The activists have to take into consideration the present power structure, social welfare delivery mechanism, nature of people's problems, human rights and the nature of welfare state. In social action, change agents may be the activists/leaders themselves or the supporters. One can use various strategies to bring a social change. These include power strategy (creating desired behaviour through authority, force), persuasive strategy (creating desired behaviour through logical, emotional and moral appeals, for example, family planning programme).

To bring a change in people's lives, advocacy can be one of the effective methods. Depending on the nature of the issue, different forms of advocacies can be used. There are several forms of advocacy. Each one of them has different approaches. A few of them are discussed below.

Social justice advocacy basically deals with power relations and tries to bring a just society. They focus on 'what should be', rather than 'what is'.

1. **Mass advocacy:** This mainly includes action taken by a large number of people (for example, demonstration).

2. **Interest-group advocacy:** This is done through lobbying. It may not always succeed especially in influencing political decision makers. This requires resources and very effective organization.

3. **Legislative advocacy:** As a part of process of creating change, it relies on the state legislative process to create a change.

4. **Media advocacy:** Media is used as a resource to advocate local people.

Following are some of the social action strategies which were used in India:

1. **Civil disobedience:** People refuse to obey civil laws. This is called passive resistance. They break the law as they feel the law is unjust. They want to call attention to injustice and wish to bring amendment. They willingly accept to pay any penalty such as imprisonment for breaking the law. The best example of this is independence movement of India.

2. **Hunger strike:** This includes fasting voluntarily as a means of protest. Hunger strikes have worked as a weapon to bring the desired social change. This has tremendous strength and brings pressure on decision-makers (power holders). Much social action concerning social welfare is aimed at changing social legislation.

3. **Direct action:** In the last few years, 'direct action' is the most commonly used strategy to bring community change. Direct action normally refers to a fairly high degree of personal involvement. Usually, it uses conflict and confrontation as its strategies. They identify their target as an enemy. Hence, the people who are involved in direct action behave militantly. There is often a high degree of hostility against organizations. Their attack is on the comfort, status or prestige enjoyed by these organizations.

Direct action is illegal. It involves unlawful activities. Still, direct action is most commonly used action. It is a kind of civil disobedience. The direct actionist violates law because s/he believes that particular law is unconstitutional or unjust or violates his/her religious or ethical values and convictions. For example, a member of a minority group may refuse to obey an ordinance, which may establish discrimination and segregation in the use of public accommodation. Sometimes, the direct actionists disobey the law/violate as a symbol of protest. Staging a sit-in (*dharna*) during assembly to fulfil certain demands is an example of this. *Anganwadi* workers get their demands fulfilled using this strategy. In *Narmada Bachao Andolan*, the highways were blocked to stop the dam work. These are non-violent actions. Demonstration is one of the non-violent direct actions.

Non-violent direct action may have two contrasting purposes. One is to show the strength. Here the intention is to mobilize people and demonstrate the people's power to achieve the desired goal. Another purpose is based on Gandhian philosophy. Bringing moral pressure on the opponents by observing fasting, lying down in front of a car of a minister to fulfil demands, blocking a road and getting arrested, etc. are some of the strategies which are used by activists. This approach stresses more on goodwill rather than hostility towards opponents. A contemporary instance of this type of approach is Anna Hazare's fast in Ram Leela Maidan, New Delhi for Lok Pal Bill (August 2011).

NEED FOR DIRECT ACTION

One cannot really explain the need for direct action. It is possible that the social activists realized that they cannot attain their goals of social change through social action. They might have thought that direct action would be more effective as it involves more propaganda. Its impact on public is stronger in comparison to other actions. In some cases it is the personal drive and emotions of the activists that leads them to direct action method. Some activists are emotional, impatient and adventurous, who want to draw public attention, and want to project themselves as heroes. Hence, they opt for this model. Whatever the reason may be, the direct action model involves the following tactics/methods.

Demonstrations

1. **Marches and parades:** This is a walk carried out on the roads usually to draw the immediate attention of the people for a particular cause. It has a definite planned route, which creates potential impact on the people.
2. **Picketing:** People stand at a particular spot and express their views on the problem, do *nishedh* and give slogans.
3. **Fraternization:** The activists or their representative/s go out of the way to talk with the police or authority or other opponents in a friendly way and try to convince them that their cause is just.
4. **Leafleting:** Means distributing leaflets on the issues and expressing one's side.

Non-cooperation

1. **Strike:** This is perhaps the most popular method generally used by various unions to get their demands fulfilled. There are variations in this method. For example, in token strike, people go off the work for a short period of a few days or for a few hours. In pen down strike, strikers do attend the office, but do not do any work.

2. *Hartal*: This is also a very common practice in India. It involves staying at home for a full day or more, without going on job, leaving offices/factories totally empty.

3. **Boycott:** This refers to refusal of doing a particular work and trying to bring the management in difficult position.

Interventions

1. **Sit-in:** The demonstrators sit in front of the factory/gate/entrance of the authority and shout slogans.

2. **Reverse strike:** This method is usually used in western countries. Examples are related to agricultural workers who work for more than the stipulated time duration in support of their demand for pay increases.

3. **Nonviolent interjection and obstruction:** Here, the body is used to obstruct another person's work to bring pressure, for example, strikers lay down in front of the car of the factory owners to get their demands fulfilled.

The above list is not exhaustive. Some other forms of **direct action** include disrupting meetings, boycotts, walk out, protest, blocking traffic and civil disobedience, etc. Direct action should take place within the law. But, there are times and instances when law is used to abuse the inherent rights of the people and the only option left is to violate it to draw the attention of authorities to get justice.

Saul Alinsky is one of the most popular actionists who strongly believed and successfully used the direct action model. Details about him and his work are discussed in Annexure I.

Following paragraphs give brief information on some of the social actions that took place in India.

WOMEN'S MOVEMENTS

During post-independence, women's movements were based on the issues which directly affected their lives. These included rape, sexual harassment in the workplace, and violence against women—in the family and in public spheres as well. They opted for different strategies such as demonstrations, processions, public meetings, signature campaigns, public mass petitions, and so on. They struggled at micro as well as macro levels, at lower court and the Supreme Court, respectively. They also used pressure tactics against police and political leaders to arrest and punish the culprits. Women groups also conducted campaigns on several issues such as legal maintenance, guardianship and custody of children, uniform civil code, thirty per cent reservation, and so on. They have protested against sex determination tests, compulsory family planning practices and the state policy on reproductive health and population policy. These protests, campaigns and movements have resulted in the enactment of new laws/legislations, and/or changes in legislations to give justice to women. The examples include 73rd Amendment in *Panchayat Raj* Act, Prevention of Domestic Violence Act (2007), PC&PNDT (Pre-conception and Pre-Natal Diagnostic Technics) Act. Implementation of all these laws and prevention of their misuse is in the hands of society.

Today, the process of social transformation has taken a different turn. Many middleclass women are educated, working and actively participating in politics. Women are working in all the spheres—aeronautics, science, research, industry, commerce, politics, aviation, engineering, medicine, etc. Overshadowing the positive indicators, there are certain distressing negative indices which demonstrate that disparity and discrimination against women continues. For example, female mortality rate, declining sex ratio, higher dropout rate among girls, higher illiteracy rate, proportionally unequal increase in the enrolment of girls in higher education, higher number of women working in the unorganized sector, marginalization of women in the country's workforce and continuous increase in the crimes against women are the examples of social gender bias. Globalization, too, has adversely affected women. It has created new imbalances and disparities, eventually leading to women's exploitation and oppression.

Following are some of the movements where women have taken certain actions collectively and forced government to enact certain legislations.

The *Chipko* Movement

This is a world famous movement of women in the hills of Uttaranchal. It was initiated in 1972–1974. This is an excellent example of powerful impact of women's initiative against power brokers, contractors and government officials. Women succeeded in defending the forest against destruction for commercial purposes. They hugged the trees to protect them against the contractors and their fellers. Women united on this front and acted entirely on their own. Except in Raw (*Chamboli* district), where the protest was against a timber contractor, in all the other cases, the protest was against their cash hungry men who were not bothered about either the forest or their women (who had to walk many miles to collect their daily load of fuel and fodder).

Tehri Garhwal is a hilly region in the state of Uttaranchal. The trees in this region prevent the soil from erosion due to heavy rains and also provide grass to cattles. The decisive agitation started in December 1972. The contractor was an influential person. He used both political power and police force. But, women were very determined. They did not care for their own lives in their bid to save the trees. *Chipko* (hugging the trees) movement saved about 40 acres of oak forest. Now, there is a ban on commercial felling. People have rights on forest produce like dry twiges and leaves (1980).

Anti-liquor Movement in Andhra Pradesh

Rural women in Andhra Pradesh made history. Illiterate women, mostly labourers, were exploited by local landlords. They became involved in this movement. These socially and domestically oppressed women were mostly from the lower caste (SC&OBC) strata. Many of them were sexually exploited as well. Suddenly, they revolted against all oppressors including their husbands, the *mandal* officers, the police inspector, the collector, and superintendent of police, Home Minister and the Chief Minister. Their demands were very simple—'no drinking or selling of liquor'.

The movement against the sale of arrack (liquor) started in Nellore district. Initially, women went to police station to register the complaints. But, police did not pay any attention. Many attempts were made to suppress the agitation by the police intervention, which went to the extent of selling arrack not only under police protection, but even in the police stations. Many brutal attacks were made by state on agitating women. Apparently, the movement started spontaneously. It was initially responded by the state with a kind of indifference under a cynical hope that it would fizzle out. But women were very determined. They had decided to continue their fight till they got justice by stopping the production and selling of liquor.

Background

By 1990–1991, Andhra Pradesh occupied first rank in the country in arrack consumption with 111 million litres (30 UP) per annum. 70–80 per cent of the excise growth was accounted for the revenue from arrack, the poor people's drink. Thus, the substantial burden of the regressive excise duty was borne by the poor. The number of arrack shops increased from 7,159 in 1969–1970 to 22,803 shops in 1987–1988 but declined to 16,436 in 1990–1991 (Reddy and Patnaik, 1993). In 1986, selling arrack in polythene sachets, under the name *Vanuni Vahini* (a mythological name) began. They were available in two sizes—90 ml and 45 ml. Arrack in sachets made it more convenient for the distributors to distribute it. It was delivered at doorsteps by peddlers on foot and by bicycle. This became very convenient for the drinkers as they did not have to go to the arrack shops. This also increased drinking habits among men folk and destroyed family life. Men started drinking day-night due to its easy availability. The increasing arrack consumption resulted in increasing price of arrack. Much of the hard-earned wages of the entire family were spent in buying arrack.

As men used to spend the entire earning in arrack, women of the household had to struggle to manage the family, provide for the subsistence of the children and the household. After doing all this, they were beaten and abused by their drunken husband. On the other hand, they did not get any political support. The picture was bleak as there were very few hopes of transformation for the better life. But the women decided to take a collective stand and started movement against liquor and after many initial hurdles finally succeeded in getting law passed in their favour.

The Movement

Total Literacy Campaign (TLC) was completed and Post Literacy Campaign (PLC) started. Lakhs of neo-literate, mainly women, became functionally literate. In Nellore, Chittoor and elsewhere, the neo-literate women in the villages pledged to fight against the "arrack-demon" in the concluding sessions of the *Akshara Jyoti* programme. Since then, a new momentum has been unleashed by the women. To their credit, it can be said that they have converted a women's movement into a people's movement.

The anti-liquor mass movement not merely raised a women question but also targeted its attack on the nexus between the so-called 'people's representatives', police and arrack contractors. When the women were demanding prohibition on arrack for a dignified survival, the people's representatives in the state government were busy in talking about the impending revenue loss in view of the prohibition.

Majority of the women involved in this movement were agriculture labourers. Many of them were the only bread winners of their family. The village committees were formed in different villages. They were invariably led by the women of the poorer *dalit* households. These committees did not have any representation from any political parties. Many local NGOs, who believed and were concerned about women's welfare, started extending their support to this movement. In Nellore district alone 36 voluntary organizations were involved (Reddy and Patnaik, 1993). Due to this, women got additional strength. They started pressurising their men to take oath in the village temples to stop drinking arrack. They also decided to punish men in case they violated the oath. The punishment included payment of heavy fine to the temple and abandoned their families from the village. In a few cases, the women themselves physically forced their husband and stopped them from visiting arrack shops. In some villages, women started guarding the arrack shops by sitting in front of them and preventing the sale of arrack. As stated earlier, these women were agriculture labourers, their work was seasonal.

They were missing the season by keeping watch at the arrack shops. They were losing their wages and there was not even a thin possibility of getting any compensation for wages. Their men folk were habitual drunkards at the cost of the wages earned by the women.

They also started preventing peddling of sachets by bicycle or foot. While doing this, many of them were beaten by the *goondas*. They knew these tactics were temporary. They wanted some permanent solution. The season of transplantation was nearing and they had to go farms for their earnings. They knew that once they turn their backs, these men will again indulge in drinking.

As mentioned by Reddy and Patnaik, in most of the villages, women formed squads to face the *goondas* of landlords. The women squads discovered three instant instruments of struggle—broom, chilli powder and fin. They countered the threat from police and the drunken males with broomsticks and chilli powder. They attacked the contractors' dens and set fire to the barrels and sachets. These attempts symbolically aimed at purification of their villages by burning the 'arrack demon'. The messages against the ill-effects of arrack on the household economy and against the nexus of police and arrack contractors were spread through graffiti, street plays, rallies, door-to-door campaigns and public meetings in the villages. The women squads also prevented auction sales being organised by the excise department. In Nellore alone, they have stalled auction sales 36 times. This was true of almost all district auction counters. As a result, many women were arrested and police had filed false cases against them. More and more such repressions were launched, the nexus between bureaucracy, police and arrack contractors was revealed before the agitating women. No wonder, the district collectors engaged in such auction sales were sarcastically labelled as 'Indian Arrack Sellers' (IAS).

Women realized that the state and police were not giving any positive response. So, they decided to focus at the village level. They unanimously decided to drag the drunkards on streets and clean shave their heads. The arrack dealers were brought in *chowrastas,* garlanded with *chappals,* and onions and were made to ride a donkey through the village.

In one group, more than hundred women would go to the nearby police station to tell the inspector the bitter truth, 'you are licking the feet of sara contractor'. They used to go to the local landlord, whose very presence spelt terror to them not so long ago, and say 'stop trading with our men's blood and our honour'. They went to the collector, and said 'either stop auctioning the contractor or dare to drive your car over our bodies'. They went to the Chief Minister with a letter written in the blood of a young woman to demand 'ban liquor or burry us all'. From local to state level, women used all the tactics to bring pressure on decision makers to stop the arrack production and selling. They fought against all odds including the power structures.

In some villages, the landlord-contractor *goondas* attacked women campaigners, but they retaliated with *lathis*. Landlords, their drunken *goondas* and even the police realized that these women were not docile anymore and were incarnated as "Durga/Kali".

They used the strategies of protests, *dharanas*, human road blocks to stop the collector and the SP from reaching the place, where arrack auction was supposed to take place. The women suffered the daily ordeal at their drunken men's hands. They were beaten and cheated on a regular basis. Women struggled at both the fronts—home and state. Their struggle at home front was more significant. As usual, they requested their men not to drink. Since most of these habitual drinkers had already become psychological wrecks, they did not care. The women decided to mete out symbolic punishment. Even this collective decision could have been resisted by men but for the fact that they saw how each wife has now become a *kalika*—the wife who was eating his beatings every day was now facing police officers, collector, and ministers including the Chief Minister. The local landlord-contractor who was a terror to them became 'adanavadu' (it's only him) both at the collectorate and village. All this shattered the confidence of 'drinking husbands' who used to beat their wives. They did not take any help from the men in the village. Women were very confident in their own leadership, and strengths.

Nellore movement succeeded in stopping the liquor auction. In a state where the class movements and *dalit* movements have been paving newer ways, the anti-liquor movement, started and led by women, has shocked many patriarchs irrespective of their caste, class and status (Kancha ilaiah, 1993).

When we look at this movement, we realize the two distinguished sides. One is the power structure which was numb. Here, the state, particularly the police, contractors, henchmen and the political parties ignored the movement. On the other side, the courageous, determined and strong women organized themselves against all the odds. The police tried their level best to prevent women in organizing public meetings by denying permissions whenever and wherever possible. They even provided support to the arrack contractors and their *goondas*. They did not take any action against these *goondas*, even if they abused and attacked the agitating women. Some of them even attacked the vulnerable poorer households as well. The government was just passing the time with verbal assurances and not taking any concrete steps. It tried its level best using delay tactics hoping that one day the movement will dissipate. The dark side of this whole issue is that the ruling as well as the opposition party did not bother to take any action against the arrack contractors and distributors. The women used a number of strategies and tactics to stop the production and selling of arrack. They also used different types of punishments for drunken male folks such as beating them with brooms, torturing, shaving the heads and parading, refusing food to drunken husbands, throwing chilli powder on the faces of contractors who supplied arrack. These tactics were part of the movement. They were the result of their sufferings and suppressions of all these years. This prolonged suffering, absence of love and affection, daily drunken brawls and destruction of the family life forced women to come out on the street and fight for their right—Right to live with dignity.

PUBLIC INTEREST LITIGATION

Social action is a viable method for achieving healthy social transformation and development. One of the legitimate strategies used under social action is Public Interest Litigation (PIL). The concept of PIL is not new for Indians. Nowadays, it is used to protect the interests of the common people and also of a weaker section due to which it has come into limelight.

Courts were accessible only to the rich and influential people. The marginalized and disadvantaged groups continued to be exploited and denied basic human rights. The emergence of PIL is a great hope for the disadvantaged and common people as well. PIL emerged as a result of informal nexus of proactive judges, media persons and social activists. It does not deal with a range of 'single dispute'. PIL deals with group problems. In other words, it is for collective rights, involving a question of injustice pertaining to a group.

The Black' Law Dictionary explains PIL as follows:

'Public Interest Litigation means a legal action initiated in a court of law for the enforcement of public interest or general interest in which the public or class of the community have pecuniary interest or some interest by which their legal rights or liabilities are affected.'

Aspects of PIL

The aspects of PIL are as follows:

1. **Remedial in nature:** The remedial nature of PIL departs from traditional *locus standi* rules. It has indirectly incorporated the principles enshrined in Part IV into Part III of the Indian Constitution.

2. **Representative:** It is a creative expansion. It allows a third party to file a corpus petition on behalf of an injured/affected party, as s/he cannot approach the court himself/herself.

   This makes the Indian PIL unique as compared to the American PIL.

3. **Non-adversarial litigation:** It includes two aspects, namely:

   (i) *Collaborative litigation:* In this, the effort is made from all sections of society. The affected party (claimant), the court, common people and the government official, all come together to see that the basic human rights get implemented practically, so that a large number of people get justice. PIL helps the executive to discharge its constitutional obligations. The court assumes three different functions other than that from traditional determination and issuance of a decree.

(a) *Ombudsman:*   The court receives citizen complaints and brings the most important ones to the attention of responsible government officials.

(b) *Forum:*   The court provides a forum or place to discuss the public issues at length and provides emergency relief through interim orders.

(c) *Mediator:*   The court comes up with possible compromises.

(ii) **Investigative litigation:**   It mostly works on the reports of different people such as the registrar, district magistrate, opinions of experts, newspapers, etc.

4. **Relaxation of strict rule of locus standi:**   The rule of *locus standi* is relaxed. Any person who is the citizen of this country can become a locus standi. S/he can file a case. The main condition is s/he should not have any personal agenda or gain or private profit or political motive or any other oblique consideration.

5. **Epistolary jurisdiction:**   The High Courts as well as the Supreme Court have an authority to convert a letter by a layperson/common person into a writ petition. The access to judicial redress may be found even without a lawyer or filling formal papers.

PIL in India is emerging as an effective medium for bringing social change. In certain cases, it has become a good weapon against domination and victimization. Right to Information Act, and Noise Pollution during festivals are examples of this. PIL acts as an important instrument for the welfare of every section of society. It is a very important tool which contributes towards the development of India. PIL has been used as a strategy to combat the atrocities prevailing in society. It has proved a good instrument towards the welfare and development of the needy, deprived class of the society.

PIL seeks to draw the attention of the authorities to their constitutional and legal obligations. It enforces the judiciary system to give benefit of law to common people and not only to the fortunate few. PIL helps to get the rights, irrespective of their power, position or economic condition.

PIL in India has shown astonishing results in the last three decades. The examples of degraded bonded labourers, tortured under trials and women prisoners, exploited children, smoking in the public places and other such cases have been liberated through judicial interventions. In a landmark judgement of *Delhi Domestic Working Women's Forum* vs. *Union of India* (1995) 15CC14, the Supreme Court issued guidelines for rehabilitation and compensation for the rape on working women. In *Vishaka* vs *State of Rajasthan*, the Supreme Court has laid down exhaustive guidelines for preventing sexual harassment of working women in place of their work.

PIL has helped to bring the issue of human rights of the socially excluded people on the surface. It has focused on the accountability of government towards these people. PIL has helped to bring some sensitivity in power structure. Now, people at the grass-roots level have some hopes of getting justice.

Evolution of PIL

The Indian PIL is an improved version of PIL of USA. It is an effort which provides legal representation to previously unrepresented groups and their interests. It was realized that the current legal system failed to provide services to significant segments of the population and their interests. Such groups include the environmentalists, consumers, racial and ethnic minorities, etc. During the emergency period (1975–1977), Indians have witnessed the failure of judiciary system in maintaining the law and order. The lawless situation repressed thousands of innocent people, resulting in total deprivation of civil and political rights.

The post-emergency period gave an opportunity to the Supreme Court judges to express their disregards in providing access to justice to the poor. It was Justice V.R. Krishna Iyer and P.N. Bhagawati from the Supreme Court who recognized the possibility of providing access to justice to the poor and the exploited people by relaxing the rules of standing. Media has played an extraordinary important role in post-emergency period. The investigative journalism brought in light many cases of governmental lawlessness, repression, and custodial violence. This drew the attention of lawyers, judges, social activists and common man as well. This resulted in the emergence of PIL. The first reported case of PIL in 1979 dealt with inhuman conditions of prisons and undertrial prisoners.

Features of PIL

PIL helps to protect the human rights in the following ways:

1. **By creating a new regime of human rights:** It has expanded the meaning of fundamental right to equality, life and personal liberty. The PIL provides the right to speedy trial, free legal aid, dignity, means and livelihood, education, housing, medical care, clean environment, right against torture, sexual harassment, etc. These new reconceptualized rights provide legal resources to activate the courts for their enforcement through PIL.

2. **By democratization of access to justice:** This is done by relaxing the traditional rule of *locus standi*. Any public spirited citizen or social action group can approach the court on behalf of the oppressed classes. The court's attention can be drawn even by

writing a letter or sending a telegram. This is called epistolary jurisdiction.

3. **By fashioning new kinds of reliefs:** Under the court's writ juris-diction, the court can award interim compensation to the victims of governmental lawlessness. The grant of compensation in PIL matters does not preclude the aggrieved person from bringing a civil suit for damages. In PIL cases, the court can fashion any relief to the victims.

4. **By judicial monitoring of state institutions:** This covers the functioning of jails, women's protective homes, juvenile homes, mental asylums, and the like. Through judicial invigilation, the court seeks gradual improvement in their management and administration. This has been characterized as creeping jurisdiction, in which the court takes over the administration of these institutions for protecting human rights.

5. **By devising new techniques in fact-finding:** In most of the cases, the court has appointed its own socio-legal commissions of inquiry or has deputed its own official for investigation. Sometimes it has taken the help of the National Human Rights Commission or Central Bureau of Investigation (CBI) or experts to inquire into human rights violations. This may be called investigative litigation.

PIL and Social Change

In the past few decades, PIL has worked as an important instrument of social change. It is working for the welfare of every section of society. It is used for the purpose of getting justice. This legitimate instrument has proved to be beneficial, especially for India. PIL has been used as a strategy to combat the atrocities prevailing in society. One can say that it is an institutional initiative towards the welfare of the needy class of society. The examples include banning smoking in public places, rehabilitation and compensation for the rape on working women, preventing sexual harassment of working women in place of their work, etc.

When and How to File a PIL

PIL can be filed in any High Court or directly in the Supreme Court. It is not necessary that the petitioner himself/herself had suffered some injustice or has personal grievance to litigate. Any socially aware member of a society or an NGO dedicated to the welfare of a society can file a case for public cause. Such case may be a breach of public duty or due to a violation of some provisions of the constitution. PIL assures public participation in judicial review of administrative action. It has made judicial process more democratic.

PIL has emerged as one of the most powerful tools for promoting social justice and for protecting the rights of the deprived and marginalized, poor people.

In PIL cases, if the petitioner is not in a position to provide all the necessary evidence, either because it is voluminous or because the parties are socially and/or economically weak, courts have appointed commissions to collect information on facts and present it before the bench.

The Indian Constitution has given equal rights to all citizens, irrespective of caste, class, religion, race, gender and other considerations. Under Directive Principles, the government should provide a minimum standard of living to all its citizens, which is obligatory on its part. But the reality is different. There is a certain section of the society which is deprived of all these rights. Hence, anyone who files a PIL must find out the main issue/problem. Then, follow the following steps:

1. One has to make an informed decision to file a case.
2. The person/s who takes initiative must consult all the affected people/groups who are possible allies.
3. Be careful in filling a case because of the following reasons:
    (i)   Litigation can be time-consuming.
    (ii) Litigation can be expensive.
    (iii) Litigation can take away decision-making capability/strength from communities.
    (iv) An adverse decision can affect the strength of the movement.
    (v)   Litigation involvement can divert the attention of the community away from the real issues.
4. Once you have taken a decision to file a case, then follow these steps:
    (i)   Collect all the relevant information.
    (ii)   Be meticulous in gathering detail for use in the case. If you plan to use photographs, retain the negatives and take an affidavit from the photographer. Retain bills.
    (iii) Write to the relevant authorities and be clear about your demands.
    (iv)   Maintain records in an organized fashion.
    (v)   Consult a lawyer on the choice of forum.
    (vi)   Engage a competent lawyer. If you are handling a matter yourself, make sure you get good legal advice on the drafting.
    (vii) A PIL can be filed only by a registered organization. If you are unregistered, please file the PIL in the name of an office bearer/member in his personal capacity.
    (viii) You may have to issue a legal notice to the parties/authorities concerned before filing a PIL. Filing a suit against the

government would require issuing a notice to the officer/ department concerned at least two months prior to filing. (http://www.ngosindia.com/resources/pil_sc.php)

The Supreme Court has now accepted its role in welfare state. For effective implementation of PIL, it has adopted certain strategies. One can simply approach the court for the enforcement of fundamental rights by writing a letter or postcard to any judge. Based on the true facts and concept, that particular letter/s will be converted into writ petition. The court has realized that PIL is for the benefit of the have-nots. PIL has proved a boon for the common man. By introducing PIL, the court has brought legal aid at the doorsteps of the millions of Indians.

To conclude, PIL is still in the experimental stage. It is the first attempt to break away the legal system perpetuated for centuries. PIL focuses on reaching the justice to unreached people. It has brought change both substantial and structural. It has radically altered the traditional judicial role. PIL has enabled the courts to bring the justice within the reach of a common man. It develops a new jurisprudence of the accountability of the state for constitutional and legal violations adversely affecting the interests of the weaker sections of the society.

Narmada Bachao Andolan is a good example, where PIL was used for the rights of tribal and rural people and also for the cause of ecology/ ecosystem. It is discussed in brief in the following paragraphs.

Narmada Bachao Andolan (NBA) symbolizes the struggle for a just and equitable society in India. The *Sardar Sarovar* Project (SSP) came into light due to *Narmada Bachao Andolan*. But the antecedents of the Project can be traced way back in 1946. In 1946, for the first time, the idea of harnessing the Narmada's water was proposed. The Provinces did not agree to this proposal. On October 6, 1969, the Narmada Water Disputes Tribunal (NWDT) was set up by the Government of India to resolve this conflict between three states, namely Maharashtra, Gujarat and Madhya Pradesh. It submitted its report in 1978. This was followed by actual implementation of the Project.

The Narmada Valley Project (NVP) is the single largest river valley project in India. The NVP includes construction of thirty major dams; SSP is one of them, 135 medium and 3000 small dams to harness the waters of the Narmada to provide water and electricity, which are desperately required for the purposes of development. The SSP is the second largest dam of the NVP as far as the area submerged and population displaced is concerned. Its construction started in 1961. In 1985, it received funding from the World Bank and the work progressed fast.

The *Sardar Sarovar* dam is intended to provide water for irrigation, drinking and power generation. This is done at the cost of submerging of thousands of hectares of land, belonging to the poor and mostly the tribal people. The people to be affected by such displacement are peasants and agricultural workers; however, the overwhelming majority of them are tribal people. Most of them are dependent on primitive methods of agriculture, gathering forest produce and grazing livestock in the forests. The government offered a meagre compensation package for those who are displaced [Project Affected People (PAP)]. Several recent studies have shown that the government did not provide proper resettlement and rehabilitation facilities to these displaced people.

Nimar, a village from Madhya Pradesh, is the first village where two-thirds of the displacement will occur due to dam. In Maharashtra, Anjanvara village will be affected very badly.

The government claims that they have plans for rehabilitation and alter the lives of PAP. The history shows that the resettled people have never been provided with just compensation and rehabilitation for any large dam built on their land in India. Further, the researches show that the government has not bothered to consult, or even inform, the people (whose land will be submerged) about their fate. In Anjanvara, the first information about the dam came from the Central Water Commission Surveyors, who came to place stone markers to indicate the reservoir level (Baviskar, 1995).

The first stirrings of protest against the SSP started in 1978 in *Nimar*. It was known as *Nimar Bachao Andolan*, where people were mobilized around the issue of displacement. This campaign was mostly supported by merchants and farmers in *Nimar*. They took a rally. The second attempt to oppose the construction of dam took place in 1985. At the same time, Medha Patkar started working in the SSP submergence zone villages in Maharashtra. In 1987, Patkar came to *Nimar* and started mobilization to oppose the SSP. The *Andolan* mainly focused its efforts on collective action against two major dam projects of the NVP, namely SSP and *Narmada Sagar*. Opponents of the dam believe that its planning is unjust, is abusing of human rights and displacement of many poor and underprivileged communities. They also believe that water and energy can be provided to the people of the Narmada Valley, Gujarat and other regions through alternative technologies and planning processes, which can be socially just and economically and environmentally sustainable.

Medha Patkar established *Narmada Bachao Andolan* in 1989. People from all sectors joined this *Andolan* including environmental and human rights activists, scientists, academics and project-affected people with a non-violent approach.

Initially, the *Andolan* started to organize people to agitate for their adequate rehabilitation. However, in later stage, they realized that the government does not have proper resettlement plan for PAP. Activists realized that all the displaced people were given compensation only for the immediate standing crop and not for the displacement and rehabilitation. Then, the *Andolan* changed its track and took a firm stand to reject the project in totality.

The NBA became a social movement consisting of tribal people, *adivasis*, farmers, environmentalists and human rights activists against the *Sardar Sarovar* Dam being built across the Narmada River. Medha Patkar and the local people organized a 36-day long, solidarity march among the neighbouring states of the Narmada valley from Madhya Pradesh to the *Sardar Sarovar* dam site. This march was resisted by police and many were arrested.

The campaigning against SSP took place at all levels. They used all the strategies, which can be categorized into three levels, namely:

1. Participation of city-based NGOs—They disseminated information about the movement through press briefings, newsletters and films, by lobbying, collecting funds for the valley and by organizing events to express solidarity with the struggle in the valley. The rural-based NGOs shared their human resources by sending their members/representatives to participate in *Andolan*.
2. At the national level, *Andolan* formed a committee which comprised representatives of different organizations, interested in rights-based approach.
3. *Andolan* could succeed to reach out of the country's NGOs. Western NGOs helped to pressurize the international funding to withdraw its support from the project. In 1989, three US-based environmental NGOs urged the United States' Congress to compel the World Bank to stop funding the SSP. They lobbied and succeeded. The World Bank took an unprecedented decision.

Medha Patkar did 22 days fast that almost took her life. In 1991, her actions led to an unprecedented independent review by the World Bank. The Morse Commission, appointed in June 1991 at the recommendation of World Bank President Barber Coinable, conducted its first independent review of a World Bank project to review the environmental and detailed displacement issue of the project. The team submitted its detailed report in 1992. It clearly mentioned how the project has violated its guidelines. The international NGOs continued their pressure on the World Bank for its support to the project. Ultimately, in March 1993, the Bank stopped its funding to SSP (Baviskar, 1995).

The *Andolan* has brought many important issues, such as land acquisition and forcible eviction, state repression, right to life, etc. on the surface to grab the attention of people.

The *Andolan* was supported by many celebrities ranging from film stars (Amir Khan) to the Supreme Court Justices, prominent social workers (Baba Amte). The *Andolan* used diverse tactics for different audiences. It used coordinated strategy to fight the dam at all levels—international financial institutions, the national and state governments and most powerful of all—the public opinion. The people from submergence area were continuously protesting since 1988. They mobbed the World Bank team, demonstrated, and launched relay hunger strikes. While doing this, many were beaten and arrested by the police from time to time. But nothing stopped them. Fiery speeches, torchlight processions and tribal dances, a pledge opposing the displacement, rallies with slogans such as *Vikas Chahiye Vinash Nahin!* (we want development, not destruction!) were organized. The other tactics used were—non-cooperation, blocking traffic on national highway, non-violent satyagraha, indefinite hunger strike, morchas, demonstrations, petitions, etc. to draw the government's attention for justice. Mass media was aggressively used, by screening of several documentary films and similar forms of action became part of Andolan to make people aware of the consequences of this project. The songs echoed the valley—*Narmada ki ghati me ab ladai jaari hai, chalo utho, chalo utho rokna vinash hai* (Struggle is on in the Narmada valley. Rise up, destruction has to be stopped...)

The insensitive authorities reacted very strongly to the action by arresting and using lathi-charge on people. Other pressure tactics included misinformation, threats, and the ever-increasing height of the dam itself acting as the most ominous threat, police force, intimidation and even rape were used by the authorities. These tactics have played a significant role in contributing to the fear and insecurity among people (Bhatia, 1993). The whole environment was coercive. Other coercive actions by government included closure of local schools, cutting of trees and deforestation on which the livelihood of people was dependent. All this made the survival of people difficult. But the activists and PAP did not bother and continued their struggle. This mass movement created a new era in society, which affected the policy making process. This brought the issue of land displacement and rehabilitation of the displaced people on national and international front. People became aware of their own rights and fought for them following the non-violent methods, which resulted in the constructive change in the system at bureaucratic, judicial, social and political levels. The common and affected people—farmers, labourers, and fishermen realized their strength and could bring change which affected their life.

Corruption at higher level in India is rampant. There are some laws, especially to tackle corruption at lower levels. But there is no specific law which can check corruption at higher levels. Hence the need for Lokpal Bill came. There is Central Vigilance Commission (CVC) which handles corruption charges against officers. Such mechanism is necessary to reduce/ stop corruption at the higher level.

An anti-corruption law known as Citizens' Ombudsman Bill, which is popularly known as Jan Lokpal Vidheyak, is proposed. The main aim of this Bill is to eradicate/nail out corruption totally and redress the complaints.

Lokpal Bill has been introduced eight times in Parliament since 1968. The first Jan Lokpal Bill was introduced in Parliament in 1968 by Mrs. Indira Gandhi, in the 4th Lok Sabha and passed. But it could not be passed in the upper house of Parliament—Rajya Sabha. Since then, the Bill was introduced in the Parliament nine times—1971, 1977, 1985, 1989, 1996, 1998, 2001, 2005 and 2008. All the eight versions have been very weak.

In 2010, the social activist Anna Hazare took up this issue. Along with other like-minded people, an organization called "India Against Corruption" (IAC) was established. They drafted Jan Lokpal Bill. It has proposed that the Jan Lokpal would be an anti-corruption institution at the central level. It would work as an independent powerful institution like Election Commission. It would control corruption in the central government machineries and redress the complaints of the central government's offices, departments and institutions. Similarly, 'Lokayukta' would be set up in the states as anti-corruption institutions. The government has also drafted this bill by constituting a ten-member Joint Committee of ministers and civil society activists. The Lokpal Bill, 2011 was introduced in Parliament on August 4, 2011. The Bill seeks to establish the office of the Lokpal to investigate and prosecute cases of corruption. The Bill has been referred to the Standing Committee on Personnel, Public grievances, Law and Justice. The report of the committee is being awaited.

The Bill provides for establishment of the Lokpal for enquiring into complaints of corruption against certain public servants.

Thus, we see that social action is a very powerful tool for bringing a positive and desired change in the society. The community worker should be well versed with the procedures of social action so that s/he can help people to fight against any kind of suppression and get justice. The community worker should have deeper understanding of the roles that s/he has to play. The next chapter deals with this aspect in detail.

Review Questions

1. Define social action. How is it used for bringing social change?
2. Illustrate in detail the models of social action.
3. Explain the role of a community worker in social action.
4. What are the different forms of advocacies used in social action?
5. Explain the different strategies used in social action.
6. Explain direct action model. What different tactics were used in direct action model? Comment on their effectiveness.
7. What tactics were used in anti-liquor movement of Andhra Pradesh?
8. What tactics were used in *Narmada Bachao Andolan*?
9. How was PIL evolved? Give features of PIL.
10. What procedure one has to follow for filing a case under PIL?
11. How does PIL help in bringing a social change? Illustrate.
12. '*Lokpal* Bill will help in reducing corruption.' Comment.

10

Roles of a
Community Worker

The community worker has to work in different types of communities such as tribal, rural or urban (division based on geographical locations) or communities classified on the basis of different religions, castes, occupations, etc. S/he has to be equipped with certain skills to perform different roles, depending on the issues or problems s/he is dealing with. The community worker should be endowed with good communication skills, problem-solving skills, skills in mobilization of resources, planning and implementation, monitoring and evaluation, etc. Some of the important roles of a community worker are as follows. The list is not exhaustive. You can also add to it.

1. **Guide:** The main role of a community worker in community organization is that of a guide. The community worker helps the community to achieve its goals of development to solve its problems and to fulfil its needs. Instead of taking any decision/s on behalf of a community, he provokes a community to find its needs/or problems and helps them take certain actions. The community worker should never manipulate people. S/he may stimulate feeling of needs, encourage discussion/s and may suggest benefits of the programme.

The community worker can provide information, knowledge on issues related to the life of local people. For example, the health status of community women is very poor. In such a situation, the community worker should be able to provide information about health schemes, how to get services of PHC (Primary Health Centre), indigenous medicines, help from ASHA (Accredited Social Health Activist) workers, etc. This will definitely help the community worker to build a rapport with the community members.

The community worker always believes in the process by which a community may gradually develop its capacities and recognize its problems, so that people can find and develop strategies on their own. The community worker should accept the community people as they are. S/he should try to become a part of them. The community worker should not identify himself/ herself with any particular group or party. S/he should respect the rights, cultures, traditions, beliefs of the community people. S/he just gives direction to the community people to work on the needs/problems, tries to build and sustain their tempo till they achieve their goals. The community worker should always remember that s/he is there to facilitate the people to overcome their problems.

The community worker always encourages discussions, asks probing questions which lead to in-depth discussions. S/he should always focus on the ultimate goal of development to be achieved. His/her main concern is to make the community aware of its needs and to find the means by working together cooperatively. The community worker guides a community to work collec- tively with mutual understanding, cooperation and to come to a common consensus to solve problems. Sometimes s/he may unconsciously interfere, use undue influence, or take decisions on behalf of a community. At some point of time, s/he may consciously take certain decisions by taking calculated risks. While doing all this, s/he should always remember that the sole object is the development of a community.

2. **Initiator:** There are certain communities which believe in *status quo*. They never want to change themselves. If somebody tries to change them, they resist it with a strong and rigid defense mechanism. In such a situation, the role of community worker is that of an initiator. S/he does not offer any help, but just stimulates a sense of need and discontentment. S/he makes them aware of the problematic conditions and suggests them the means to improve their conditions.

Once the community worker takes initiative, s/he forces the community to re-examine the situation. S/he starts considering the alternative ways to overcome the present conditions, and thus stimulates the community to find solutions to their problems. This leads to growth and development of a community.

The community worker strongly believes that unless the community members begin to strive, to move, to achieve, they will not grow. Hence, s/he takes initiative to create such conditions which stimulate them.

Sometimes the community is so accustomed to the condition in which they live that they never feel that these conditions are inconsistent and unhealthy. In such a situation, the community worker may take initiative. But s/he should not impose interpretations or understanding of the condition on them. The community worker can just interrogate, exchange views, introduce to facts and explain the procedure of how to go about. S/he can initiate a process by conducting discussions. The community worker should be aware of the nature of the community. S/he should be aware of ignorance of people, vested interests of a few people, rigid beliefs and customs of people, aggression and hostility, inconsistent behavior, etc. S/he should accept the community as it is and work consistently towards its development.

3. **Communicator:** The community worker should be a good communicator as s/he has to share information, knowledge of different issues to the community people. This information enables the community people to take action to fulfil their needs, to solve their problems. There should be transparency between the community worker and the people. One misunderstanding may collapse the whole project. Hence, the communication between the community worker and the people should be open. Whenever required, the community worker can organize group meetings, focus group discussions, *melawas* (public meetings), or individual contacts and transfer the information. This transparency helps to establish rapport with people and develops healthy relationship. People extend their cooperation in community work.

The community worker can use different media such as puppet show, street play, role play, exhibition, slide show, film show, use of audio-visual to disseminate the information. Depending on the issues, availability of resources and local conditions, the community worker can choose any method for communication.

4. **Enabler:** The community worker facilitates the process of social change. S/he enables the people to focus on discontent. The community worker helps people to realize, understand and to be vocal about their needs or problems or discontents. The community worker should allow people to express their suppressed feelings. S/he should listen to them patiently, interrogate skillfully, enable them to locate the exact problem and help them to find solutions by themselves. The community worker, as an enabler, should initiate and facilitate the process by which discontents can be identified. This helps to bring people together, organize them and overcome their discontents.

The community worker supports people in all situations. Instead of having an approach of 'do not worry, everything will be all right', the community worker should ask 'how much are you willing to sacrifice to overcome this problem', or 'how much cooperation are you willing to extend, by forgetting interpersonal clashes? The community worker, as an enabler, should have right judgement of the situation. S/he should try to visualize the forthcoming anxiety and the way to deal with it. Accordingly, s/he can encourage the people to take responsibility for action.

As an enabler, the community worker helps the community to realize its potentials and strengths in cooperative work. In other words, the community worker facilitates the process through listening and questioning, gives consistent support and encouragement to people. S/he facilitates local efforts and does not take a lead. S/he does not provide any readymade answers or solutions to the problems of community, but he just stimulates people. In other words, the community worker facilitates and accelerates the right action, which leads towards development. It is a time-consuming process. For this, the community worker requires to be patient and have good listening skills. S/he should understand the deeper feelings of the people.

5. **Counsellor:** The community worker initiates the process of community organization. Coming together and extending cooperation to each other may be a new thing for local people. Sometimes stressful situations arise. People do not come to a common consensus. This may lead to conflict situation. In such situations, the community worker should play the role of counsellor. A group of people may need to be counselled. The community worker should listen to them patiently and try to resolve the issues as early as possible, so that friendly work environment remains intact.

6. **Motivator:** The community worker enables the people to find their discontentment. S/he should continuously stimulate people to sustain the process. Sometimes it takes such a long time to achieve a goal that people get restless and start losing interest. Usually, many hurdles come in between and people get tired, as they do not see any results. They just struggle and struggle. In such situation, the community worker plays the role of a motivator. S/he should encourage people to understand the situation and respond to it tactfully.

7. **Advocate:** This role is very important if the community worker is adopting the social action model of community development. S/he represents the whole community to get the services for the marginalized people. S/he raises issues and challenges the power structure. S/he tries to bring solutions to discontent generating issues. Sometimes the voice of the marginalized people is not heard. The community worker represents the needs and problems of these people, builds up required support, and does networking to increase the pressure on power structure (oppressor). Here, the community worker fights for the rights of others. In the role of advocate, the community worker helps the community to get access to services, so that they can improve their quality of life. In this role, s/he argues, negotiates and confronts the concerned authorities, on behalf of community and helps them in getting justice.

8. **Mediator:** In community organization, it is very difficult to come to a common consensus about the needs and problems faced by

people. The community has different groups based on religion, caste, power, educational background, and so on. When the process of organization starts, conflicts may arise. The community worker should act as a mediator between these groups, intervene the disputing people and try to resolve the problem. S/he can help them to reach compromises, reconcile differences and find out solution, which mutually satisfies both the parties. S/he should remain impartial.

9. **Catalyst:** The community worker facilitates the process of organization. S/he tries to empower the people, so that people can work independently to solve their problems and needs. S/he tries to develop local leadership and enables people to acquire the skills of decision making. Slowly, s/he hands over the situation to people. But, the community worker is always there in the background, whenever required, to help them. S/he plays the role of catalyst when situation demands. S/he enables people to work independently and work towards their own needs.

10. **Innovator:** The community worker should use different innovative approaches to deal with situations. This will enable people to try out new ways and means to deal with their needs and problems. This will also improve the capacity of people. People will understand that instead of using routine techniques, if innovative techniques are used, they can find better solutions easily and quickly.

11. **Collaborator and networker:** Community organization requires collaboration and networking. Getting cooperation from other organizations helps in solving the problems. If different organizations working for the same cause collaborate, it increases their strength, and human and material resources get utilized at the optimum. The collaborative strength helps to bring social change much faster.

12. **Expert:** The community worker should provide statistical data, research findings, technical experience, resource material, which people need while dealing with their discontent. S/he may help the people in analyzing and diagnosing the problem. Sometimes, people are unable to understand the root cause of their problems. Here, the community worker can act as an expert and guide people to work together to solve common issues.

The community worker also needs to keep updated information, knowledge about different government schemes, policies, etc. S/he should be able to provide this data to local people, as and when required. S/he should be able to guide the people in getting financial assistance, both from government departments (including ward offices of municipal corporations, *panchayat* offices) or non-governmental agencies. S/he should guide them about how to approach these organizations, how to draft a letter or project proposal, preparation of a budget, etc. to make their official spade work easy.

13. **Evaluator:** The community worker should be a good evaluator. Without bringing any subjectivity, s/he should be able to evaluate the process of cooperative work. S/he should evaluate the interaction, cooperation of people and its effects on them. S/he should present these facts to the community. This will help the people in future when they work together. This will increase understanding and ability of the people. The function of the community worker in community organization is to facilitate the community organization process. While doing this, s/he may play the role of an expert, counsellor, initiator, facilitator and innovator. Community organization is one of the important methods of social work. The community worker must possess certain qualities and skills for working with the communities. The exact role of the community worker keeps on changing with the changing context. It depends on the type of the community, the issues, the resultant conflicts, and the availability of resources. An efficient community worker adopts and adapts the role according to the changing situations. Most of the time, s/he has to perform multiple roles to enhance the process of community development.

To perform the above-mentioned roles efficiently, the community worker has to maintain records. This documentation is very crucial for any organization's proper functioning. The next chapter deals in detail with this.

Review Questions

1. What are the different roles a community worker has to perform while working with a community?

2. 'The community worker should be a good counsellor and mediator.' Illustrate.

3. Explain the different roles performed you by during your field work placement.

11
Records

Record is a document which is maintained in all the organizations. There are a variety of records maintained in organizations depending on the type and requirements. Some of them are named as accounts records, minutes, reports: monthly, quarterly, bi-yearly and annual reports, inward and outward registers, attendance register, dead stocks, etc. Some records come under the category of personal records such as service book and diary. Some are official and administrative records such as minute book, accounts register, inward and outward register, etc. In addition to these records, the social organizations have other records as well, such as case work files, proposals written to funding agencies, and so on. Overall, the functions of these records are as follows:

1. It gives an account of something that has taken place.
2. It gives details of person/s involved in a particular activity/ programme/meeting or things happened in a department.
3. It gives factual description, analysis, instructions, directions, opinions, decisions, recommendations and suggestions.
4. It helps to plan future activities.

Each organization, working for the people, must decide what type of records are to be maintained to meet its needs. It is essential for all the organizations to maintain the records relating to work plan and work progress reports.

Records can be maintained in different formats such as textual-reports, charts, graphs, maps, blueprint, audio-cassettes, audio-visual form, films, CDs, DVDs, slides, micro film, or photographs, micro-cards, etc. The intention behind preparation of these records is that they can be seen or heard in future as well. Some of these records such as annual reports may be published, but most of the other records are usually unpublished and are used only in the office and by the related persons.

Records are maintained in almost all organized sectors—government and non-government organizations, business, religious institutions, educational institutions, sport clubs, and so on.

Maintaining records properly is very important for any organization. In long term, it helps us a lot especially for ready reference. As we know, each community is unique. Each has its specific problems. So, the approaches of every organization vary immensely. The type of work also varies from survey to fund raising and organizing different activities to taking steps to change the social legislations (in case of social action), if needed. Hence, we cannot force the organizations to maintain a particular type of records (as in case work) in the name of essential records. It is up to the organization to decide what to record and what not to record. Unfortunately, some organizations take disadvantage of this situation. They do work and do not keep proper records.

As stated earlier, in this chapter we discuss the important types of records maintained in the social organizations working for the communities, and their purpose. This is an open-ended list. One can add to it as per one's requirements.

PURPOSES OF RECORD MAINTENANCE

Following are the purposes of record keeping in an organization working for community development:

1. Records help to perform the tasks accurately, which results in good performance. The persons involved in the tasks get an idea about the actions that need to be taken. They get all the information through the recorded facts and opinions. This helps in proper planning of an action and its execution. We need to have this information background as planning cannot be done in a vacuum.

2. Records are maintained to know the progress and development of an activity/project and for further planning. This ultimately helps to improve the services of the agency and results in welfare of the people.

3. Records are very helpful to seek cooperation of the local people, both from the organization and from outside agencies and people as well. If the person involved in the task leaves or gets transferred, and a new person takes over, records help him/her to know what has happened earlier and what needs to be done, without wasting much time. Records help to improve the effectiveness and efficiency of personnel working on that task/s.

4. Records help in monitoring the tasks/activity. These help the supervisor to understand the problems and the solutions for them.

5. Records also tell us the stages when the problems occurred especially while implementing a particular activity and the steps that were taken. In future, if the organization wants to replicate the same activity in other communities or same community, precautions can be taken while planning the activity itself to avoid the problems. So, there will no wastage of time, money and human resource.

6. Records help the funding agencies and top authorities of the organization to know under what circumstances the work has been carried out, what were the problems faced, and their solutions, how the development took place, how was the participation of people, whether the funds were utilized adequately and if not, then their justification.

7. Records can become an important guidance for other agencies performing similar type of work.

8. Records can be helpful for researchers.

TYPES OF RECORD

Some of the types of records are discussed at length in the following sections.

Administrative Records

There are no specific administrative records essentially to be maintained by every organization working with communities. It depends on administrative problems and the type of community they are working for, what records are to be maintained. Common administrative records include agendas, minute books (such as board of management, executive committee, staff meeting, community level committees, advisory board, grievance committee, purchase committee, etc.), job descriptions and specifications, personal files/service books, leave rules, scrap books of newspaper cuttings, field level reports containing types of problems faced across and actions taken, progress reports, mailing list, list of experts, financial records, and other such types of records.

Process Recording

The community worker has to maintain a diary where s/he can record the happenings in the field in brief. Diary is a narrative record of what happened. This helps to prepare process records afterwards. The process record contains details of things happened in the community. The process record not only emphasizes on what happened but also elaborates on how and why it happened. It informs about the steps taken by the worker. It also explains the way the community development principles were used by him/her. Such records give a better understanding about the working in different situations. It also helps to understand the community, its intergroup relationships, community politics and power structure in a better way.

Process record helps to understand the problems faced by the community worker, how s/he has handled them, why s/he took certain steps, was his/her strategy correct. In other words, it is a self-study process through which the worker can learn the things in a much better way. This experience enriches him/her and the supervisors as well.

The drawback of process recording is that it is time-consuming. It tends to be highly subjective. The selection of the content (field happenings) and the methodology is decided by the person. It is possible that some of the important happenings might be overlooked and are not recorded. Sometimes personal biases might result in misinterpretation of certain actions, behaviours, motivation and attitudes of people. Hence, at times it becomes difficult to find out what exactly had happened. Sometimes, the community worker gets habituated in making process record. S/he may believe that the steps s/he had taken to solve the problem worked last time, so will work in all situations. This may result in the loss of his/her creativity and spontaneity of taking new steps and strategies while working with people.

Diary

For keeping day-to-day happenings in a narrative manner, the community worker can write a diary. There is no standard or specific way/style/method to write a diary. It has flexible style that gives freedom to a worker. One can write it according to one's convenience, time and pace. Important events that took place, factual information, its interpretation and own opinion may be noted down in a diary. It should be written more objectively. Ideally, the diary should be written daily and should be updated regularly.

Remember, it is a valuable record. No matter however time-consuming it may be, each worker must maintain it. It helps to analyze the situations/problems and for further study.

Day Sheet

This is very useful for a community worker. In one glance, it gives a clear picture of the work done. This also helps in further planning. The worksheet contains the following information (Table 11.1). One can add to it or delete, as per one's requirement.

Table 11.1 Worksheet

Sr. No.	Time		No. of hours	Tasks performed/ activities	Target group	Venue	Problems faced, if any	Output/ remarks
	From	To						

Agency Log

This can be maintained on a daily or weekly basis. It informs about important events, developments that took place within a day or in a week. There is a difference between log and diary. Log includes very selective happenings, whereas diary is much comprehensive. It can include changes in structure—organizational and/or administrative, committees, personal; it also informs about the meetings held, publications, and other developments.

Scrapbook of Publications

This contains a sample of every printed material prepared by an organization such as printed record forms, pamphlets, brochures, handouts, posters, booklets, etc. They are entered in a chronological order. They are also given numbers. The scrapbook should show a table of contents. Scrapbook can be used as a good reference material.

Minutes

Minutes are important records of any organization. These give an account of the happenings in an organization. Minutes act as a major tool in the process of community organization. These should be written and maintained very carefully as they reflect the work done by the community worker and other personnel. The minutes should be signed. They should be put in next forthcoming meeting and approved, which increases its authenticity. All minutes should contain the date when it was conducted, its venue, time, list of participants attended and absent (if it is close ended), agenda and the decisions taken. It should give a summary of the discussions. It should be self-explanatory. It should clearly mention why such action was taken by giving certain examples. If certain decisions were kept pending, this should also be mentioned along with the reasons/justifications. Minutes should be written in a simple and understandable language. There should not be any ambiguity. It should contain factual information. It should be reasonably concise and complete.

Usually, the secretary writes minutes. Minutes should be written immediately after the meeting. The person who writes minutes must attend the meeting. It becomes difficult for a person to write minutes without attending meeting. S/he should be very attentive during the meeting and should note down all the details of happenings. While writing minutes, s/he can take help of other members who have attended the meeting, if necessary. It is also possible to record whole discussion of the meeting, with prior permission of the chairperson and members. The minutes once ready can be presented to a few members and checked whether all points are covered correctly or not. Then they can be put up in the forthcoming meeting for its approval. The copies of minutes should be distributed to all the members of the committee. Suggestions, changes should be made, if necessary and approval be sought. Once the minutes are approved, they should be signed by the chairperson/ secretary. Then it becomes an official document. A separate file should be maintained for approved minutes. They become very important documents for the organization.

REPORT WRITING

The community worker has to write different types of reports. Each report should mention the name of the committee or subject on which the report is written, date and to whom the report is addressed. It should be well organized. If necessary, appropriate headings and sub-headings can be used. Wherever necessary, tables can be given. At the end, it is better to give summary, conclusion and recommendations. If the report deals with a particular problem, it must follow an analytical approach, which should include the following steps:

1. Nature of the exact problem and the situation.
2. Its duration, its background.
3. The people affected by this problem. Also, if possible, write about their attitudes, beliefs, and prejudices.
4. Location of the problem.
5. Nature of the problem.
6. Root cause of the situation/problem.
7. Consequences.
8. Strategies to be adopted.
9. Initiators.
10. Organized efforts by people.
11. Personnel/experts required.
12. Utilization of the existing resources.
13. Approximate expenses and the funding sources.

The report should mention plans to overcome the situation, methods used to implement the plan (action taken) and results.

PROJECT RECORD

The agencies can take up different projects. Records of each project should be maintained separately. Mostly, such project records include information in a chronological order, different meetings held, conferences, workshops, seminars organized, interviews conducted, correspondence, memoranda and publications. Sometimes, if more information is there, like photos, charts, tables, this can be given in appendices, at the end of the report.

WORK PLAN

Work plan is a comprehensive written plan for the execution. It is for a specified period. It contains tasks, divided into small tasks explaining what is to be done, who will do it (committees, experts, local people, and resource persons) and how it is to be done (strategies).

Need for a Work Plan

Work plan is essential to improve the services of an organization. It increases the organization's effectiveness, efficiency and economy of operation. It also helps the understanding of the personnel working in the organization. The staff understand what the agency is doing and what is expected from them. Work plan helps to seek optimum participation of the employees at all the stages—from planning to execution. It helps to know the progress of work and check whether one is on the right track or not, moving towards achieving the objectives or not.

Content of the Work Plan

The work plan should give answers to six couplings, that is, what, why, who, where, when and how. In general, it should explain the following things:

1. Brief description of nature of activities to be performed (what).
2. Purpose of the activities to be performed. It justifies the activities (why).
3. Write briefly who will carry these activities. It may be only community people or community people along with the representative of organization or a committee specially constituted for this purpose to carry the task, other agency support. This should explain who is responsible to carry the task (who).
4. This should specify the geographical area where the activities will be carried out. Sometimes the organization works in different areas, has its branches at different locations, and hence it is necessary to specify this (where).
5. Time framework should be mentioned in the work plan. Otherwise, the duration will be unnecessarily prolonged (when).
6. It is important to mention different strategies to carry out the tasks successfully. The method/s you adopt should be clearly mentioned. The financial aspect should be covered in it. For example, if one wants to record the happenings through video, or want to pay field visits outside the state/country. This requires additional funding. Hence, there is a need to mention funding and expected expenditure (how).

In addition to the above list, one should mention if additional staff is required, number of people, time duration. Give the list of equipment required, if any. We must cover the maintenance part of the equipment. Once the work plan is ready, it should be discussed with all the staff members and if required, can be revised according to their suggestions.

WORK PROGRESS REPORT

Work progress report is prepared on the basis of the work plan and the actual work done. This gives boost to those who are actually working on the tasks. This facilitates for further action, to improve services as well. The work progress report contains three major parts, namely what happened, what is the current situation and what steps need to be taken. The report covers all types of activities undertaken, major developments taken place during that period. This helps in interpretation and analyzing different issues.

Work progress report can be prepared at regular intervals—quarterly or biannually. It helps to give direction for further work. Sometimes it is also helpful to close down the project. In many agencies the community worker has to submit such type of progress reports to the immediate boss or an employer. In a few cases, the organizations have to submit the progress reports to the donor agencies/funding agencies. Depending on the progress, they get further funding. Hence, it is an important record from the organization's point of view. The basic purpose of the progress report is to improve the services of an organization. This gives direction to an organization. The progress report helps to improve the efficiency of human resources. It enriches the monitoring system that guides the workers for better performance with good result.

Following are the general guidelines to write a progress report. One can definitely adapt it as per the requirement.

1. Title, name of the agency, name of the project.
2. Name of the person who is submitting the report.
3. Date of the beginning of project.
4. Period covered under the report.
5. Date on which the report is submitted.
6. Summary of the work done—it should highlight the important events that took place during the above-mentioned period, present status and further steps required to be taken (recommendations).
7. Special activities conducted such as campaigns, seminars, conferences, delegations, *pada yatras, morchas,* public meetings, *dharanas,* etc.
8. Major contacts—This refers to other agencies, government departments, politicians, local leaders, funding agencies/donors, and

universities. This information should be given date wise. One can mention how these contacts were made, whether personally, telephonically or through written correspondence. It should also mention the purpose of contact and its outcome.

9. Details of meetings held—Mention whether it was held at the community level or at the level of the community worker's parent organization, or at the level of other organizations. All the details must be mentioned including the date, time, duration, venue and purpose of the meeting, the number of people attended, programme/agenda and its outcome.

10. Other activities carried out such as consultations, speeches, etc.

11. Publicity—Coverage in media–print and/or electronic, hand bills, pamphlets, posters, brochures and other material prepared and disseminated, number of copies and further details one feels relevant should be mentioned clearly.

12. Changes related to committee members, venue of work, target group (if occurred, but not mentioned in the original work plan) should be mentioned.

13. Problems faced and the strategies used to overcome them should be reported.

14. Current problems/challenges must be explained.

15. Further help, if needed from the organization, in the form of human resources, material resources or financial resources should be mentioned clearly.

The progress reports may be quarterly or biannually or annual, depending on the requirements of the organization. It is very useful for a community worker as it gives an insight to carry out the work further. Diary, worksheets, minute books and work plan help in writing the progress report. Progress report should be written promptly at the end of each report period, as required and submitted to the authorities. This definitely gives direction to an organization as well as to the work.

To summarize, we can say that it is the choice of each organization to select the types of records to be maintained. The records are very important documents which give a clear picture of the work done by an organization. They guide in planning future activities for achieving the goal of community development.

Review Questions

1. Explain the importance of maintaining different types of records.
2. What is the purpose of records?
3. What records a community worker should maintain? Justify.

4. Illustrate the importance of diary maintaining and monthly reports.

5. Explain the importance of minutes of a meeting.

6. Explain the necessity of a work plan. What should be the contents of this?

7. Give different aspects of the work progress report.

8. How do records help in community development process?

Saul David Alinsky (1909–1972)

Saul Alinsky's work is an important milestone which inevitably becomes a reference point when we discuss community organization and development. Following paragraphs describe Alinsky and his work.

Saul was born in Chicago on January 30, 1909. Since childhood, he was interested in dynamics of power and the interactions between those who are denied resources and those who deny. In 1930, he graduated from the University of Chicago. He stayed on for two more years, and studied criminology. He worked as a social worker and dealt with juvenile delinquents from 1933 to 1936. During this period, he studied social problems like discrimination, unemployment, poor-housing and poverty very closely. He was also involved with fund raising and organizational work for various reform movements.

Saul Alinsky established the Industrial Areas Foundation in 1939. He moved to the back of yards of the Chicago district and started working for the poor working class. His approach included uniting local people around immediate grievances in their neighbourhoods and in protesting vigorously. He emphasized on recruiting and training local people as 'organizers' to take lead in the communities.

With the help of labour and religious leaders, he formed Back of the Yard Council—a citizen's organization. The purpose behind its establishment was to act as a pressure group for social improvement. It used peaceful direct action tactics. The Council succeeded in improving conditions of people staying in neighbourhood (Mike Seal). Very importantly, the people who participated realized the realities of political and economic power. They also realized their own ability to use power to achieve their own legitimate right. (www.infed.org/thinkers/alinsky.htm).

Alinsky established the Industrial Areas Foundation (IAF) in 1940. During World War II, he worked as a consultant to various government agencies. After World War II, he again started working for poor and power-less neighbourhoods. He always believed in developing indigenous leadership and self-help. He was passionate for radical democracy. He believed that one should never go outside the expertise of one's people. If this happens, the result will be confusion, fear and collapse of communication.

RADICALISM

Alinsky always believed in working within the system. It is very necessary to work with the system to bring changes in the system. He stressed on people's participation. Radical change can happen only when the large number of people involved in it needs to be in favour even passively. He said, usually people are afraid of change. Unless they feel fully 'frustrated, defeated, lost, futureless in the prevailing system that they are willing to let go of the past and change the future, revolution will not take place'.

He felt that people should not underestimate themselves in a democratic system. He knew the government system and its harassment. But he strongly believed that the system had the potential to be reformed. Unless people crave for the need desperately, they would not act for change.

TACTICS FOR RADICALS

1. Power is not only what you have, but what the enemy thinks you have. Alinsky thinks that if one has mass support, one should flaunt it. If one does not have support, one should make a lot of noise. If one cannot make a big noise, make a big stink.
2. Never go outside the experience of your people—If people do not have experience of a particular action or tactic, the result will be confusion, fear and sometimes failure.
3. Whenever possible, go outside of the experience of the enemy— Look for different ways which can create and increase insecurity, anxiety and uncertainty.
4. Make use of the energy to live up to their own book of rules—Allow enemy to be lethargic. Attack suddenly and manage to get the law changed.
5. Ridicule is man's most potent weapon—It is almost impossible to counteract ridicule. It infuriates the opposition, which then reacts to your disadvantage.
6. A good tactic is the one that your people enjoy.
7. A tactic that drags for too long becomes a drag—Man can sustain interest in any issue for only a limited time.
8. Keep the pressure on—Saul Alinsky says not to rest on one's laurels if one has a partial victory. For Alinsky, action comes from keeping the heat on.

9. The threat is usually more terrifying than the thing itself. Give such threats which are horrifying. Threat should be such that the opponent has to accept the demands, just by imagining about threats and its effects.

10. The major premise for tactics is the development of operations that will maintain a constant pressure upon the opposition. Such pressure is necessary in order to get reaction from the opponent. He argued that 'the action is the reaction'.

11. If you push a negative emotion hard and deep enough it will break through into its counter side. Every positive has its negative. Essentially, this is to not to give up and to be afraid to concentrate on the negative aspects.

12. The price of a successful attack is a constructive alternative. This is the other side of the previous rule. If one does push the other party through to changing, one has to offer some kind of solution.

13. Pick the target, freeze it, personalize it and polarize it. This is perhaps Saul Alinsky's most controversial rule and is counter to the common idea that we should not make things personal when pursuing the changes. Do not target one individual.

These principles and rules are a practical toolkit to bring change. They have a great potential to motivate those who are engaged in community work and education.

Saul Alinsky was a committed organizer and activist. He was an influential writer. He is the author of two famous books namely *Reveille for Radicals* (1946) and *Rules for Radical* (1972) which are treated as bibles of community organization and development. His ideas and thoughts are still relevant for those who would like to work to bring a change. They are useful for those who are engaged in power structure and wish to work for the rights of deprived section of the society. Saul Alinsky died on June 12, 1972 in Carmel, California.

References

Ahuja, Sangeeta. 1997. *People, Law and Justice Casebook on Public Interest Litigation.* Vol. I. New Delhi: Orient Longman.

Aiken, Michael and Mott, Paul E. (Eds.). 1970. *The Structure of Community Power.* New York: Random House.

Anderson, M. (Ed.). 2007. Do No Harm Checklist: www.cdainc.com.(http://www.cdainc.com/cdawww/project_home.php)15.9.2011.

Anderson, M. (Ed.). 2007. *Do Not Harm.* Checklist:www.cdainc.com.

Arthur, Fink E. 1978. *The Fields of Social Work.* New York: Holt Rinehart and Winston.

Asthana, Pratima. 1974. *Women's Movement in India.* Delhi: Vikas.

Bahuguna, Vimla. 1990. The Chipko Movement. In *A Space Within the Struggle: Women's Participation in People's Struggle*, edited by Sen Ilina. New Delhi: Kali for Women.

Battem, T.R. 1962. *The Non-Directive Approach in Group and Community Work.* London: Oxford University Press.

Baviskar, Amita. 1995. *In the Belly of the River: Tribal Conflicts over Development in the Narmada Valley.* New Delhi: Oxford University Press.

Bhatia, Bela. 1977. Forced Evictions in the Narmada Valley. In *The Dam and the Nation: Displacement and Resettlement in the Narmada Valley*, edited by Dreze Jean, Samson Meera, and Singh Satyajit. New Delhi: Oxford University Press.

Bienen, Henry. 1968. *Violence and Social Change.* Chicago: University of Chicago Press.

Cary, Lee J. 1970. *Community Development as a Process.* Columbia, USA: University of Missouri Press.

Chambers, R. 1983. *Rural Development: Putting The Last First.* Harlow, UK: Longman.

Chambers, R. 1997. *Whose Reality Counts? Putting the First Last.* London: Intermediate Technology.

Chambers, R. 2002. *Participatory Workshops: A Source Book of 21 Sets of Ideas and Activities.* London: Earthscan.

Community Mobilization in the Context of Globalization: Challenges to Social Work. 2000. Reading Material. UGC Refresher Course. Mumbai. Department of Urban and Rural Community Development, TISS.

Cox, F.M. and others (Eds.). 1974. *Strategies of Community Organization.* Illinois: F.E. Peacock Publication.

D'Souza, Anthony. 1987. *Leadership.* Bombay: Better Yourself Books.

Dan, Chekki A. (Ed.). 1987. *Community Development Theory and Methods of Planned Change.* New Delhi: Vikas.

Dan, Chekki A. 1979. *Community Development.* New Delhi: Vikas.

Dantwala, M.L., Sethi, Harsh, and Visaaria Pravin (Eds.). 1998. *Social Change through Voluntary Action.* New Delhi: Sage.

Dayal, Rajeshwar. 1966. *Community Development Programme in India.* Allahabad: Kitab Mahal.

Desai, Neera and Patel, Vibhuti. 1985. *Indian Women: Change and Challenge.* Bombay: Popular Publication.

Desrochers, John CSC. Wielenga, Bastiaan, and Patel, Vibhuti.1991. *Social Movements: Towards a Perspective.* Bangalore: Centre for Social Action.

Donatella, Della Porta and Mario Diani. 1999. *Social Movements: An Introduction.* UK: Blackwell.

Dunham, Arthur. 1970. *The New Community Organization.* New York: Thomas Y. Crowell Company.

Freire, P. 1970. *Pedagogy of The Oppressed.* New York: Continuum.

Gandhi, P.K. (Ed.). 1985. *Social Action through Law—Partnership for Social Justice.* New Delhi: Concept Publishing Company.

Gangrade, K.D. 1971. *Community Organization in India.* Bombay: Popular Prakashan.

Gangrade, K.D. 1976. *Dimensions of Social Work in India.* CSE Studies. New Delhi: Marwah.

Green, Gary Paul and Anna Haines. 2002. *Asset Building and Community Development.* New Delhi: Sage.

Guide to community mobilization programming, Mercycorps (mercycorps.org) 21.9.2011.

Handbook for Non-formal Adult Education Facilitators, UNESCO PROAP, Bangkok, 2001.

Herbert, J. Ruhim and Irene S. Ruhim. 2001. *Community Organizing and Development.* Massachusetts: Allyn and Bacon.

Hersey, P. and Blanchard, K.H. 1972. *Management of Organizational Behaviour: Utilizing Human Resources*, 2nd ed. New Jersey: Prentice Hall Inc.

Hersey, P. and Blanchard, K.H. 1977. *Management of Organizational Behaviour: Utilizing Human Resources*, 3rd ed. New Jersey: Prentice Hall Inc.

Hillman, Arthur. 1950. *Community Organization and Planning.* New York: Macmillan.

http://christcollegemsw.blogspot.com/2008/03/community-organization-notes.html22.11.2011.

http://faizlaw   journal.blogspot.com/2007/12/public-interest-litigation.html 5.1.2012.

http://psychosocial.actalliance.org/default.aspx?di=64184&subject=Community%20mobilisation15.6.2011.

http://psychosocial.actalliance.org/default.aspx?di=6504915.6.2011.

http://psychosocial.actalliance.org/default.aspx?di=6505015.6.2011.

http://psychosocial.actalliance.org/default.aspx?di=6505115.6.2011.

http://psychosocial.actalliance.org/default.aspx?di=6505215.6.2011.

http://psychosocial.actalliance.org/default.aspx?di=6505415.6.2011.

http://psychosocial.actalliance.org/default.aspx?di=6570315.6.2011.

http://psychosocial.actalliance.org/default.aspx?di=6643415.6.2011.

http://www.crossroad.to/Quotes/communism/alinsky.htm26.1.2012.

http://www.google.co.in/search?tbm=isch&hl=en&source=hp&biw=939&bih=562&q=PRA+Maaping-matrix.ranking&gbv=2&oq=PRA+Maaping-matrix.ranking&aq=f&aqi=&aql=&gs_l=img.3...645l12229910l23625l26l26l0l19l0l0l1l25l738l4 j3l7l0.frgbld. On 05.04.2012.

http://www.infed.org/thinkers/alinsky.htm 26.1.2012.

http://www.jstor.org/stable/4399756 on 09/03/2012.

http://www.mercycorps.org/sites/default/files/CoMobProgrammingGd.pdf 15.7.2011.

http://www.ngosindia.com/resources/pil_sc.php 5/9/2012.

http://www.scribd.com/doc/17169418/approaches-to-community-development on 5/23/2011.

http://www.sscnet.ucla.edu/southasia/History/SocialPol/spmove,html5.3.2012.

http://www.supremecourtonline.com/articles/public-interest-litigation.php 5.3.2012.

http://www.tysknews.com/Articles/dnc_corruption.htm26.1.2012.

http://www2.unescobkk.org/elib/publications/nonformal/19.8.2011.

International Foundation for Education and Self-Help (IFESH), Training Manual, (1999): http://www.ifesh.org/— http://psychosocial.actalliance.org/default.aspx?di=64185&ptid=66401.

Jain, Shobhita. 1984. *Women and People's Ecological Movement: A Case Study of Women's Role in the Chipko Movement in Uttar Pradesh. Economic and Political Weekly,* 19(41), Oct. 13.

Joshi, Vidyut. 1977. Rehabilitation in the Narmada Valley: Human Rights and National Policy Issues. In *The Dam and the Nation: Displacement and Resettlement in the Narmada Valley*, edited by Jean Dreze, Meera Samson, and Satyajit Singh. New Delhi: Oxford University Press.

JSTOR, *Economic and Political Weekly*, Vol. 27, No. 45 (Nov. 7, 1992), pp. 2406–2408_files dated 9.3.12.

Krishna, Sumi. 1996. *Environmental Politics: People's Lives and Development*. New Delhi: Sage.

Kumar, Radha.1999. From Chipko to Sati: The Contemporary Indian Women's Movement. In *Gender and Politics in India*, edited by Nivedita Menon. Delhi: Oxford University Press.

Lingam, Laxmi. 2002. Taking Stock: Women's Movement and the State. In *Social Movements and the State*, edited by Ghanshyam, Shah. New Delhi: Sage.

Lowry, Nelson. 1960. *Community Structure and Changes*. New York: Macmillan.

McMillan, Wayne. 1945. *Community Organization for Social Work*. Illinois. USA: The University of Chicago Press.

Mishra, Anupam and Tripathi, S. 1978. *Chipko Movement: Uttarakhand Women's Bid to Save Forest Wealth*. New Delhi: People's Action for Peace and Justice.

Mott, Paul E. 1970. Power, Authority and Influence. In *The Structure of Community Power*, edited by Aiken, Michael and Mott, Paul E. New York: Random House.

Moving forward together (stories from the women's movement), 1999. Banglore. UMA Prachar, Institute of Social Studies Trust.

Mukherji, B. 1961. *Community Development in India*. Bombay: Orient Longman.

Murphy, Campbell G. 1954. *Community Organization Practice*. Cambridge: Houghton Mufflin Company. The Riverside Press.

Nisbet, Robert A. 1965. *Community and Power*. A Galaxy Book. USA: Oxford University Press, Inc.

Pandya, S.R. and Dave, Shastri Pratima (2004): *Personality Development and Communicative English*. Mumbai: Himalaya Publishing House.

Pankajam, G. 2000. *Extension—Third Dimension of Education*. New Delhi: Gyan Publishing House.

Parasuraman, S. 1977. The Anti-Dam Movement and Rehabilitation Policy. In *The Dam and the Nation: Displacement and Resettlement in the Narmada Valley*, edited by Jean Dreze, Meera Samson and Satyajit Singh, New Delhi: Oxford University Press,

planningcommission.nic.in/plans/planrel/fiveyr/7th/hindi/7th_fypv1.pdf 28.3.2012.

psycosocial@actalliance.org17.8.2011.

Rahim, A. (1986). *Managing Conflicts in Organizations*. New York: Praeger.

Ralph, M. Kramer. 1975. *Readings in Community Organization Practice.* New Jersey: Prentice Hall Inc.

Rao, M.S.A. (Ed.). 2004. *Social Movements in India: Studies in Peasant, Backward Classes, Sectarian, Tribal and Women's Movements.* New Delhi: Manohar Publishers and Distributors.

Ray, Raka. 1999. *Fields of Protest: Women's Movements in India.* New Delhi: Kali for Women.

Reddy, D. Narasimha and Arun, Patnaik. 1993. Anti-Arrack Agitation of Women in Andhra Pradesh. *Economic and Political Weekly,* 28(21), pp. 1059–1066.

Ross, M.G. 1955. *Community Organization: Theory and Principles.* New York: Harper & Row.

Ross, M.G. 1958. *Case Histories in Community Organization.* New York: Harper & Row.

Ross, M.G. 1967. *Community Organization: Theory, Principle.* New York: Harper & Row.

Ross, Murray and Benn, Lappin. 1967. *Community Organization: Theory, Principles and Practices.* New York: Harper & Row.

Rothman, J. 2001. Approaches to Community Intervention. In *Strategies of Community Intervention,* edited by Rothman, J., Erlich, J.L. and Tropman, J.E. Itasca, II: Peacock.

Rothman, Jack, Erlich John and Tropman John. 1987. *Strategies of Community Intervention: Strategies for Community Organization.* Micro Practice. Michigan: F.E. Peacock Publisher.

Ruopp, Phillips (Ed.). 1953. *Approaches to Community Development. A Symposium Introductory to Problems and Methods of Village Welfare in Underdeveloped Areas.* The Hague, Bandung: W. Van Hoeve.

Sangvai, Sanjay. 2000. *The River and Life: People's Struggle in the Narmada Valley.* Mumbai: Earthcare Books.

Sethi, Rageev. 1996. *Tips for Effective Leadership.* New Delhi: Beacon Books.

Shah, Ghanshyam. 2004. *Social Movements in India: A Review of Literature.* New Delhi: Sage.

Sharanagat, Sitaram, B. 1996. *Gramin Sahabhagi Mulyavalokan.* Pune: AFARM.

Siddiqui, H.Y. 1997. *Working with Communities.* New Delhi: Hira Publications.

Singh, Prabhakar. 1982. *Community Development Programme in India— Organization, Working, Achievements.* New Delhi: Deep & Deep Publications.

Soloman, D.D. 1962. *Evaluating Community Programmes.* Canada: Centre for Community Studies.

Sower, Christopher. 1957. *Community Involvement.* Glencoe Illinois: The Free Press.

Taking the Experience from PIL in India, Pan Mohamad Faiz.

Thomas, K.W. 1976. Conflict and Conflict Management. In *The Handbook of Industrial and Organizational Psychology*, edited by Dunnette, M.D. Chicago: Rand McNally.

Thudipara, Jacob, Z. 2007. *Urban Community Development*. Mumbai: Rawat Publications.

Towards People-centred Development. Report of TISS Diamond Jubilee conferences on Movements and Campaigns for the Empowerment of Marginalized Groups. Nov. 1–4, 1996, TISS, Mumbai. 1997.

Tripathi, Dutta Shiva. 1988. Social Movements and Development—A Search of Paradigms. In *Social Movements for Development*, edited by Srivastava, S.K. and Srivastava, A.L. Allahabad: Chugh Publications.

Udeshi, J.J. 1974. *Community Development: Costs and Benefits*. Bombay: University of Bombay.

Warren, Roland L. (Ed.). 1962. *Community Development and Social Work Practice*. New York: NASW.

Watson, Craig M. 1996. *Dynamics of Leadership*. Bombay: Jaico Publishing House.

Wielenga, Bastiaan. 1991. Ecological Movements: Struggle for a Sustainable Society. In *Social Movements Towards A Perspective,* edited by John Desrochers csc, Bostiaan Wielenga, and Vibhuti Patel. Banglore: Centre for Social Action.

www.accu.or.jp/litdbase/pub/dlperson/pdf2003/RP_Oyasu0112.PDF.

www.fao.org/docrep/003/x5996e/x5996eob.html#Top 30.7.2011.

Index

Shriniketan experiment, 12
Situational leadership, 148
Social
    action, 156
        elements of, 161
    action model, 67
    mapping, 104
    planning model, 66
    work approach, 75
Social Security Act, 4
State charities aid association, 2

Task goals, 70
Task related conflict, 128
Training, 55
Trust building, 57

Women's movements, 164
Work plan, 192
    content of, 192
    need for, 192
Work progress report, 193
Workers alliance, 4